Michael Wedel
Pictorial Affects, Senses of Rupture

Cinepoetics

—

Edited by
Hermann Kappelhoff and Michael Wedel

Volume 6

Michael Wedel
Pictorial Affects, Senses of Rupture

On the Poetics and Culture of
Popular German Cinema, 1910–1930

DE GRUYTER

ISBN 978-3-11-076375-1
e-ISBN (PDF) 978-3-11-061355-1
e-ISBN (EPUB) 978-3-11-061237-0
ISSN 2569-4294

Library of Congress Control Number: 2019933926

Bibliographic information published by the Deutsche Nationalbibliothek
The Deutsche Nationalbibliothek lists this publication in the Deutsche Nationalbibliografie;
detailed bibliographic data are available on the Internet at http://dnb.dnb.de.

© 2021 Walter de Gruyter GmbH, Berlin/Boston
This volume is text- and page-identical with the hardback published in 2019.
Typesetting: Integra Software Services Pvt. Ltd.
Printing and binding: CPI books GmbH, Leck
Cover image: Frame enlargement from the film "Zweimal gelebt"
(1912, dir. Max Mack) by Marian Stefanowski

www.degruyter.com

Acknowledgments

The first idea for what has now taken the shape of this book goes back to a time when I was discovering the German films held in the Desmet Collection of the Nederlands Filmmuseum (now Eye Filmmuseum Amsterdam) as a graduate student at the University of Amsterdam in the early 1990s. For years to come, my enthusiasm for the legacy of the pre-Weimar period of German cinema has found its intellectual home in the communities of early cinema scholars in Amsterdam and at the annual Giornate del Cinema Muto in Pordenone, Italy. Among the Amsterdam group, I am particularly grateful to Thomas Elsaesser, Michael Punt, Ivo Blom, Alison McMahan, Wanda Strauven and the late Karel Dibbets; among the Pordenone regulars I especially want to thank Heide Schlüpmann, Kristin Thompson, David Bordwell, Tom Gunning and Rick Altman, who have taken an interest in my work and offered commentary and advice on various occasions. As the book was shaping up into its present form, I have profited immensely from the stimulating intellectual environment provided on a day-to-day basis by my colleagues at "Cinepoetics – Center for Advanced Film Studies," Freie Universität Berlin, and at the Department of Media Studies of the Filmuniversität Babelsberg KONRAD WOLF. In completing the manuscript, I had the fervent collegial support of Eileen Rositzka, who guided the process of completion and, in doing so, more than once performed overnight formatting miracles on the text and the illustrations. Mary Hennessy, who was of invaluable assistance in copy-editing the text and whose incisive comments helped to improve much more than just language and style, worked similar wonders.

A shorter version of Chapter 1 appeared in *The Titanic in Myth and Memory. Representations in Visual and Literary Culture*, eds. Tim Bergfelder and Sarah Street (London and New York 2004). Parts of Chapters 2 and 3 originate from earlier versions published in *A Second Life. German Cinema Cinema's First Decades*, ed. Thomas Elsaesser (Amsterdam 1996). Chapter 4 expands on material that was first published in *A New History of German Cinema*, eds. Jennifer M. Kapczynski and Michael D. Richardson (Rochester and New York 2012). Another version of Chapter 6 was published in *Film 1900. Technology, Perception, Culture*, eds. Annemone Ligensa and Klaus Kreimeier (New Barnet 2009). Chapter 7 builds on research first published in *Film History* 11:4 (1999) and in *New Perspectives in Sound Studies*, eds. Dominique Nasta and Didier Huvelle (Brussels 2004). Chapter 8 appeared in slightly different form in *NECSUS – European Journal of Media Studies* 1:1 (2012). An earlier version of Chapter 9 was included in *Mind the Screen. Media Concepts According to Thomas Elsaesser*, eds. Jaap Koijman, Patricia Pisters and Wanda Strauven (Amsterdam 2008).

https://doi.org/10.1515/9783110613551-201

Contents

Part 2: **Synchronizing the senses**

Introduction

Film, history and historicity

This book is not a history of German cinema between 1910 and 1930. Far from providing a full account of the trends and tendencies representative of the overall course of German cinema during this period, it addresses a set of questions that take the project down a much more fractured and staggered route. Instead of offering a full-blown macrohistory, it proposes to study the minuscule forms of historicity emerging from a multiplicity of transformative moments and movements occurring over these two decades. In terms of the material covered – the historical breaks and political upheavals broached, the films and filmmakers mentioned, the genres and modes of production discussed, the contexts and frameworks established – this book aspires to be suggestive rather than comprehensive.[1]

In another sense, and despite its obvious limitations in scope, this book's objectives can be seen as a work not only of film history but of film historiography. The idea behind the writing of this book was to define and flesh out a number of key aesthetic shifts and cultural force fields that not only underpinned but actively drove broader developments within German cinema and that have dynamically shaped our sense of its meaning and relevance. Insomuch as the concept of "historicity" as defined by Philip Rosen can serve as a heuristic tool to grasp "the particular interrelations of the mode of historiography and the types of construction of history related by it," the term is used here to mark an alternative approach to the empirical, "real" pastness of the German cinema.[2] Focusing on what François Hartog calls "regimes of historicity," which are historically specific, ever-shifting orders that organize our sense of space and time, this approach is both reflexive and experience-oriented. It is reflexive insofar as it is attentive to the constructedness of any sense of history and seeks to explore the tensions and frictions that become visible when zooming in on moments of crisis, modulation and reversal. It is oriented towards the experiential insofar as these tensions and frictions in the construction of a historical past themselves

1 Compared to the overall views e.g. taken in Sabine Hake: *German National Cinema*. 2nd ed., New York 2008, or Stephen Brockman: *A Critical History of German Film*. Rochester 2010.
2 Philip Rosen: *Changed Mummified. Cinema, Historicity, Theory*. Minneapolis and London 2001, XI.

https://doi.org/10.1515/9783110613551-001

mark shifts and contradictions in the experiential economy of a given time, both lived and remembered.[3]

The premise of the following chapters is that the signatures of these shifts and tensions in the modalities of experience become visible in the aesthetic articulation and cultural agency of cinema. They argue that taking a closer look at a number of particular cinematic and cultural constellations – 'particular' here meant both in the sense of 'distinct' and 'notable' and in the sense of 'discrete' and 'partial' – brings into much sharper focus the horizons of historicity against which – in all their kaleidoscopic diversity – any history of the German cinema is written.

In the writing of this history, moments of political discontinuity such as the end of World War I, the inauguration of the first German Republic, the deterioration of Weimar democracy after 1930 and the National Socialist Party takeover in January 1933 may serve as didactically useful and heuristically essential principles of organization, according to which historical evidence can be presented. At the same time, they also often serve as convenient turning points from one interpretative system to another. The more or less neat integration of film history into the overriding order of a political chronology necessarily suggests a 'totality' of historical reality; its underlying assumptions can appear both epistemologically and ideologically problematic. Representing film history according to pre-given patterns of political periodization runs the risk of overlooking the complex formations of much more subcutaneous layers of continuity and small-scale, gradual modulation within the field of film culture.

At the center of the present book is thus not the desire to grasp the totality of German cinema in the years between 1910 and 1930. Instead, its core interests lie in the 'contingency,' 'singularity' and 'particularity' of the historical phenomena on which it attempts to shed light. With Michel Foucault and Michel de Certeau, these interests share a "fascination with limits" grounded in the notion that any method of writing history, understood as "work on the margins,"[4] is primarily concerned with the analysis of "situations" and the study of the interweavements, bifurcations and dispersions through which the respective borderlines become decipherable and potentially meaningful.[5] Viewed from this perspective, individual films can be regarded as threshold regions of the historical, in which aesthetic modes and cultural meanings converge, thwart each other and then disperse. Accordingly, the common question bracketing all of the following

---

3 François Hartog: *Regimes of Historicity. Presentism and Experiences of Time*. New York 2017, 16–18.
4 Michel de Certeau: *The Writing of History* [1975]. New York 1988, 40 and 43.
5 Michel Foucault: *The Archaeology of Knowledge* [1969]. New York et al. 1976, 168 and 176.

chapters is not – at least not primarily – how the aesthetic production and poetic logic of a given film (or group of films) *relates to history* but how it dynamically situates itself *within history* and negotiates its own historicity. Slightly modifying Siegfried Kracauer's well-known axiom, the chapters of this book attempt to think "History" through the films, not above them.[6]

Along with Kracauer, my approach aligns with Jacques Rancière's considerations of the "historicity of film."[7] In opposition to a linear conception of historical time, Rancière shares Walter Benjamin's "vision of history as the co-presence of several temporalities in one temporal frame."[8] In opposition to a view of history driven by faith in human progress and informed by the division of the past into a sequence of identifiable periods – which, for Rancière, are nothing more than manifestations of institutional and historiographical hegemony – he posits the "distribution of the sensible" as a paradoxical force shaping our sense of history and proposes that we look at it as an intricate meshwork of dynamically overlapping and diverging "lines of temporality."[9] From Rancière's perspective, writing history means making visible the temporal distortions and intertwinements that occur within normative systems of conventionalized practices and social procedures:

> The visibility of a form of expression as an artistic form depends on a historically constituted regime of perception and intelligibility. This does not mean that it becomes invisible with the emergence of a new regime. [...] At a given point in time, several regimes coexist and intermingle in the works themselves.[10]

In this sense, the historicity of a film is determined by the singular place and the singular form its conditions of visibility and presence take on when

---

6 Cf. Siegfried Kracauer: *History. The Last Things Before the Last* [1969]. Princeton 1995, 192. For a more comprehensive elaboration on Kracauer's historical thinking in relation to the aesthetics of film, cf. Michael Wedel: Grausame Geschichte. Kracauer, *Visual History* und Film. In: Bernhard Groß, Vrääth Öhner and Drehli Robnik (eds.): *Film und Gesellschaft denken mit Siegfried Kracauer*. Vienna 2018, 107–119.
7 Jacques Rancière: Die Geschichtlichkeit des Films [1998]. In: Eva Hohenberger and Judith Keilbach (eds.): *Die Gegenwart der Vergangenheit. Dokumentarfilm, Fernsehen und Geschichte*. Berlin 2003, 230–246. For a more detailed account of Rancière's notion of historicity in relation to film, cf. Michael Wedel: Film als Rhythmus der Gemeinschaft. Zu einer Denkfigur bei Rancière. In: Drehli Robnik, Thomas Hübel and Siegfried Mattl (eds.): *Das Streit-Bild. Film, Geschichte und Politik bei Jacques Rancière*. Vienna 2010, 145–160.
8 Jacques Rancière: *Ist Kunst widerständig?* Berlin 2008, 75.
9 Rancière: *Ist Kunst widerständig?*, 75.
10 Cf. Jacques Rancière: *The Politics of Aesthetics. The Distribution of the Sensible*. London and New York 2005, 50.

different temporal modalities relate to and encompass each other in the field of the aesthetic.

Historical poetics: Effects and affects

With regard to film, the following chapters seek to locate Rancière's field of the aesthetic in expressive forms that define the historical conditions of possibility for the emergence of different (and often coexisting) regimes of experience and in the configurative space between poetics and culture. In many of his writings (not least about film), Rancière has himself suggested a close connection between poetics as a practice and mode of thinking on the one hand and the aesthetic as a cultural and political agent on the other. Connecting the two concepts remains an intricate theoretical and methodological maneuver, especially when it comes to film.[11] One reason for this difficulty is disciplinary. Within film studies, the most influential model of a poetics of cinema was developed to provide explanations for the establishment and stabilization of exactly the normative systems of conventionalized practices and social procedures that Rancière considers subject to the intervention of the aesthetic regime.

David Bordwell's programmatic outline of a poetics of cinema is based on the theoretical premise that any given film is structured by thematic and stylistic principles that organize its "phenomenal" particulars and materials into a whole of artistic form in order to achieve certain effects. He outlines two interrelated areas of poetics, one analytical and one historical. Whereas *analytical* poetics centers on the question: "What are the principles according to which films are constructed and through which they achieve particular effects?," *historical* poetics asks: "How and why have these principles arisen and changed in particular empirical circumstances?" The overriding goal of both lines of inquiry is to understand how "cinema turns materials circulating in the culture into significant

---

11 Cf. Jacques Rancière: *Film Fables*. Oxford and New York 2006; *The Intervals of Cinema*. London and New York 2014. Cf. also Jacques Rancière: *The Names of History. On the Poetics of Knowledge*. Minneapolis and London 1994; *Aesthetics and Its Discontents*. Cambridge and Malden 2009; *Mute Speech. Literature, Critical Theory, and Politics*. New York 2011. The conceptual relation between poetics and aesthetics in Rancière is further complicated by the fact that "poetics" in an Aristotelian mimetic sense is sometimes understood synonymously with the "representative regime of art" while in other instances it is considered to form part and parcel of the aesthetic regime of modernity. On his use of poetics as a concept cf. the contributions to the section "Poetics" in: Jean-Philippe Deranty (ed.): *Jacques Rancière. Key Concepts*. Abingdon and New York 2010. Also cf. Davide Panagia: *Jacques Rancière's Sentiments*. Durham and London 2018, ch. 2.

experiences for viewers" and how "those experiences both shape and are shaped by a variety of cultural forces."[12]

In the context of its neo-formalist research framework, a Bordwellian poetics of cinema, focused as it is on "film's constructional principles and effects," studies the "constitution, functions, purposes and historical manifestations" of cinematic form.[13] It proceeds according to a logic of poetic meaning-making that begins with material particulars and moves up to compositional patterns, tying these patterns to creative purposes and practices and relating the latter to competing systems of principles that set historically and culturally specific norms and standards for the ways that spectators might make sense of a given film or group of films. To the extent that Bordwell's model posits a causal or at least functional relationship between the domain of filmmaking and the perception and understanding of films, it is conceived as "a poetics of *effect*."[14]

Indebted as my own approach is to the notion of historical poetics (and the methods of what is referred to as the New Film History,[15] to which Bordwell's model has made a major contribution), I propose that we think about the impact of film not only in terms of calculated effects on processes of cognitive understanding, but also in terms of a "poetics of affect," emphasizing the fact – which Bordwell mentions – that cinematic spectatorship involves not just capacities of mental cognition, but also the "*embodied* mind engaging with the film."[16] In this respect, my approach is more closely aligned with one version of the aesthetics and poetics of film that has been developed by Hermann Kappelhoff with recourse to phenomenological film theory and in close dialogue with Rancière.

Kappelhoff argues that "cinema spectators [...] embody film images so that the world of the film becomes fused with a spectator's world as though the audience participated with the film in a shared *reality*."[17] From this theoretical perspective, cinema "may be imagined as a medium that makes the historical basis or our sense and perception faculties visible to us, our ways of sensing and our self-experience explicit without presenting history as truth or history

---

12 David Bordwell: *Poetics of Cinema*. New York and London, 2008, 23.

13 Bordwell: *Poetics of Cinema*, 23.

14 Bordwell: *Poetics of Cinema*, 54.

15 For an overview of the premises and methodologies of the New Film History, cf. Thomas Elsaesser: The New Film History as Media Archaeology. In: *CiNéMAS* 14:2–3 (2004), 75–117; James Chapman, Mark Glancy and Sue Harper (eds.): *The New Film History. Sources, Methods, Approaches*. London 2009.

16 Bordwell: *Poetics of Cinema*, 44 (emphasis added).

17 Hermann Kappelhoff: *The Politics and Poetics of Cinematic Realism*. New York 2015, ix.

as making sense."[18] Cinema's historicity is not defined, then, by lending filmic representations to historical events that can only be made sense of in retrospect. Instead, in the modern regime of aesthetics, of which Rancière like Kappelhoff believes cinema is the central vehicle,

> the sensory-physical relation to the world, the bodily being-in-the-world, is determined by forms of perceptual sensations, of affects, and of speaking positions derived from the historically contingent arrangement of a commonly shared world of the senses. [...] Aesthetics, therefore, designates the connection between an arrangement of art and an idea of thinking itself. And in this connection it is related to the historicity of a community, founded solely in the positions and relations in which we determine how we experience our reality, how we communicate with one another about this, how we describe and process it, in short, how we can think our reality.[19]

As Kappelhoff makes clear, "the idea of aesthetics [...] is in no way identical to concrete poetics and aesthetic concepts of film; rather it is realized in ever new proposals about the relationship between poetics and politics."[20] It is on the level of the concrete aesthetic concepts of (a) film, its mode of expressivity and the experiential reality it assumes, that a poetics of affect becomes operative in a twofold way:

> It encompasses on the one hand dramaturgy, the design and arrangement of the complex of scenes, which follow the calculation in order to shape a particular course of feeling in the spectator's process of perceiving what is represented; on the other hand, it includes the rhetorical strategies to provoke and model specific emotional reactions by introducing techniques of calculated affecting. The term *affect dramaturgy* is aimed at the circumstances that individual scenes can be assigned to specific qualities of affect with particular expressive patterns of pathos and staging strategies, and that these qualities, in and of themselves and in their succession, follow a calculation to affect the spectator. While *affect rhetoric* means a calculation of representation, which is capable of introducing expressive modalities of the film image compliant with the standards of a particular intention to affect.[21]

Kappelhoff's outline of a poetics of affect is sensitive to the culturally diverse and historically dynamic "*affect-economic function* of media practices."[22] In notable contrast to Bordwell's understanding of the term, "practices" here refer to

---

18 Kappelhoff: *The Politics and Poetics of Cinematic Realism*, xiii.
19 Kappelhoff: *The Politics and Poetics of Cinematic Realism*, 7.
20 Kappelhoff: *The Politics and Poetics of Cinematic Realism*, 17.
21 Hermann Kappelhoff: *Front Lines of Community. Hollywood Between War and Democracy.* Berlin and Boston 2018, 103.
22 Kappelhoff: *Front Lines of Community*, 103.

the procedures and protocols in processes of reception as much as production. As the nodal point where both dimensions coincide, it is only in their specific constellation of reciprocity that a distinctive kind of experience is brought forth – as is, in the final analysis, the film itself as an aesthetic object with an identifiable index of its historicity. In the expanded context of its "affect-economic function" the concept of "*poiesis*" figures here as a special kind of "poetic making" and cultural practice, historically tied to cinema and directed toward the generation and administration of feelings and perceptual sensations.[23]

Film culture and popular cinema

With the advent of technical media and film at the end of the 19th century, cinema emerged as one of the public institutions chiefly responsible for the generation and distribution of affects in society.[24] In performing this task, popular cinema (just as popular culture more generally) has known its own dynamics of development, embedded in a variety of traditions and media practices. The history of these practices is, of course, hardly independent from the social and political frameworks within which they operate, but neither is it necessarily in tune with the chronological patterns of social and political change. Whereas most historians of German cinema tend to divide their material according to a strict political chronology, the present book accounts for popular cinema's cultural obstinacy and genuine historical momentum by cutting across two periods that are usually kept apart: Weimar cinema and early German film, or more precisely, the pre-World War I period of late Wilhelmine cinema.[25] Instead of adhering to the grate of

---

23 Cf. Hermann Kappelhoff: *Kognition und Reflexion. Zur Theorie filmischen Denkens*. Berlin and Boston 2018.

24 Cf. Friedrich Kittler: *Grammophone, Film, Typewriter*. Stanford 1999; Francesco Casetti: *Eye of the Century. Film, Experience, Modernity*. New York 2008.

25 As separate periods in the history of the German cinema, both eras have been studied extensively, in recent years with an increasing emphasis on popular genres, counterweighing the traditional bias towards the German art films and *Autorenfilme* of the 1910s and 1920s and their prominent directors. For the two authoritative accounts available in English, cf. Heide Schlüpmann: *The Uncanny Gaze. The Drama of Early German Cinema*. Urbana-Champaign et al. 2010 (first published in German as *Unheimlichkeit des Blicks. Das Drama des frühen deutschen Kinos* in 1990); and Thomas Elsaesser: *Weimar Cinema and After. Germany's Historical Imaginary*. London and New York 2000 (first published in German as *Das Weimarer Kino – aufgeklärt und doppelbödig*. Berlin 1999). That many of the celebrated classics directed by Robert Wiene, F.W. Murnau or Fritz Lang at the time were, as a general rule, not removed from but a vital part of the popular genre system is addressed in several chapters below.

Germany's political history, the time frame of this book spans two major transformations in the film industry and in film culture that had far-reaching implications for the media practices associated with cinema and its "affect-economic function": German cinema's transition from short-film programs to feature-length narrative films around 1910 and its transition from 'silent' to sound film in the years around 1930.

What characterizes these two points of transformation? Given that Germany was a net importer of films, one key to understanding the transformations of German cinema before World War I is the way films were traded. Patterns of distribution constituted one major factor in both production and exhibition. Until 1906/07, the short form of the films entering the market can be attributed to German cinema's origins in the exceptionally well-developed culture of the *Varieté*. Cinematic presentation was thus tailored along the solidly established lines of the program structure of popular variety entertainment.[26] In most cases, an introductory piece of music was followed by an *actualité* (factual film) and then a drama sandwiched between two humorous numbers. After a break, this structure was repeated, but the tension was heightened by the appeal of the 'great attraction' (which could be fictional or non-fictional) and the concluding earthy ("derbkomisch") comedy. The short length of the films, which usually ranged between 200 and 300 meters, meant that non-fiction material dominated the screens and that the majority of fiction films before 1907 were comic episodes.

The establishment and proliferation of permanent cinemas – the mushrooming of the *Ladenkinos* – aroused aggressive competitive practices in the commercial sector.[27] As a consequence of over-ambitious cinema building projects, admission price wars and the accelerated turnover of frequent program changes, the German film industry found itself in a deep crisis that lasted from 1906 to 1909. A feverish second-hand trade in complete programs among cinema owners was both a precondition for and an inevitable result of the attendance boom. However, the insatiable demand for films only sucked in cheap imports and choked domestic productions, which were unable to compete in terms of cost. Due to the trade and barter system among exhibitors, the few existing distribution companies (only five in 1907) were unable to consolidate into an autonomous branch of the film industry or serve as a sorely needed link between production

---

26 Cf. Corinna Müller: *Frühe deutsche Kinematographie. Formale, wirtschaftliche und kulturelle Entwicklungen 1902–1912*. Stuttgart and Weimar 1994, 11–23; Josef Garncarz: *Maßlose Unterhaltung. Zur Etablierung des Films in Deutschland 1896–1914*. Frankfurt a. M. and Basel 2010, 17–68.
27 The following summary of decisive changes in the distribution sector around 1910 is based on Müller: *Frühe deutsche Kinematographie*, especially ch. 4.

companies and theater owners. Instead, exhibitors themselves set up local and regional distribution networks, which, from 1908 onwards, were structured around a film rental system that was priced according to the running times of a complete program and referred to as the *Staffelmieten-System*, with the consequence that older films were recycled and new ones suffered rapid devaluation. The first attempt to break up this system was the (short-lived) marketing ploy of the *Terminfilm*: individual films with limited release dates that were heavily advertised in advance in the trade press. Introduced in 1909 in the hope of cashing in on the thirst for novelty attractions and exclusivity, this measure failed to establish itself as a profitable practice. The undeveloped production sector was simply unable to deliver quality products with short turnarounds. The *Terminfilm* did, however, encourage a rapid rise in the number of specialized distribution companies (22 in early 1910). Following the lead of the French company Pathé-Frères and its push towards vertical integration, the German distribution and exhibition sectors stabilized around 1909/10 with the introduction of twice-weekly program changes and the transition from selling to renting. Only then did the trade of single films (instead of pre-set programs) gain a foothold in the German market, and the short film variety program, as a distinct historical phase, came to an end.[28]

Late in 1910, the unexpected success of the American boxing film JACK JOHNSON VS. JIM JEFFRIES (1,880 meters), distributed exclusively by Paul Davidson's Projektions-AG 'Union' (PAGU), and the Danish production AFGRUNDEN (THE ABYSS, 850 meters), starring Asta Nielsen and distributed exclusively by Ludwig Gottschalk's Düsseldorfer Film-Manufaktur, pointed to the financial potential of the single feature-length film when marketed under conditions of restricted access and sole distribution rights. What would come to be known in other countries as a zoning and clearance agreement, guaranteeing an exhibitor the exclusive rights to a film for a specific period of time in a specific geographical area, became known in Germany as the *Monopolfilm* (monopoly film). As elsewhere, it proved the single most important factor in changing the early film business, leading to a revolution in virtually every aspect of the industry. A local monopoly allowed exhibitors to charge higher admission prices at the box office, which in turn allowed distributors to advance capital to producers who could invest in higher production values and operate with larger budgets.

---

28 Cf. Corinna Müller: Variationen des Kinoprogramms. Filmform und Filmgeschichte. In: Corinna Müller and Harro Segeberg (eds.): *Die Modellierung des Kinofilms. Zur Geschichte des Kinoprogramms zwischen Kurzfilm und Langfilm (1905/06–1918)*. Munich 1998, 43–75.

The feature film as a commodity traded under monopoly conditions improved profits in all three areas of the film business, boosting domestic production and allowing the German film industry to consolidate from within. The *Monopolfilm* also created the first star system, with actresses like Asta Nielsen and Henny Porten achieving fame solely on the basis of their work in the cinema, bolstered by advertising campaigns that focused on single films rather than mixed programs. The new product also encouraged various innovations in exhibition, such as exclusive premieres and the building of the first *Lichtspieltheater*, large halls that seated hundreds of customers, foreshadowing many of the characteristics of the future *Kinopalast* (cinema palace) of the 1920s.[29] Once the distribution practices of the *Monopolfilm* had been established as the norm in 1910/11, the domestic production sector expanded substantially. In the following years, the German film industry gradually moved toward international standards. By 1913, it had a flourishing star-and-genre cinema sector as well as an art cinema or *Autorenfilm* culture well before the beginning of the war and the closing of the borders to French imports.

Comparable to the emergence of the feature-length dramatic film in the early 1910s, the transition from 'silent' to sound film in the years around 1930 was one complex and contingent phenomenon of the transformation of film culture. Far from constituting a linear progression toward perfecting the medium's expressive means, dictated by technological availability and feasibility, German cinema's conversion to sound was an uneven process driven by the proprietorial and economic considerations of the Tobis-Klangfilm trust, backed by the electrical industry and in collaboration with some of the major film-producing studios like Ufa. This process was also repeatedly hindered by smaller companies and theater owners, who were unable to raise the money needed to adapt their studios and theaters to the new industrial sound standards, including the considerable license fees that had to be paid to patent holders.[30] Ufa, the largest German studio and the first to carry out the transition from silent to sound film production in September 1929, was still deeply in debt by the summer of 1932, owing 2.25 million Reichsmark to the Klangfilm consortium.

In the production sector, the conversion to sound film technology (both sound-on-disc and sound-on-film) had been by and large completed by 1931 (in 1930 there were still 45 silent films produced in German studios, while in 1931

---

29 Cf. Anke J. Hübel: *Big, bigger, Cinema! Film- und Kinomarketing in Deutschland (1910–1933)*. Marburg 2011, 172–213.

30 Cf. Wolfgang Mühl-Benninghaus: *Das Ringen um den Tonfilm. Strategien der Elektro- und der Filmindustrie in den 20er und 30er Jahren*. Düsseldorf 1999; Corinna Müller: *Vom Stummfilm zum Tonfilm*. Munich 2003.

this number was down to two). The transition took considerably longer in the exhibition sector and was much more fragmented: in April 1929, 30 cinemas in 24 cities were equipped with Tobis sound projectors. Of the total of 5,071 German film theaters, only 233 or four percent had installed Tobis sound projectors and speakers by the end of 1929, a number that would rise to 35 percent by the end of the following year, to 51 percent by August 1931 and to 68 percent by September 1932. The homogenization of the – rapidly shrinking – exhibition sector began to show only in December 1932, when the number of silent cinemas had decreased to 815 compared to 4,256 converted theaters, which now made up 84 percent of the total number. In March 1935, there were only two theaters without sound equipment left.[31]

The first part of this book addresses some of the consequences and contradictions arising from the historical transformations that took place after 1910, affecting the German film industry in its entirety by challenging its aesthetic premises and changing the cultural role ascribed to cinema in Germany. The individual chapters in this first part each offer close readings of individual films within their respective cultural contexts. The expressive registers and "pictorial affects" of the melodramatic mode[32] constitute the common ground on which the chapters discuss the strategies of cinema's aesthetic and discursive re-positioning from the early 1910s to the early 1920s.

Analyzing one of the earliest cinematic treatments of the Titanic disaster, chapter 1 reconstructs the poetic and discursive strategies of topical event cinema as well as the shifting aesthetic and moral grounds it had to navigate in 1912. The uncanny proximity between the cultural legitimacy of the *Autorenfilm* and the blunt commercialism of the *Sensationsfilm* that emerges in this chapter remains a central concern in chapters 2 and 3, which are devoted to the question of how the directors Max Mack, in his film ZWEIMAL GELEBT (LIVED TWICE, 1912), and Franz Hofer, in his 1916 reworking of Goethe's Volkslied *Heideröslein*, mobilized the cultural traditions and affective potentials of melodrama to

---

31 For a concise overview and critical assessment of the technological, economical and jurisdictional premises of the German film industry's conversion to sound, cf. Michael Wedel: Klärungsprozesse. Tobis, Klangfilm und die Tonfilmumstellung 1928–1932. In: Jan Distelmeyer (ed.): *Tonfilmfrieden / Tonfilmkrieg. Die Geschichte der Tobis vom Technik-Syndikat zum Staatskonzern.* Munich 2003, 34–43.
32 Here understood less as a generic formula than, with Christine Gledhill, in the sense of a specific mode of aesthetic articulation and form of "cultural work," providing a medium of interchange and overlap between genres and cultural classifications. Cf. Christine Gledhill: Rethinking Genre. In: Christine Gledhill and Linda Williams (eds.): *Reinventing Film Studies.* London and New York 2000, 221–243.

cinematically reflect subjective states of psychological crisis and moral insecurity within an increasingly porous fabric of gender relations and social divisions.

Having already played a key role in the establishment of the long dramatic feature as the prime product of the German film business, the Danish actress Asta Nielsen has become a center of interest in debates over cinema's social impact (as discussed in chapter 3), popular appeal and cultural value. Chapter 4 sheds light on a critical moment in Asta Nielsen's career around 1920, when new filmmaking standards – epitomized in Germany by Ernst Lubitsch at the time – put pressure on the affective economy of her acting and concomitantly threatened to destroy the careful construction of a "phantasmatic intimacy" between the actress and her audience. Building on the insight that metaphorical and allegorical constructions play a prominent role in the affective poetics of almost all the films discussed in the first four chapters, the chapter concluding the first part of the book reconsiders the central contribution made by cinematic metaphoricity to the modulation of atmospheres and affects with regard to the early work of F.W. Murnau, with his idiosyncratic oscillation between expressionist fantasy and melodramatic *Kammerspielfilm*.

The chapters in the second part of the book, "Synchronizing the Senses," trace another, closely related historical trajectory within popular German cinema, likewise resulting from the transition to feature-length dramatic films in the early 1910s. Looking at developments and debates relating to the technological possibilities of implementing a 'third dimension' in the spatial arrangement of cinema's affective economy, chapters 6, 7 and 8 investigate the cultural traditions (but also ideological and political implications) of ideas and practices aimed at transcending the division between screen and audience, either through the use of music and sound or via the plasticity of 'haptic visuality' that directly affected the senses of the spectators.

Chapter 6 takes the metaphor of film as a "plastic art in motion" (Ricciotto Canudo) as its point of departure to draw our attention to contemporary experiments in stereoscopic film and explore their impact on the notion of cinematic expressivity that informed popular filmmaking's modes of direct audience address long before the advent of what came to be known as expressionist film after 1920. Chapter 7 focuses on one particular genre, the German music film, between 1914 and 1929, reconstructing the experiential and affective horizons that technical systems for synchronizing visual and acoustic perception opened up for contemporary audiences. By 1929/30, the time had come to redefine the ways in which the techniques and technologies of the genre of the musical film could be applied in the film industry in order to synchronize the acoustic and the visual.

As Chapter 8 sets out to show, the process of redefining the technical conditions of the 'audiovisual pact' also shifted aesthetic and ideological horizons. Within the context of Universal's efforts to adapt their early sound films to the German market, this chapter takes the production history and controversial reception of the German version of Universal's ALL QUIET ON THE WESTERN FRONT (IM WESTEN NICHTS NEUES, 1929/30) as a paradigmatic example of 'crisis historiography' in order to situate Universal's import strategy within the heated political climate of the late Weimar Republic. Like the other chapters in the book – including its epilogue – my critical re-assessment of the German version of Lewis Milestone's film seeks to reveal how "senses of rupture" become tangible as markers of cinema's historicity: the splits and fissures in the poetic texture and affective economy of the films themselves become indicative of the breaks and continuities, pressures and tensions that existed within (and often beyond) the culture of which they were part.

Part 1
Pictorial affects

1 Cinematic Titanic: Early German cinema and the modern media event

1.1 Event and attraction: Early cinema and after

Recent scholarship has repeatedly emphasized a secret affinity between the early "cinema of attractions" and Hollywood's post-classical event cinema. In his seminal essay on early cinema aesthetics, Tom Gunning argues that early cinema's "ambiguous heritage" reveals itself not only in the artistic practices of avant-garde cinema, but also in the commercial cinema of spectacle:

> The cinema of attractions expends little energy creating characters with psychological motivations or individual personality. Making use of both fictional and non-fictional attractions, its energy moves outward towards an acknowledged spectator rather than inward towards the character-based situations essential to classical narrative.[1]

Gunning qualifies any easy comparison between early cinema aesthetics and post-classical Hollywood, however, by arguing that contemporary Hollywood cinema's special effects are "tamed attractions."[2] They are "tamed" insofar as the attractions they offer are specifically cinematic, whereas the "unique event" by which early films "incite visual curiosity" and supply "pleasure through an exciting spectacle" can also be documentary.[3] Gunning is not the first film historian to point out that early cinema's historically-defined audience appeal used a mode of spectatorial address that reached beyond the purely filmic. Shaped for collective reception by an audience addressed as physically present at the site of exhibition (rather than as imaginary, artificially 'isolated' spectators), the appeal of early cinema was often inextricably bound to the audience's specific "pre-knowledge," activated via extra-filmic referentiality in both choice of story material and exhibition practice.[4]

Beyond the manifold formal analogies between early cinema and post-classical event cinema, the event cinema of the early 20th century also corresponds

---

1 Tom Gunning: The Cinema of Attractions. Early Film, Its Spectator and the Avantgarde. In: Thomas Elsaesser with Adam Barker (ed.): *Early Cinema. Space, Frame, Narrative.* London 1990, 56–62, here 59. This essay was first published in *Wide Angle* 8:3–4 (Fall 1986), 63–70.
2 Gunning: The Cinema of Attractions, 61.
3 Gunning: The Cinema of Attractions, 58.
4 Cf. Charles Musser: The Nickelodeon Era Begins. Establishing the Framework for Hollywood's Mode of Representation. In: Elsaesser with Barker (eds.): *Early Cinema*, 256–273. Musser's essay was first published in 1984.

https://doi.org/10.1515/9783110613551-002

with that of the late 20th century in terms of its constant referral to a wider cultural framework. For Miriam Hansen, both forms of cinematic practice can be brought into significant constellation not so much in terms of constituting their own public spheres, "defined by specific relations of representation and reception," but by virtue of being "part of a larger social horizon, defined by other media, by overlapping local, national and global, face-to-face and de-territorialized structures of public life":

> Both periods are characterized by a profound transformation of the relations of cultural representation and reception [...] Both stages of media culture vary from a classical norm of controlling reception through a strong diegetic effect, ensured by particular textual strategies and a suppression of the exhibition context; by contrast, pre-classical and post-classical forms of spectatorship give the spectator a greater leeway, for better or for worse, in interacting with the film, a greater awareness of exhibition and cultural intertexts. [...] Putting early-modern and postmodern forms of media consumption in a constellation may take away some of the inevitability the classical paradigm has acquired both in Hollywood self-promotion and in functionalist film histories.[5]

It is a point of contention as to whether early cinema in Wilhelmine Germany likewise constituted the discursive horizon, the catalyst and crystallization point of the radically modern form of public experience Hansen describes.[6] Indeed, film historians have characterized early German cinema as a failed attempt to break free from the established arts and conservative spheres of interest. In these accounts, the defining features of the stylistic and institutional development of early German cinema were largely sought and found in the encroachments of the literary *Autorenfilm* and contemporary theater culture, in the pressures of the cinema reform movement and film censorship and in war propaganda and the nanny state.[7] The critical debate about early German cinema has provided some

---

5 Miriam Hansen: Early Cinema, Late Cinema. Permutations of the Public Sphere. In: *Screen* 34:3 (Autumn 1993), 197–201, here 206 and 210.

6 Cf. Miriam Bratu Hansen: America, Paris, the Alps: Kracauer (and Benjamin) on Cinema and Modernity. In: Leo Charney and Vanessa Schwartz (eds.): *Cinema and the Invention of Modern Life.* Berkeley, Los Angeles and London 1995, 362–402, here 366–367: "[t]he cinema was not just one among a number of perceptual technologies, nor even the culmination of a particular logic of the gaze; it was above all [...] the single most expansive horizon in which the effects of modernity were reflected, rejected or denied, transmuted or negotiated. It was both part and prominent symptom of a crisis as which modernity was perceived, and at the same time it evolved into a social discourse in which a wide variety of groups sought to come to terms with the traumatic impact of modernization."

7 For a critical revision of this attitude towards early German cinema, cf. Michael Wedel: Filmform und Filmformat. Bausteine zu einer Mediengeschichte des frühen deutschen Kinos. In: *KINtop* 8 (1999), 189–194.

of the terms on the basis of which scholars began to recognize the necessity of contextualizing and historicizing individual films. This recognition has not however been conceived as implying a new, genuinely modern capacity of media incorporation, nor has it transposed into a functional analysis of the aesthetic strategies in early cinema's popular genre formations.

It is in this respect that Mime Misu's film TITANIC – IN NACHT UND EIS (TITANIC – IN NIGHT AND ICE, 1912), long assumed lost, provides valuable insights. Rarely is the oft-noted correspondence between the specific forms of *Öffentlichkeit* (public sphere) created by the commercial cinema of attractions at the turn of the last century and that of the previous one been concretized to the same extent as in this case. The publicity campaign for the German release of James Cameron's TITANIC (1997) led to the emergence of Misu's film, originally known only from contemporary reports, as a film-historical reference point.[8] Even before the two films' differences and analogies could be charted in terms of the textual strategies they used to represent the Titanic disaster cinematically (i.e. a common generic identity), the films were already linked by the various media and marketing mechanisms they used to draw public interest. In both cases, at two different historical junctures, these mechanisms helped transform the cinematic representation of a historical event into 'event cinema.'

The following discussion of the media discourse in and around Misu's TITANIC – IN NACHT UND EIS is meant to bring into sharper focus the antinomies involved in mediating between the global and the local, between the competing desires for visual pleasure and collective *Trauerarbeit* (mourning work) in the context of the German public sphere of 1912.

1.2 Mapping a media event: Titanic and the cinematic imaginary

Less than two weeks after the ocean giant of the White Star Line sank in the early hours of April 15, 1912, the German film company Continental-Kunstfilm announced the May release of a filmic dramatization of the tragedy. Under the title THE SINKING OF THE TITANIC, Continental was to produce a "sea drama" that would depict "the whole disaster, including the collision with the iceberg and highly dramatic scenes on board."[9] In May, the release date was pushed back to June 22

---

8 On the biography of the Romanian-born Misu (1888–1953) and the circumstances of the rediscovery of his film, cf. Michael Wedel: *Kollision im Kino. Mime Misu und der Untergang der "Titanic."* Munich 2012.

9 *Erste Internationale Film-Zeitung* 17 (27 April 1912), 31.

and Continental issued an announcement – "in order to avoid possible misunderstandings" – that Misu's film would be "a longish drama, absolutely faultless with respect to dramatic values and technical implementation. It is therefore neither an arbitrary series of scenes (partly taken from older footage) nor is it blatant sensation-seeking."[10]

The different versions of the Titanic disaster that had already reached German cinemas did indeed include old, existing footage that was adapted only superficially to fit the requirements of the current media event – as, for example, in DIE SCHWIMMENDEN EISBERGE (THE FLOATING ICEBERGS), which the German newsreel DER TAG IM FILM produced for the week of April 23–29, 1912. This newsreel's topicality and therefore its attraction value rested entirely on a written commentary that was added to the images via intertitles, indicating "floating icebergs are extremely dangerous even for giant ocean cruisers. The Titanic collided with such an iceberg and sank, with approximately 1,500 people losing their lives."[11]

At about the same time, the T. Scherff film company of Leipzig Lindenau advertised a series of 8 ½ x 8 ½ cm magic lantern slides called DER UNTERGANG DER "TITANIC" (THE SINKING OF THE "TITANIC") that offered a "true-to-life account based on original drawings by a famous marine artist" and was "available for immediate delivery."[12] It was probably this series of lantern slides that the central cinema in Pirmasens screened on May 11, with the promise of "the greatest possible appeal." The T. Scherff film company made the slides available for sale or rent ("immediate delivery – low price") together with a "separate cabaret programme with police licence."[13]

But it was the 130-meter Gaumont newsreel KATASTROPHE DER "TITANIC" ("TITANIC" DISASTER) that gained the widest distribution in Germany and internationally.[14] Released on May 11 and distributed initially by the Martin Dentler distribution company (in 20 prints as early as the second week of distribution) and later by the German Gaumont subsidiary Elge-Gaumont, its sequence of shots was necessarily disconnected in nature given that there existed hardly

---

10 Bekanntmachung. In: *Erste Internationale Film-Zeitung* 19 (11 May 1912).
11 *Der Kinematograph* 279 (1 May 1912).
12 *Der Kinematograph* 279 (1 May 1912).
13 *Erste Internationale Film-Zeitung* 19 (11 May 1912).
14 Cf. Stephen Bottomore: *The Titanic and Silent Cinema*. East Sussex 2000, 69–105. The footage was produced by the American Gaumont newsreel ANIMATED WEEKLY. Whether another 400-meter newsreel program about the Titanic disaster produced by the British Globe Company in May 1912 was distributed in Germany, still is to be verified.

any original footage of the Titanic before being destroyed on her maiden voyage.[15] Trade advertisements delivered the following description of the newsreel:

> Captain Smith on the bridge – The Icebergs, the originators of the catastrophe – the colossal crowd of people in front of the White Star Line office in New York – Arrival of the "Carpathia" with the survivors on board – Some of the survivors from the "Titanic" – Mister Marconi, thanks to whose genial invention the lives of over 700 people were saved.[16]

It was less the content of the Gaumont newsreel than the way it was exhibited that created controversy among German film critics and theater owners. In early June, the trade journal *Lichtbild-Bühne* reported on the presentation of the Gaumont newsreel in Katowice. This "actuality footage" had, they reported, already

> done the rounds of all top-class picture palaces in all big towns. [...] They must use every such event to fill their coffers, every dreadful, terrifying and even hideous event. [...] The public everywhere wants "to have been there." They are like the fairy tale character that never learns the meaning of fear. They see the "Titanic" leave port. Then they see an "iceberg." Finally, they see the Carpathia entering New York harbour carrying the "Titanic" survivors.[17]

At the screening of Gaumont's KATASTROPHE DER "TITANIC" in Katowice, the audience was asked to sing "Nearer My God to Thee," which – according to the Titanic legend already established[18] – the ship's orchestra had played as it was going down: "Every member of the audience gets a free copy of the words."[19] For cinema owner Fred Berger, the cathartic effect of the audience's collective intonation of the hymn was the central argument in his defense against accusations of emotive sensationalism by the German press.[20]

Exhibitors in other countries made similar attempts to bring an emotional charge to the newsreel footage at hand through the use of dramatizing intertitles,

---

15 Bottomore: *The Titanic and Silent Cinema*, 89.
16 *Erste Internationale Film-Zeitung* 19 (11 May 1912); cf. *Der Kinematograph* 280 (15 May 1912).
17 Die Rache einer Tageszeitung: Der "Oberschlesische Kurier" und seine gerechte Abfuhr. In: *Die Lichtbild-Bühne* 23 (8 June 1912), 20, 25.
18 For press coverage of the Titanic disaster in Germany, cf. Barbara Driessen: *Tragödie der Technik, Triumph der Medien. Die Berichterstattung über den Untergang der Titanic in der zeitgenössischen deutschen und britischen Presse*. Münster 1999. About the question what the ship's band might have played when it was going down, as well as about this particular facet of the Titanic myth, cf. Ian Jack: Leonardo's Grave. In: *Granta* 67 (Autumn 1999), 7–38.
19 Die Rache einer Tageszeitung, 20.
20 Die Rache einer Tageszeitung, 20.

Fig. 1.1: Final shot from the Gaumont newsreel KATASTROPHE DER "TITANIC."

commentaries and, above all, musical accompaniment.[21] The shot of drifting ice-bergs – inserted into the Gaumont newsreel between old footage of Captain Smith on the bridge (filmed the previous year on the Olympic, the Titanic's sister ship) and images of the throng of people outside the White Star Line office in New York after the announcement of the disaster – along with its emotive final shot of waves on the open sea backlit by the setting sun (Fig. 1.1), did however also serve to add a strong notion of causality to the succession of individual scenes. This structuring process clearly removes the film from the simulation of a continuing present characteristic in favor of the "mimesis of the act of observing" exercised in so many early non-fiction films.[22] Within a processual logic of "before and after,"

---

21 Bottomore: *The Titanic and Silent Cinema*, 90–104.
22 Cf. Tom Gunning: Before Documentary. Early Nonfiction Films and the "View" Aesthetic. In: Daan Hertogs and Nico de Klerk (eds.): *Uncharted Territory. Essays on Early Nonfiction Film*. Amsterdam 1997, 9–24, here 15.

the iceberg image evokes a spatio-temporal proximity to the absent event, while the last shot of the film, accompanied by the audience's singing, links the imaginary place of the event with the time and place of the film's reception.[23]

From this kind of practice in newsreels, one perceives an effort, on one hand, to overcome discursively the absence of authentic images of the event itself and, on the other, to find a form of representation that placed the event into a direct, affective relationship with what is seen in the cinema. Both tendencies press against the generic conventions of the non-fiction genre and indicate a strong demand for fully dramatized, fictional treatments of the event, an approach that the film industry would not take very long to adopt.

The first completely dramatized film version of the sinking of the Titanic was released to the German market as early as the beginning of July 1912. It was the American Standard production SAVED FROM THE TITANIC, under the German distribution title of WAS DIE TITANIC SIE LEHRTE ("What the Titanic Taught Her").[24] The lead performer and heroine of the film was actress and Titanic survivor Dorothy Gibson, who is also believed to have collaborated on the script. Within a framing story showing the anxiety of relatives upon hearing news of the accident and the return of the heroine to her home, the film used a long flashback to depict the events as recounted by Dorothy to her parents and fiancé. According to written sources of the day, the film (now assumed lost) used original documentary footage of the Titanic in its main story. In another scene within the flashback, the collision with the iceberg was reconstructed.[25]

The nested narrative technique of the flashback lent this first filmic fictionalization of the Titanic disaster a complex structure in which the main character's diegetic narration to her relatives doubles the filmic narration of the event to a cinema audience. In its emphasis on the act of narration itself and the fact that the experiences of a survivor were being visually recreated, SAVED FROM THE TITANIC signaled, on the one hand, the freedoms of a *cinematically* dramatized representation of the event. On the other hand, it lent the filmic representation authenticity and credibility, bolstered by the use of documentary footage within the subjective flashback. By integrating newsreel footage, SAVED FROM THE TITANIC

---

23 The final shot of the film is commented on in an intertitle reading: "Oceano Nox – O waves! Of what tragic events you can tell!" I refer here to a German release print of the Gaumont newsreel (length: 119,3 metres) held by the Bundesarchiv-Filmarchiv in Berlin. I am grateful to Jeanpaul Goergen (Berlin), who made me aware of the existence of this print.
24 The film was submitted to the censorship board in Berlin on 6 July 1912. Cf. Herbert Birett (ed.): *Verzeichnis in Deutschland gelaufener Filme. Entscheidungen der Filmzensur 1911–1920.* Munich et al. 1980, 53.
25 Bottomore: *The Titanic and Silent Cinema*, 111.

'quoted' from its cinematic predecessors only to underscore its departure from existing, non-fiction Titanic films: here, for the first time, one of the many 'silent' survivors from the newsreels was given a 'voice,' brought before a camera and appearing on the screen not as an object 'on show' but as the narrator of 'her story.'

The market presence of (externally dramatized) non-fictional footage and of a first dramatic film about the sinking of the Titanic only increased the time pressure on Misu and his collaborators. While the shooting of Misu's film was in full flow by the first week of June, there were already opinions voiced in the German trade journals to the effect that public interest in cinematic representations of the disaster had been largely exhausted:

> And can it [the audience, M.W.] imagine finally that it has "been there too," has shared that fearful experience? No, for the audience must see, unless it is completely stupid, that it has been taken for a ride. And that's why "icebergs" have disappeared from films too. There was no horror in them; they don't attract audiences any more.[26]

Against this background, Continental's repeated postponements of the release of Misu's film would have read like very bad news for cinema owners. On June 12, Continental announced that, because of the "abnormally great technical difficulties that we had to overcome in the artistic elaboration of the Titanic film" and because of the "quite extraordinarily high expenditure demanded by this production," the premiere of the film would have to be postponed from June 22 to July 27, the beginning of the new season.[27] There followed more ads in which Continental assured readers that the film would be released on this date "punctually [...] with excellent advertising material"[28] – yet even so on July 27, instead of the film, there appeared only further announcements for an August 17 release.[29]

The deck scenes were shot in May 1912 in Hamburg and Cuxhaven, "with a real ship and the kind collaboration of the totally real sea," as Misu informed interested journalists.[30] The shoot probably took place on the Auguste-Viktoria, a ship of the Hamburg-Amerika Line, which along with the two sister-ships of the White Star Line was one of the few ocean cruisers with four funnels. In

26 Die Rache einer Tageszeitung, 20.
27 Bekanntmachung. In: *Erste Internationale Film-Zeitung* 19 (11 May 1912); 25 (22 June 1912); *Die Lichtbild-Bühne* 23 (8 June 1912); 25 (22 June 1912), 2–3; *Der Kinematograph* 285 (12 June 1912); 287 (26 June 1912).
28 *Die Lichtbild-Bühne* 26 (29 June 1912), 2.
29 *Die Lichtbild-Bühne* 30 (27 July 1912), 2.
30 *Berliner Tageblatt und Handelszeitung* 288 (8 June 1912).

return for permission to shoot, the Auguste-Viktoria is named in the film, which was good publicity, and shown on screen, supposedly from the point of view of the Titanic. The long shots of the collision with the iceberg and the sinking of the Titanic were filmed using a miniature model on the Grüpelsee, a lake near Berlin. According to Emil Schünemann, one of the film's cinematographers, Max Rittberger, the head of Continental and not only a famous figure skater, but also an engineer by profession, made the single-sided, eight-meter long model ship himself (Fig. 1.2).[31]

Fig. 1.2: Miniature model of the Titanic.

The shooting of other parts of the film was also put to good promotional use during the first week of June in Berlin in the back courtyard of the Continental main office. Numerous journalists from the daily and trade papers were invited and reported in detail:

> In thoughtless naivité a loafer wandered into the courtyard, and in the very same moment he sprang back terrified, for a powerful detonation shattered the air. "The boiler has exploded! Help! I'm dying!" echoed hollowly across the courtyard. Water, steam, fire, smoke and everything imaginable filled the air. One saw terrifying accidents across the disaster site, and while the heart skipped a beat and caused a paralytic terror, an apparently insane foreman called out: "More fire! The other boiler must also explode! Let the people drown!

---

31 Gerhard Lamprecht: Interview mit Emil Schünemann, 6 January 1956. A tape recording is archived in the collection of the Deutsche Kinemathek – Museum für Film und Fernsehen, Berlin.

More water!" In the background, two cameramen worked implacably at their cranks, and since I recognized the capable and brilliant director Mime Misu in the water under his stained makeup, and despite his missing clothes, I realized that this disaster was a planned one. One also saw that today's filmmaking demands exceptional realism.[32]

Although a comparison of Misu's surviving photographs with the extant film prints does not permit certain identification, the press reports suggest that Misu himself played the role of Captain Smith.[33] The future film director Otto Rippert, outfitted in a stick-on beard, can be identified with certainty as the actor playing the millionaire Isador Strauss. Other main roles were taken by Anton Ernst Rückert (as J.J. Astor) and another Continental director, Waldemar Hecker. Siegfried Wroblensky handled costumes, props and sets, and Willy Hameister shot the scenes in Hamburg and Cuxhaven, while in Berlin and the surrounding area, two cameras were sometimes used, manned by Emil Schünemann and Viktor Zimmermann.

A press screening took place in Berlin during the first week of July. Schünemann reports that most of the critics present left before the end, disappointed.[34] The *Lichtbild-Bühne* correspondent, however, reported his positive impressions: "We must admit that the 'Continental-Kunstfilm' has treated this very difficult matter, which due to its tragic character could have led to a sensation-seeking mode of representation, with laudable delicacy."[35]

The film's official premiere finally took place on August 17, at the beginning of the new season. Continental had already paved the way with a full-fledged marketing campaign. Cinema owners were told in the trade press that "this film will be delivered, if so desired, without the name 'Titanic' and with the title IN NIGHT AND ICE only.[36] Continental promised "full houses"[37] and was convinced "that you, without exception, know the value of this sea drama about the tragic sinking of the 'Titanic.'" The film was, they said, "likely to be nominated as the top item of the coming week's program."[38] A last advertisement for TITANIC – IN

---

32 Besuche in Berliner Kino-Ateliers. In: *Die Lichtbild-Bühne* 24 (15 June 1912), 18.

33 Also see the report in *Berliner Tageblatt und Handelszeitung* 288 (8 June 1912): "A couple of half-naked fellows, covered with sooty marks, wet, their hairstyle muddled, are waiting for the signal of the director, in order to receive the despairing messages of the Captain who is, equipped of course with a white stick-on beard, still conferring in his navy-blue uniform with the cameramen at the cinematographic apparatuses."

34 Lamprecht: Interview mit Emil Schünemann.

35 Der Untergang der Titanic. In: *Die Lichtbild-Bühne* 28 (13 July 1912), 18, 23.

36 *Erste Internationale Film-Zeitung* 25 (22 June 1912); *Die Lichtbild-Bühne* 25 (22 June 1912), 2–3; *Der Kinematograph* 287 (26 June 1912).

37 *Die Lichtbild-Bühne* 26 (29 June 1912), 2–3.

38 *Die Lichtbild-Bühne* 28 (13 July 1912), 1.

NACHT UND EIS appeared on August 31, 1912.[39] The "great success" which the film was said to have enjoyed up to then was confirmed by a cinema owner from Pirmasens, who wrote that his Union-Theater had "not since DIE WEISSE SKLAVIN [THE WHITE SLAVE] seen such crowds as we have in the last few days." The fact that the film was distributed in the provinces barely two weeks after its Berlin première – and "on very favorable terms" – does however testify to the film's initial box-office difficulties in Germany. Continental's admission that they were forced, "due to the now daily arrivals of bookings, to offer extremely advantageous conditions for repeat bookings" seems paradoxical given that the monopoly distribution system during this period used a scale to dictate a weekly decrease in rental fees.[40]

It was not until mid-October that Continental was able to report the sale of 148 prints (certainly a remarkable figure), mostly abroad.[41] The film was released in the Netherlands at the end of September and in France at the beginning of October. Not until the end of that month was TITANIC – IN NACHT UND EIS finally shown in the USA under the distribution title SHIPWRECKED IN ICEBERGS.[42]

While the film seems to have had a successful career abroad – Schünemann looks back on it as "very big business" because it had been seen "all over the world"[43] – its success at home was probably rather limited. As early as the beginning of November, German distribution companies released TITANIC – IN NACHT UND EIS on the domestic market as part of a 2,000-meter long compilation of hits "at the lowest rates."[44] Also striking is the minimal amount of press coverage that the film received in Germany. The only detailed treatment of Misu's film still available today was written by the critic Walter Thielemann and published in an Austrian journal under the title "Education in Entertainment Form? Critical Observations on Some Recent Hits." Thielemann took the film to task for "giving the audience an entirely false impression of the events on board and creating unrest among the German people." He expressed regret

---

39 *Die Lichtbild-Bühne* 35 (31 August 1912), 19.

40 *Die Lichtbild-Bühne* 35, 19. What in other countries became the zoning and clearance agreements, guaranteeing an exhibitor exclusivity of a film for a specific period in a specific geographical area, became known in Germany as the *Monopolfilm* (monopoly film). For a detailed account, cf. Corinna Müller: *Frühe deutsche Kinematographie. Formale, wirtschaftliche und kulturelle Entwicklungen 1902–1912*. Stuttgart and Weimar 1994.

41 *Die Lichtbild-Bühne* 41 (12 October 1912), 37; *Erste Internationale Film-Zeitung* 41 (12 October 1912), 74–75.

42 In the US, the film was licensed in the category "non-fiction." Cf. Bottomore: *The Titanic and Silent Cinema*, 121.

43 Lamprecht: Interview mit Emil Schünemann.

44 *Die Lichtbild-Bühne* 45 (9 November 1912), 50.

about the fact that the film speculated on the sensation-seeking taste of the masses, and he described its representation of the disaster as tasteless "kitsch."[45] Thielemann's verdict, intended to discredit Continental's rhetoric of enlightenment, brings into sharp relief the cultural battleground on which Misu's project took its place. It may also explain some of the reservations the German press had against this film.

1.3 Looking back to the future: Media modernity and the paradoxes of time

The first intertitle of Misu's film signals the cultural conflict that characterized the film's conception. The words "In Night and Ice. Sea drama. True to life and based on authentic reports" are meant to authenticate the following representation of a 'true' event, but they also signal the 'structuring absence' of the event itself, a constituting lack of representation at the center of the media discourse.[46] When adapting the disaster to the screen, Misu had recourse only to reports in the press and cinema.

In this sense, the sinking of the Titanic qualifies as one of the archetypal "modernist events" of the 20th century in which the *opposition* between fact and fiction is radically undermined, as Hayden White has argued: The 'historical' event dissolves as an object of verifiable knowledge and becomes identical, as if of the same ontological order, with the meanings assigned to it. No longer the point of departure from which the historical significance of the event – its 'myth,' 'legend' or 'moral' – can be deduced, the 'facts' disseminated about a historical event appear in the media as a function of the meanings ascribed to it.[47]

According to Stephen Kern, the new communication technology of wireless telegraphy, with which the Titanic sent its SOS calls, together with the modern mass media, created an impression of 'simultaneity' between the event and its mediatized dissemination and interpretation.[48] A similar impression regarding changing perceptions of time and space would become characteristic of radio,

---

45 *Lichtbild-Theater* 40 (3 October 1912), 8.

46 For similar reasons, the historian Frank Bösch calls the sinking of the Titanic a "placeless event." Cf. Frank Bösch: Transnationale Trauer und Technikkritik? Der Untergang der "Titanic." In: Friedrich Lenger and Ansgar Nünning (eds.): *Medienereignisse der Moderne.* Darmstadt 2000, 79–94, here 84.

47 Hayden White: The Modernist Event. In: Vivian Sobchack (ed.): *The Persistence of History. Cinema, Television, and the Modern Event.* New York and London 1996, 17–38.

48 Stephen Kern: *The Culture of Time and Space, 1880–1918.* Cambridge, Mass. 1983.

television and the internet in the second half of the 20th century. Historians of the Titanic have documented and described how journalists picked up on the myth-making potential of the last telegraphically transmitted message ("Sinking by the head. Have cleared boats and filled them with women and children"), working it into dramatic headlines even before the first witnesses on the Carpathia had reached New York. "By the time the survivors reached shore," Stephen Biel writes, "the myth was firmly in place and their testimony could only confirm what the press and the public already knew."[49] In Hayden White's terminology: the 'facts' followed the fiction.

Originating from the wireless signal, the channels of mass media coverage quickly filtered the circulating tropes and narratives for symbolic meanings. They recoded and 'authenticated' some of the information as 'facts' through rhetorical strategies and stylistic devices, lending them different degrees of institutional legitimacy and media-specific levels of credibility: Newspapers were more trustworthy than novels, photographic representation more faithful to 'reality' than pictorial representation, and so on.

The sense of simultaneity and the uprooting of 'historical reality' through rhetorical devices such as narrativization and dramatization has become a hallmark of modern mass media, which have capitalized on the double matrix across which the truth value of a given historical event is transformed into a commodity value. Daniel Dayan and Elihu Katz provide an entire catalogue of criteria to define a media event, each of which, we will see, apply to Misu's film. Apart from its live character ("simultaneity") and transformational quality ("aesthetization"), a media event transmits an event that occurred in a remote location outside the media sphere; it is pre-planned, announced and advertised; it is characterized by a norm of reception which integrates a very large audience; it takes the form of a "ritual" or "ceremony" through its "monopolistic interruption" of everyday routine; and it is a "festive viewing" of history in the making and celebrates not conflict, but the reconciliation of a proclaimed "historic meaning."[50]

It is against this media scenario that Misu's film becomes readable as a multi-layered palimpsest. At the time of shooting, there was already a distinct, hierarchically ordered narrative surrounding the sinking of the Titanic. Within this emerging narrative pattern, certain figures and their fates were moved into the foreground, marking them as recognizable 'protagonists' and fashioning them into tragic heroes. Within a very short time, binding iconographic models

---

49 Steven Biel: *Down with the Old Canoe. A Cultural History of the Titanic*. New York and London 1996, 25. Cf. Richard Howells: *The Myth of the Titanic*. London 1999.
50 Daniel Dayan and Elihu Katz: *Media Events. The Live Broadcasting of History*. Cambridge, Mass. and London 1992.

of representation had been formed on which every new portrayal of the tragedy had, if not to reproduce, than at least to reflect.

Following the general logic of modern media events, whose cultural surplus in the market is primarily measured not by the represented event, but by the representational strategies deployed to depict it,[51] the first act of Misu's film adopts the documentary aesthetic of newsreel reporting. In long shots and pans, we are shown the ship in the Southampton docks, the boarding of passengers and loading of cargo, the closing of the side hatches and the ship's departure. The opening sequence also simulates a newsreel aesthetic by picking passengers out of the crowd who will later be protagonists in the drama, including the Strauss couple and the Astors. Their departure (Fig. 1.3) is signaled immediately beforehand by two intertitles: "A millionaire who will go down with the Titanic boards the ship with his young wife. (Front, he wearing a cap, she a scarf)" and "Another well-known millionaire embarks with his young wife (Front, with a floppy hat.) The young woman was saved while her husband drowned, because he could only think of helping others." While the two intertitles borrow from newsreel reporting the gesture of 'showing' and the practice of guiding the audience's attention via verbal descriptions, they deviate decisively from this representational formula in their allusion to the audience's prior knowledge.

Fig. 1.3: Departure.

These intertitles presuppose that the audience is in a position to identify the figures portrayed on screen, from both the information about their destiny and from the appearance of the actors, who are appropriately made up and costumed. Furthermore, the prophetic commentaries of the two intertitles establish

---

51 Dayan and Katz: *Media Events*, 17–18.

a temporal structure for the narrative that marks not only a departure from the present tense of the "view aesthetic" characteristic of non-fictional genres ("this is..."), but also from the instantaneous present of contemporary sensational melodramas and adventure films, with their concentration on physical action – into the paradoxical narrative tense of the future in the past ("it will have been").[52] Comparable to the nested narrative perspective in SAVED FROM THE TITANIC, Misu's exposition thereby installs a knowing mode of narration and reception, in which the spectator is meant to identify the people portrayed, but not (yet) to identify with them.

Only towards the end of the first act do we find elements of narrative integration and filmic fictionalization alongside the documentary gestures with which the film refers to the pro-filmic event. With the appearance of Captain Smith as the main character in the film, the function of the camera's look tends to shift in favor of a subjectivization of filmic space. The sequence is first introduced by the intertitle "On duty on the bridge," which is the last of a series of titles describing exemplary ritual acts such as "Letting down a boat in port," "The stewards bring the suitcases on board," and "The lateral doors are closed water-tight." A medium long-shot of the First Officer looking out to sea through his telescope follows, a shot that is clearly distinguished from the long-shot pans that precede it. Here, for the first time, the film activates an invisible space beyond the frame of the image, which is, through a cut to the passing Auguste-Viktoria, immediately re-inscribed into the space of the image (Fig. 1.4).

Fig. 1.4: Re-inscribing and subjectivizing off-screen space.

---

52 On the "view aesthetic" of early non-fiction films, cf. Gunning: Before Documentary; on the aesthetics of early actuality films and newsreel items in Germany, cf. Uli Jung: Aktualitäten und Wochenschauen. In: Uli Jung and Martin Loiperdinger (eds.): *Geschichte des dokumentarischen Films in Deutschland*, vol. 1.: *Kaiserreich, 1895–1918*. Stuttgart 2005, 230–252.

The use of masking to simulate the telescope establishes a link between the observing person and the observed object, identifying the shot as the representation of the character's subjective view. It is crucial, however, that the subjectivization of the camera's perspective is first introduced in the context of a paratactic, un-dramatized structure, which places the documentarizing 'reading' evoked up to that point into a contradictory relationship with the unfolding narrative. The point-of-view pattern certainly allows the spectator to share the view of the character concerned, but the un-dramatized nature of the sequence of shots also makes the imaginary look of the First Officer through the telescope legible as an integration of the spectator's look and mode of reception (which until this moment has been documentary-oriented) into the diegetic world of the film.[53]

This integration becomes all the more evident when Captain Smith steps on the bridge immediately afterwards and picks up the telescope. His view of two other passing ships again duplicates, without any change of perspective, the previously dominant frontal camera view on events that were presented in a documentary manner. Unlike the narrative resolution of point-of-view patterns in classical narrative cinema,[54] there remains here a dialectical uncertainty as to whether the camera has assumed the position of the fictional character and thereby anchors the spectator's look within the diegetic world, or whether the representation of the character's subjective perception adopts and doubles the previously established non-fictional 'view,' thus figuring as the fictional agent of the spectator's documentary interest.

The fundamental ambivalence of the camera's look, oscillating between narrative absorption and documentary attraction, remains characteristic for the narrational process of the film. In a second key sequence constructed in parallel to this first one, a distinct difference is marked by the discovery of the icebergs. At the beginning of the sequence, we once more see the First Officer on the bridge looking off screen through a pair of binoculars. A masked shot shows the sea lying calm. After cutting away into a passenger cabin and into the ship's café, the action jumps back to the deck. In a diagonal low-angle shot we see a sailor, also looking at the sea through a telescope, who suddenly starts gesticulating wildly. The following shot of icebergs reveals the cause of his excitement. This shot can, however, only be ascribed to the sailor because of the telescope masking and narrative context, not the camera's perspective. The

53 On the use of subjective shots in early European cinema, cf. Elena Dagrada: *Between the Eye and the World. The Emergence of the Point-of-View Shot*. Brussels 2015.
54 Cf. Edward Branigan: *Point of View in the Cinema. A Theory of Narration and Subjectivity in Classical Film*. Berlin, New York and Amsterdam 1984.

sailor is shown once more, before we return to the First Officer on the bridge. He looks (and listens) at first diagonally upwards towards the sailor in the crow's nest, then forward again through the binoculars, where – from the same perspective of the sailor – he discovers the icebergs (Fig. 1.5).

Fig. 1.5: Discovering the icebergs.

From the masked shot of the icebergs, the film cuts back to the First Officer, who is now also gesticulating and looking through the telescope. An intertitle interrupts the shot to explain the narrative meaning of what has been seen and to interpret the reaction of the First Officer: "Some massive icebergs, lying ahead of a big ice field, are so near that a collision with the ship seems inevitable." In the second part of the shot the First Officer puts the binoculars down and turns his line of sight towards Captain Smith who reappears in the frame. The Captain looks through the binoculars, discovers the icebergs and initiates the following course of action by signaling to the machine room "Full-steam to aft."

It is notable how subtly the film's narrational structure is modified in this sequence, disappointing the spectator's expectations of documentary-style shots: the first look through the binoculars goes literally into the void, the field of vision, doubly coded, by the interest of both the characters and the spectators, is emptied of all narratively irrelevant objects, in order to be newly semantically defined and take over its function as the trigger for a causal chain of events. While the view of the icebergs is narratively integrated, its meta-diegetic quality as an 'excessive signifier' nevertheless remains in its paradoxical position within the filmic space. In the fictional sphere of action, otherwise coherently organized by the First Officer's view of the crow's nest and the approaching captain, the perspectively identical, 'impossible' views of all three protagonists of the icebergs forms an erratic element. This positioning within the spatial structure can be understood as a sign retaining the autonomy of a documentary camera-view that reinscribes into the fiction the attraction of the icebergs known to the audience from newsreel compilations. At this point in the film, the cinematic process of representation pursues a double agenda whose central interest rests not primarily on coherent narrative action but on a *mise-en-abyme* of the 'act of seeing' itself.

As in all subsequent filmic representations of the Titanic disaster, the discovery of the icebergs marks a decisive point of transition in the film's narrational logic. In Misu's film, the sequence serves to mediate between a narratively situated and action-oriented desire for visual information articulated via the gaze of the characters and the desire of the audience, reaching beyond the narrative 'to see what actually happened.' The central poetological operation of the film evolves around the paradoxical coexistence of two different desires, two different visual and temporal axes: the retrospective look of the spectator and the subjective, action-oriented look of the characters, directed 'forward' in time. In resolving but not neutralizing the split between narrated time and the time of the narration, Titanic – In Nacht und Eis arrives at a radically modern, and genuinely cinematic, narrative temporality which makes the spectator 'look back into the future.'[55]

---

55 On the modern, 'alienated' experience of time, and the role of cinema in this epistemological shift, cf. Leo Charney: *Empty Moments. Cinema, Modernity, and Drift.* Durham and London 1998; Mary Ann Doane: *The Emergence of Cinematic Time.* Cambridge, Mass. 2003.

Alternating montage, another central element of filmic narration, is used in the film in a similarly paradoxical manner. Throughout most of the film, alternating montage is its main formal characteristic. But it is similarly paratactically used to introduce various sites of action that will not be dramatized until the second part of the film. Thus, the constant scene changes at first serve only to take the audience on an imaginary tour around the Titanic: the alternating montage is not, in the beginning, principally dictated by dramatic principles but follows instead the serial logic of a 'viewing.' Again, a documentary 'view' is established and maintained in parallel with the subjective look of the characters, above all the Strausses and the Astors, as when a "Viewing of the boat-deck by the above-mentioned passengers" (intertitle) takes place in the first act and we get to see the "Passengers' on-board pastimes," we visit the radio and machine rooms, and we are able to witness the passengers in various luxury cabins dressing for dinner ("Toilette in the luxury apartments for the ship-board soirée") as well as the "Evening entertainment in the elegant Café Parisien." The shifting ground on which this sequence of 'factual views' rests is, however, hinted at in the film in two ways: by announcing in intertitles the future fate of each character as she or he appears (with the exception of Captain Smith) and by leading all of the characters' tours of deck past the life boats (Fig. 1.6).

Fig. 1.6: Tours of deck.

It is only with the discovery of the icebergs that the alternating montage is transformed into a dramatic means of creating plot-motivated tension at the very moment when the subjectivization of the visual space gradually transforms, or 'integrates,' into a narrative space. By inter-cutting to the Café Parisien after the discovery of the icebergs, the film establishes a crucial disparity between the knowledge of the alarmed ship's crew and that of the still-ignorant passengers, wherein not only the look but also the superior knowledge of the spectator is reflected within the narration. Not until this moment does the narrative significance of the previous jumps from scene to scene become fully visible: the alternating views of the activities of the millionaire couples Strauss and Astor and the places they spend their time initially pull the characters into an iconographic constellation, the narrative significance of which emerges only from the purely visual analogy of their paths finally crossing for the first time in the fictional space of the Café Parisien at the fateful moment of the disaster (Fig. 1.7).

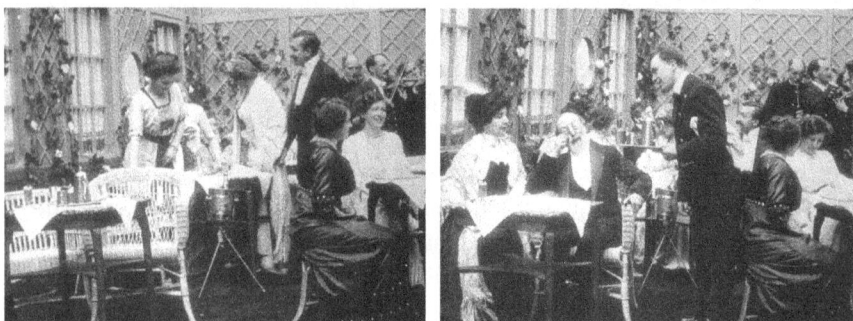

Fig. 1.7: A fateful moment.

The film spectator – because her view in time and space is always slightly displaced and because her so carefully-prepared double dose of advance knowledge is superior to that of all the characters – has at this point in the film no direct emotional participation in the fate of the characters. From this identificatory distance, the spectator can enjoy the ensuing spectacle of the collision as a fine example of cinematic representation.

In the representation of the collision itself, Misu largely foregoes any claim to authenticity in favor of the high spectacle value offered by a head-on collision. The disaster is first announced by the distancing intertitle "Collision with the iceberg and its effect above and below deck," followed by a long-shot of the model ship running into a model iceberg (Fig. 1.8). The moment of the collision is repeated another three times, the shock shown in swift succession in the Café Parisien, in the cabin of the millionaire Allinson and his family and in the machine room (Fig. 1.9).

Judged by the standards of classical narrative filmmaking, the serial resolution of the collision scene chosen by Misu might seem surprising. Misu's subtle understanding (demonstrated immediately beforehand) of how the impression of

Fig. 1.8: Collision with the iceberg.

Fig. 1.9: Repeated collision.

simultaneity can be created by parallel editing suggests that what we are witnessing is not lack of competence in narrative technique but rather a representational logic of a quite different kind. The representational logic that dominates here aims to present the spectacular climax of the film as a filmic attraction as often as possible. The repeated presentation of something that has happened only once should therefore be understood less as "action overlap" – the action overhang so often criticized in early films as inelegant – than as an "action replay" used to emphasize and intensify the experience of a singular "event."[56] The aesthetic principle of an excessive flood of stimuli, with its cumulative intensification of the experience of shock, consciously disrupts the linear structure of the narrative, but it also shatters any documentary reading of the text: the spatial expansion of the shock effect – which is, according to the intertitle, the central interest of the sequence – spreads from the fictional space of the film to the perception space of the spectator, whose established patterns of reception, both 'narrative' and 'documentary,' are severely shaken by the violent event presented as an accumulation of stimuli.[57] In the triple 'Now!' of the simultaneous traumatization, the different time planes of the narration are for the first time integrated into a common logic of experience. The serial lesion of the ambivalent aesthetic fabric stitches narrated time and narrative time into a loop of experience and repetition, the utopia of which is represented by that very 'it will have been' with which the virtual spectator's gaze goes back in time only to meet itself in the future of the fiction.[58]

At its climax, the film veers around to the presence of the spectator from whom any framework for understanding – whether narrative or documentary – has been pulled away. The spectator's own traumatic experience of the incommensurable aesthetic material must now be processed in the poetic organization of the film: after disrupting all generic fabrics of meaning, the rest of the film sets out to re-fix these unleashed affective energies, to recharge the aesthetic material with positive meaning and to re-establish the conditions of the pleasure principle.

1.4 Allegories of narration: Saving the audience

To this end, the last act of the film develops a new, far more classical narrative economy concentrated on the characters of Captain Smith and the first wireless

---

56 Cf. Thomas Elsaesser: Early Film History and Multi-Media. An Archaeology of Possible Futures? In: Wendy Hui Kyong Chung and Thomas Keenan (eds.): *New Media, Old Media. A History and Theory Reader*. New York 2006, 13–25, here 21.
57 Cf. Tom Gunning: An Aesthetic of Astonishment. Early Film and the Incredulous Spectator. In: *Art & Text* 34 (1989), 31–45.
58 On the temporality of traumatic experience, cf. Cathy Caruth: *Unclaimed Experience. Trauma, Narrative, and History*. Baltimore and London 1996.

operator, Jack Phillips, the two characters who had previously been 'spared' the shock of the collision, as there was no visual depiction of the shock on the bridge or in the radio room. Untouched by physical damage, they can act as intact representatives of their respective corporations and technologies: the White Star Shipping Line and the Marconi Telegraph Company. A production communiqué from Continental underscores this conception of the two characters in the last part of the film:

> In the midst of the confusion, as our film shows, the crew keeps perfectly calm and fulfils its duty with iron-like energy, as if nothing exceptional had happened. [...] Now the Captain himself goes over to the Marconi-station and orders the first telegrapher, Mr. Philipps, who in the meantime has returned to his to duty, to send out the first emergency signals.[59]

In alternating shots, the two main characters' efforts to save people are shown as a race against the ship's sinking (intertitle: "The ship sinks deeper and deeper"), through which a linear temporality is created that vectorizes all narrative action in a run-to-the-rescue-scenario and that satisfies the melodramatic conventions of tragic self-sacrifice, a rhetorical model that was familiar to the German public from the press. While there was unanimity about the Marconi wireless operator's "devotion to duty"[60] in the German press, the same was not true for the Captain. "Captain Smith?" Maximilian Harden asked in his journal *Die Zukunft*, with reference to the contradictory reports about Smith in the mass-circulation papers:

> Drunkard and good-for-nothing. No: noble hero of duty, as land and sea have never seen one before. At the banquet he got himself into a drunken stupor and missed his duty. In the second collision, he stood, sober and watchful, on the bridge and afterwards directed the rescue operations with majestic calm. Shot himself on the bridge. Grabbed a helplessly discarded child, carried it on his arm through the waves into a lifeboat and drowned himself with a smile.[61]

That Misu's film should follow the heroic version of the Captain's death – summarized by Harden with deadpan irony – positions TITANIC – IN NACHT UND EIS within an ideologically-determined discourse about the means and possibilities of overcoming social trauma. The poignancy of Misu's cinematic intervention

59 *Der Kinematograph* 288 (3 July 1912).
60 In treuer Pflichterfüllung. In: *Illustrierte Rundschau (Hamburger Fremdenblatt)* 95 (24 April 1912), 29; reprinted in Werner Köster and Thomas Lischeid (eds.): *Titanic. Ein Medienmythos.* Leipzig 1999, 88–89.
61 Maximilian Harden: Titanic: Report. In: *Die Zukunft* (15 June 1912), 340–354; quoted from Köster and Lischeid (eds.): *Titanic. Ein Medienmythos*, 53.

in the public debate over the Captain of the Titanic is demonstrated by the fact that the fate of this character is the only fate not shared with the spectator in advance. The prevailing uncertainty over the historical role of the Captain is thereby used to create suspense and draw the spectator into the narrative. The audience's epistemological interest brought to the narrative from outside is thus in the last part of the film transformed into an identificatory moment. This identificatory moment culminates in the film's final scene, as the Captain's actions are cross cut with the steady sinking of the ship, enforcing the notion of emotional catharsis: "The proud ship sinks into the deep and with it its greatest hero, its Captain! All honor to him!"[62]

Contemporary sources make clear that the end of Misu's film was conceived as an allegorical duel between the Captain and death. The final shot, in which death appears incarnate behind the iceberg – "And while the waves of the sea strike the iceberg, roaring and surging, we see the ghostly face of death grinning spectrally through the ice colossus, as though pitiless death were satisfied with his horrifying harvest"[63] – has disappeared from the surviving prints of TITANIC – IN NACHT UND EIS. In Continental's description of the film,[64] this allegorizing reading, which is meant to work against the traumatic experience of a contingent event, is set up much earlier than the film's ending. Even the initial discovery of the iceberg, for example, is accompanied by the words: "It moves up from behind like a white ghost!"[65]

If the first half of the film aims to achieve the dialectical synthesis of a camera-eye that would incorporate both the subjective look of the characters and the retrospective view of the spectator with a camera-I whose mysterious identity is established at the moment of the traumatic event, this synthesis is again dissolved discursively in the last act of the film: the *lecture documentaire*[66] of a paratactically-structured sequence of views emanates from the sudden shock as an allegorical reading of a melodramatic *mise-en-scène*. In their allegorical stylization, the characters of Smith and Phillips no longer function as autonomous

---

62 [Plot synopsis of Continental-Kunstfilm]. In: *Erste Internationale Film-Zeitung* 25 (22 June 1912), 33.

63 [Plot synopsis]. In: *Erste Internationale Film-Zeitung* 25, 33.

64 Promotional texts such as this one can be read as reception-guiding paratexts as proposed by Gérard Genette and would fall into the category of "publisher's peritexts." Cf. Gérard Genette: *Paratexts. Thresholds of Interpretation.* Cambridge, Mass., New York and Melbourne 1997, 16–36.

65 [Plot synopsis of Continental-Kunstfilm]. In: *Der Kinematograph* 288 (3 July 1912).

66 I am here referring to Roger Odin: Film documentaire, lecture documentarisante. In: Jean Charles Lyant and Roger Odin (eds.): *Cinémas et réalités.* St. Etienne 1984, 263–280.

agents of a linear narrative but coagulate into representatives of a constellation whose true meaning is located outside the horizon of the diegetic world.

Under the guise of narrative concretion, this superordinate framework of meaning emerges as a dramatization of the technological transformation responsible for turning the Titanic disaster into a media event: down to individual patterns of mobility, the race against time that the Captain and the radio officer each undertake via their respective apparatuses mirrors the innovative logics of locomotion and communication and of traffic and information technology that have become uncoupled during the course of modernization.[67] What is ultimately articulated via the two characters at the moment of greatest shock is a topos of technological unity – the imaginary reconciliation of what Georg Simmel referred to as "the wonders and comforts of space-conquering technology."[68] At the moment of crisis of "the one misused technology that was about to kill everyone," the existential cultural value of the other technology truly reveals itself, as Gustav Landauer put it: "The saving of several hundred people by the wireless telegraph was to give the people of our time a signal to reflect on the strength of our spirit [...]. Humanity [...] is made reality by technology."[69]

Landauer's definition, as radical as it is empathetic, of that which can be sublimated as symbolical from the telegraphic "message of the Titanic," is at the same time an accurate description of the gradual dissolution of individual life experience into the conforming economy of experience of a new community of media consumers, on whom Misu, in his own writings, based cinema's claims to artistic value and to cultural significance.[70] Only the reflexive self-integration of the individual into a collective consciousness can achieve the psychic integration of the montage of disparate 'sensations,' and allow media contingency to be experienced not as terror, as an overwhelming flood of information and sensations, but rather as an instrument of communal self-recognition.

Early narrative cinema harnessed in many different ways the altered quality of chrono-topical perception in the wake of modern transport and communication technologies to naturalize the spatio-temporal autonomy of its own medium

---

67 Cf. e.g. Johannes Rohbeck: *Technik, Kultur, Geschichte. Eine Rehabilitierung der Geschichtsphilosophie.* Frankfurt a. M. 2000, 132.

68 Georg Simmel: Die Großstädte und das Geistesleben. In: Georg Simmel: *Aufsätze und Abhandlungen 1901–1908.* Frankfurt a.M. 1995, 116–131, here 130.

69 Gustav Landauer: Die Botschaft der Titanic. In: *Frankfurter Zeitung* (21 April 1912); reprinted in Köster and Lischeid (eds.): *Titanic: Ein Medienmythos,* 82, 86–87.

70 Cf. [Mime] Misu: Kunst und nochmals Kunst. In: *Die Lichtbild-Bühne* 23 (7 June 1913, special supplement "The Film Director"), 122.

and to motivate new narrative techniques such as cross-cutting and parallel editing as means of creating suspense. Films like Pathé's A Narrow Escape or The Physician of the Castle (1908), Edwin S. Porter's Heard over the Phone (1908), D. W. Griffith's The Lonely Villa (1909), The Lonedale Operator (1911) and The Girl and her Trust (1912) or Kalem's The Grit of the Girl Telegrapher (1912) bring to the screen the overlapping rates of acceleration of information transfer and passenger transport on the model of an action-centered, melodramatic rhetoric of separation, salvation and reunion. The dramatic isolation of the character/s to be saved corresponds here to the imaginary isolation of the spectator-subject, whose virtual mobility allows the technologically-structured temporality of the narration to be experienced as the "terrors of technology," unleashed by and, at the same time, contained within the filmic representation.[71]

Misu's film, in its crucial alteration of this cinematic model of representing modern technology, aims to convert the individual concern of each spectator into a new community consciousness of collective reception. It does so by strongly allegorizing the story being told: Intertitles function as a transmission belt between sensory perception and cognitive processing, continually placing what has happened on the screen against its allegorical readability. The dynamic that unfolds between the shots is coupled with an illustrative representational mode that charges each narrative development with an anticipated meaning. The tension between diegetic and extra-diegetic meaning culminates in the shot of the final meeting between the Captain and the radio officer. In the intertitle, the meeting's place within the causal chain of the narrative is removed for the emphatic visualization of the solidarity between the two technologies that the characters represent: "Since there is no longer hope of salvation, the Captain releases the first radio officer from his duties. Both are now firmly decided to go down with the ship and are concentrating only on saving the passengers." Pictorial *mise-en-scène* and melodramatically over-acted gestures coalesce into the arabesque of an allegorical tableau, before they dissolve back as an over-determined plot figuration into the flow of the narrative structure (Fig. 1.10).[72] Once more the characters in the film are unmasked as double agents within and beyond the

---

71 Cf. Tom Gunning: Heard over the Phone. The Lonely Villa and the de Lorde Tradition of the Terrors of Technology. In: *Screen* 32:2 (Summer 1991), 184–196. Also cf. Lynn Kirby: *Parallel Tracks. The Railroad and Silent Cinema*. Exeter 1997.

72 Far from being barely 'theatrical' and incompatible with 'realist' demands of narrative filmmaking, the acting style in this film therefore carries an important function within the double agenda it pursues throughout. On acting styles in early cinema, cf. Ben Brewster and Lea Jacobs: *Theater to Cinema. Stage Pictorialism and the Early Feature Film*. Oxford and New York 1997, 79–138.

Fig. 1.10: An allegorical tableau.

film's diegetic horizon. Their movements 'play out' the composition's figurative, performative dimension against its narrative significance.

The film adds another layer of meaning to this double semantic of visual space. Parallel to the visual space, the film establishes an imaginary sound space, which undergoes a crucial perspectivization in the final act. Throughout the film, this sound space accompanies individual scenes via linking musical motifs with the ship's orchestra. On deck, when casting off, and in the Café Parisien, the ship's orchestra is a constant visual element in the background of the image. The audience's attention is specially directed to this element at the beginning. The intertitle "The stewards' orchestra plays 'Home Sweet Home'" is to be understood also as a direction to musicians playing in the cinema, to bring the event portrayed into line acoustically with the collective experience of the audience.

Toward the end of the film this imaginary sound space – which corresponds with the audience's acoustic perception space, thanks to the way sound and image were synchronized during exhibition – is consciously subjectivized within the narrative space.[73] By introducing a shot of survivors of the disaster with the

---

73 I am here adopting James Lastra's definition of the term "synchronization." Lastra contends that "any fixed or purposeful relationship between sound and image legitimately may be thought of as synchronized. From this perspective 'lip-synch' is only one, rather banal, possibility." Cf. James Lastra: *Sound Technology and the American Cinema. Perception, Representation, Modernity*. New York 2000, 94.

words (in intertitles) "From the boats in the water, full of saved passengers, one can hear the stewards band on board playing 'Nearer My God to Thee!'" and then firming up the musical concordance by revealing the hymn's musical notation and lyrics, the film aims at the very identificatory moment previously denied by the ambivalent construction of the space of the visual perception of the individualized spectator-subject. It is thus not the perspectival identity of a shared individual look of spectator and character that enables the collective audience to feel itself part of the community of 'survivors'; it is the 'shared' sound perspective in the acoustic perception space that allows the audience to join in with the hymn (Fig. 1.11).[74]

Näher, mein Gott, zu Dir, näher zu Dir:

Fig. 1.11: A shared sound perspective.

Through the creation of a common auditory space, the 'salvation' of the audience is itself inscribed into the central plot motif of the last act, the saving of individual passengers by the Captain and the radio officer. The duel between death and technology becomes the site of a final allegorical transformation, with which the film symbolically integrates the conditions of its own public reception into the fictional space of the narrative. When at the end the Captain,

---

74 Reports on screenings of TITANIC – IN NACHT UND EIS in the Netherlands document the importance of an accurate creation of the accompanying sound space and of the participation of the audience. In the Netherlands, the exhibition of the film was accompanied by lecturers and vocal soloists, who encouraged the audience to join in the choral "Nearer, My God, to Thee." Cf. *Nieuws van de Dag* (7 and 14 October 1912). I am grateful to Ivo Blom for drawing my attention to these documents.

himself drowning, saves a passenger from going down, the film seems to have come full circle: with the same move with which Misu – both as Captain Smith and as director of the film – integrates the individual into the collective of survivors, the narrative sinks with its last agent back into the public space of its exhibition.

Thus, TITANIC – IN NACHT UND EIS produces only the appearance of narrativity in order to form and to reflect a design for a cinematographic public sphere at the point of convergence of different film genres, iconographic models and semantic planes. It is on this point, and not via a one-dimensional generic relationship, that Misu's Titanic project meets Cameron's. Both of them aim in their aesthetic intention "for the enjoyment of illusion, but not for the illusion of a real event"; in both films "it is not the chronology of a past event [...] that has become the object of an aesthetic adaptation but the difference between different time planes – the remembered and the present time, the narrated time and the time of the filmic perception"; and in both films "it is not the mode of the illusionistic present tense of the representation of the event but a cinematographic image, able to connect immanently the different time planes, that forms [...] the center of the audio-visual construction."[75]

Beyond any notion of cinematic primitivism, which is often assumed to be the case in early German cinema, Misu's version of an 'event cinema' reveals itself, in its reflection of the media integration of cultural representation, as a paradigmatic example of the complex interplay between technological modernization and aesthetic modernism. What philosopher Hans Blumenberg once described in terms of a precarious positioning of the spectator vis-à-vis (media) enactments of catastrophic events as a basic constellation of the modern experience of reality applies also to Misu's cinematic adaptation of the Titanic disaster:

> Clearly, the pleasantness that is said to characterize this sight [of other people who are in peril on the storm-tossed sea] is not a result of seeing someone else suffer but of enjoying the safety of one's own standpoint. [...] However, the spectator, too, no longer represents the exceptional existence of the sage, on the edge of reality; rather he has himself become an exponent of one of those passions that both move and endanger life.

---

75 Hermann Kappelhoff: And the Heart will go on and on: Untergangsphantasie und Wiederholungsstruktur in dem Film TITANIC von James Cameron. In: *Montage AV* 8:1 (1999), 85–108, here 88–89.

It is true that he is not personally involved in adventures, but he certainly is helplessly at the mercy of the attraction of catastrophes and sensations. His non-involvement is not that of looking on but that of a burning curiosity [...]. Through the move from sea-shore to theater, [the] spectator is withdrawn from the moral dimension; he has become "aesthetic."[76]

76 Hans Blumenberg: *Shipwreck with Spectator. Paradigm of a Metaphor for Existence.* Cambridge, Mass. and London 1997, 26, 35, 40.

2 Ciphers of loss: Max Mack's (in)visible authorship

> In the photoplay, our imagination is projected onto the screen. [...] The visual perception of the various forms of expression of [...] emotions fuses in our mind with the conscious awareness of the emotion expressed; we feel as if we were directly seeing and observing the emotion itself. [...] the photoplay tells us the human story by overcoming the forms of the outer world, namely space, time, and causality, and by adjusting the events to the forms of the inner world, namely, attention, memory, imagination, and emotion.
>
> Hugo Münsterberg, 1916[1]

In 1913, just before World War I, the generic term '*Autorenfilm*' (authors' film) began to be used in Germany to describe films made with reference to well-known figures of the German literary and theatrical scene, either because of the direct participation of writers and stage actors, or indirectly, in the form of literary adaptations. In 1908, the director Heinrich Bolten-Baeckers established a 'Society for the Utilization of Literary Ideas for Cinematic Purposes,' inspired by Pathé's French *films d'art*, which entered the German market the same year.[2] It was not until 1913, however, that the first German *Autorenfilme* were released. The intervening years saw a bitter campaign waged against cinema by theatrical institutions that saw the new medium as responsible for the economic crisis in German theaters. This campaign culminated in May 1912 with an agreement to boycott cinema and to prevent theater actors from working in cinema.

Despite the institutional boycott, negotiations between the major production companies and individual artists continued, resulting in an unexpected reversal of the situation in November 1912, when the Danish company Nordisk, which had been producing authors' films – or *forfatterfilm* – for Danish audiences since 1910, announced future collaborations with such prominent writers as Gerhart Hauptmann, Arthur Schnitzler, Hugo von Hofmannsthal, Felix Salten and Jakob Wassermann, among others. In a parallel move, Paul Davidson's Projektions AG 'Union' (PAGU) signed an exclusive contract with the Verband Deutscher Bühnenschriftsteller and founded a joint distribution company.[3]

---

1 Allen Langdale (ed.): *Hugo Münsterberg on Film. 'The Photoplay: A Psychological Study' and Other Writings.* New York and London 2002, 91, 105, 129.
2 Cf. Wolfgang Mühl-Benninghaus: DON JUAN HEIRATET und DER ANDERE: Zwei frühe filmische Theateradaptionen. In: Thomas Elsaesser and Michael Wedel (eds.): *Kino der Kaiserzeit. Zwischen Tradition und Moderne.* Munich 2002, 336–347.
3 Cf. Leonardo Quaresima: Dichter Heraus! The Autorenfilm and the German Cinema of the 1910s. In: *Griffithiana* 38–39 (1990), 101–126.

https://doi.org/10.1515/9783110613551-003

Yet the first German *Autorenfilm* was not released and marketed as such until January 1913 by Vitascope. Directed by Max Mack, DER ANDERE (THE OTHER ONE) was based on a screenplay by Paul Lindau and starred the famous stage actor Albert Bassermann in the lead role. While Vitascope continued to work with Bassermann and Mack (who with the film WO IST COLETTI?/WHERE IS CO-LETTI? later the same year made the first comic detective film scripted by the well-known writer Franz von Schönthan), several other film companies contributed to this genre over the following two years: Deutsche Bioscop contracted the hugely successful writer Hanns Heinz Ewers and the stage actors Paul Wegener, Grete Berger and Alexander Moissi, resulting in films like DER STUDENT VON PRAG (THE STUDENT OF PRAGUE, 1913), DAS SCHWARZE LOS (THE BLACK LOT, 1913) and DIE AUGEN DES OLE BRANDIS (THE EYES OF OLE BRANDIS, 1914).[4] Davidson's PAGU secured a collaboration with Germany's leading theater director Max Reinhardt. Initially contracted to make four films each year until 1916, Reinhardt was in the end responsible for only two films made in 1913, DIE INSEL DER SELIGEN (THE ISLAND OF THE HAPPY ONES) and DIE VENEZIANISCHE NACHT (THE VENETIAN NIGHT). Messter-Film made three films based on works by Richard Voss, and Continental produced a series of screenplays by Heinrich Lautensack. Nordisk achieved considerable success in the German market with adaptations of Hauptmann's ATLANTIS (1913, dir. August Blom) and Schnitzler's LIEBELEI (1914). Nordisk also signed the Austrian writer Hugo von Hofmannsthal to script DAS FREMDE MÄDCHEN (THE STRANGE GIRL, 1913, dir. Mauritz Stiller) for the Swedish company Svenska Film, which premiered in Berlin in July 1913.

Although the influence of the *Autorenfilm* might seem marginal compared to the total number of films released in Germany at that time, its impact becomes clear when considered in the context of the transition to the long narrative film to which this cycle of prestige productions made a considerable contribution.[5] Set up in opposition to the popular *Sensationsfilm*, the *Autorenfilm* met some of the central demands of the *Kinoreformbewegung* (cinema reform movement), calling for a 'cultural upgrading' and 'higher artistic standards' for the multiple-reel feature film.

Apart from their literary prestige, *Autorenfilme* were promoted through exceptionally large budgets, expensive advertising campaigns and exclusive premieres. *Autorenfilme* helped legitimate the building of larger, architecturally ambitious palace cinemas, the *Kinopaläste*, or cinema palaces, signaling the industry's

---

4 Cf. Deutsche Bioscop Gesellschaft m.b.H. (ed.): *Unsere Künstler*. Berlin [1913/14].
5 Cf. Corinna Müller: Das "andere" Kino? Autorenfilme der Vorkriegsära. In: Corinna Müller and Harro Segeberg (eds.): *Die Modellierung des Kinofilms. Zur Geschichte des Kinoprogramms zwischen Kurzfilm und Langfilm (1905/6–1918)*. Munich 1998, 153–192.

intention to cater to upper middle-class audiences. The emergence of professional film criticism in Germany is also indebted to the *Autorenfilme,* whose arrival coincided with the introduction of new production facilities just outside of Berlin, the most notable examples being the new Bioscop *Glashaus-Atelier* in Neubabelsberg, PAGU's new studio buildings in Tempelhof and Vitascope in Weißensee.

While the first wave of the *Autorenfilm* has undeniably changed the course of German cinema, both in its self-definition and in the critical expectations the cultural establishment has applied to it ever since, it has often been argued that the *Autorenfilm*-cycle brought about only minor innovations in terms of cinematic narration and visual style and relied instead on the literary prestige of the subject matter or amounting to little more than 'filmed theater.' Drawing on the example of a dramatic film based on a script by a literary author before the actual wave of the *Autorenfilme* gained momentum, I want to dispute this view and point both to its cinematic potential and its close proximity to the aesthetic modes of melodrama and even the *Sensationsfilm,* addressing the senses as much as the mind by fusing, to take up Hugo Münsterberg's words from the beginning of this chapter, "the visual perception of the various forms of expression of [...] emotions [...] in our mind with the conscious awareness of the emotion expressed."

2.1 Between author and audience

In 1920, looking back on what would remain the most productive decade of his career, Max Mack was convinced that future historians would acknowledge the significance of his films for the development of German cinema.[6] By then he had directed nearly 100 films of all conceivable genres, among them some of the most successful and popular films the German cinema of the 1910s had produced.[7] Ironically, however, when critics or trade journals paid attention to these films, it often happened without his name being mentioned at all. Mack's DER ANDERE, advertised as the first *Autorenfilm* and based on a play by the then-famous author Paul Lindau, brought onto the screen for the first time one of German theater's most renowned stage actors, Albert Bassermann. For most film historians, the film's lasting significance is to be found in its cultural

---

6 Max Mack: Wie ich zum Film kam. In: *Die Lichtbild-Bühne* 21 (24 May 1919), 24: "If anybody should ever make the effort of writing a history of the German film, then a true expert of the matter will surely not want to pass by my first creations without notice."

7 For biographical information on Mack, cf. Michael Wedel: *Max Mack. Showman im Glashaus.* Berlin 1996.

references to the literary and theatrical establishment rather than in any particular stylistic elements attributable to the director. In its reference to motifs from modern psychology and literature, DER ANDERE figured, for Siegfried Kracauer for instance, as an exemplary foreboding of German cinema's symptomatic obsession with the double, from which other film historians extrapolated the crisis of the male bourgeois identity.[8] Paradoxically, it might have been the very notoriety of DER ANDERE for all subsequent retrospective histories of German cinema which blanked out the name of its director and blocked off any closer attention given to the work of one of the most versatile and prolific, but also enigmatic, directors of the 1910s.

In this sense, the still photograph (apparently inserted at a much later point in time) that opens the film and shows Lindau, Bassermann and Mack assembled around the writer's massive desk (Fig. 2.1) became emblematic for the cinema's cultural transition into the 'bourgeois' sphere of traditional cultural production.[9]

Fig. 2.1: Albert Bassermann, Paul Lindau and Max Mack.

---

8 Siegfried Kracauer: *From Caligari to Hitler. A Psychological History of the German Film*. Princeton 1947, 33–34. Also cf. Heide Schlüpmann: *Unheimlichkeit des Blicks. Das Drama des frühen deutschen Kinos*. Basel and Frankfurt a. M. 1990, 108–113.
9 Cf. Tilo Knops: Cinema from the Writing Desk. Detective Films in Imperial Germany. In: Thomas Elsaesser with Michael Wedel (eds.): *A Second Life. German Cinema's First Decades*. Amsterdam 1996, 132–141.

VITASCOPE

Der Regisseur
schlägt dem Autor
die Hauptdarsteller
für seinen Film vor.

Fig. 2.2: Conjuring up the actors.

But a variation of this opening in another of Mack's *Autorenfilme* problematizes this notion. In WO IST COLETTI?, the author Franz von Schönthan witnesses how Mack conjures up the actors in a series of trick shots which set up the action-packed scenes that follow, a *mise-en-abyme* that culminates in a repetition of this opening in front of a cinema audience within the film at the very end (Fig. 2.2).[10] The trajectory from the author to the audience in WO IST CO-LETTI? is indicative of the transformation of the literary source material into the performative space of the cinema. The agent of these complex processes of transformation is the film director. Mack himself repeatedly defined his role as a "mediator between the author and the audience."[11] According to Mack, the early 1910s were

> A period when each film was an experiment and when there was no authority in power to
> tell what the public wanted; when the problem had to be solved of expressing intelligibly
> to a new audience a vision of a story in terms of a language which was still silent and in

---

10 On these moments of cinematic self-reference in early German cinema, cf. Sabine Hake: Self-Referentiality in Early German Cinema. In: *Cinema Journal* 31:3 (Spring 1992), 37–55.
11 Max Mack: Moderne Filmregie. In: *Die Lichtbild-Bühne* 7 (1920), 13: "Between the audience and the film author a tacit agreement exists about venturing ever more deeply into the innermost problems of mind, soul, and the senses. Does it not therefore stand to reason that the director is doing his best to keep pace with them? More than that, would he not want to provide the appropriate platform on which these battles can take place? After all, the director is the born mediator between author and audience: only he can infuse with blood the poets' dreams, loosen the actors' tongues – if this bold metaphor can be applied to a silent art – and turn the receptive auditorium into the ideal spectator, a process for which Greek tragedy required the chorus."

pictures which were moving pictures without having any examples of this kind in the past to point the way.[12]

In solving this practical problem, the primary requirement of a film director consisted of having an "optical sensibility"[13] that could convey narrative information by visual means such as framing[14] and character movement.[15] In what

---

12 Max Mack: *With a Sigh and a Smile. A Showman Looks Back.* London 1943, 35.

13 Max Mack: Das Motiv: Fachwissenschaftlicher Hinweise. In: *Die Lichtbild-Bühne*, vol. 7:6 (7 February 1914), 11: "Among the many talents the modern cinematic director has to combine, pictorial vision is one of the most necessary and perhaps the most often ignored. [...] Apart from an innate pictorial predisposition there must be a trained eye, a steady apprenticeship of the look."

14 Mack: Das Motiv, 12: "In conclusion, I want to draw your attention to the eminent importance which framing has in film photography." Also cf. Max Mack: *Wie komme ich zum Film?* Berlin 1919, 21: "film is above all a matter of photography. This means: it does not bring onto the screen the beautiful soul, but the material body, the exterior world. And the problem of material appearance is the first, the central question one has to answer in order to be successful in film at all."

15 In his chapter on "Film Direction" in *Wie komme ich zum Film*, Mack has described in great detail the importance of character movement for the transformation of a literary model into the performative space of the cinema: "The director [...] has to make sure that the unity of the photoplay is preserved, that the transition between the individual scenes is continuous, that the pace of the film is kept flowing. It sounds so easy: keeping the pace flowing – but oh how difficult this is in actual practice. Let me single out just one of the many ball scenes. The script says: 'Boisterous ball atmosphere. Lissy enters in excellent mood, when suddenly she spots her husband.' That's all! The film author has done his job, however rudimentary. The general course of the action is defined – now it is a matter for the director to conjure a vivid image from these meagre words. How this is done is probably best illustrated by illustrating my own practice. First of all, the director must have an idea of the overall course of the scene, of the individual events, but not necessarily in all the minor details. Then he contacts the 'artistic advisors.' Together with the art director he discusses the location and the different spaces. They have to be appropriate for the action he is about to film in them. A ballroom isn't just a square room with a couple of doors. Things are not that simple. What one wants to conjure up is not the sight of a few dancing couples, but the atmosphere, the magic of a ball. So, I have an expensive ball staircase leading from a raised platform down into the hall. The orchestra plays in a spacious alcove. A gallery winds itself around the hall at a certain height, interrupted by a few lateral boxes. There are exits to the right and to the left, which lead to brightly-lit side rooms. Once transformed like this, you can really do something with the space. I have several choices of entrances and exits. I have a big gallery that I can use for interrupting shots. And I have a couple of lateral boxes for making all sorts of connections. – Now I let thirty, forty couples dance. Then I choose a group of ladies and gentlemen who enter the hall when I call 'one,' join the exactly defined couples, mingle to blend with the line, disengage and exit through a side door. In the meantime, my group 'two' has entered, consisting of ten waiters, all symmetrically waving their napkins and holding out in front of them champagne bottles on their trays. On another command, more couples come dancing in, appearing from other entrances, rendered in long shot. On command

follows, I shall focus on ZWEIMAL GELEBT, the first of Mack's films made in collaboration with the literary author Heinrich Lautensack, to trace some of the stylistic strategies and experimentations aimed at rendering basic narrative information in a comprehensible manner to a cinema audience – an audience that, due to censorship restrictions in Wilhelmine Germany, apparently never saw ZWEIMAL GELEBT.

2.2 Visual codification of narrative oppositions

In production at about the same time as Mime Misu's TITANIC – IN NACHT UND EIS and scheduled for release in June 1912 as one of Continental-Kunstfilm's first "art-films," ZWEIMAL GELEBT (literally: "Lived Twice") begins with a happy nuclear family – father, mother and daughter – whose happiness is destroyed on the parents' wedding anniversary,[16] when the little girl only narrowly escapes being hit by a car, and her mother (Eva Speyer) suffers a nervous breakdown necessitating that she be committed to a sanatorium. During the mother's stay at the sanatorium, the doctor in charge falls in love with her. Shortly after he has notified her husband via telephone that she will need to stay in the sanatorium for further observation, the mother suffers a serious relapse. She loses consciousness and is declared dead by the doctor who informs her desperate family via a telegram. Two days later, the doctor visits the chapel where her body awaits burial. The woman suddenly rises from her coffin, apparently recovered but suffering total amnesia. The doctor immediately seizes his chance to keep the love object to himself, and without informing her family of the turn of events, takes her abroad. Six months later, the bereaved father takes his daughter on a holiday, and as fate would have it, their paths cross. Observing the playing child, the woman suddenly regains her memory and with it, an awareness of her intolerable situation.

'five,' the couples that passed through the dancers on command 'one' to disappear in the wings have reappeared on the gallery, disturbing the whispering couples there, and throwing confetti down on the crowd. At the same time, the boxes have filled up, the waiters are once more rushing in and pour the champagne. Below in the hall, a couple has in the meantime attracted broad admiration and applause with their step dancing. People are standing in a circle around them, imitating the rhythm of every movement. The dance is coming to an end, the band is playing louder, and everyone joins for the last few steps. This is the appropriate moment to let the plot begin." Mack: *Wie komme ich zum Film?*, 68–71.

16 A piece of information not given in the film as it has come down to us, but in a contemporary plot-synopsis, cf. *Die Lichtbild-Bühne* 24 (15 June 1912), 36.

Torn between two men and two irreconcilable lives, she commits suicide by jumping from a bridge.[17]

As already indicated in the film's title, it is clear from the storyline that the film's narrative hinges on a set of oppositions derived from the main conflict between the woman's 'two lives' before and after her apparent death. This split generates several different female roles (mother/wife and patient/lover) and motivates new roles for both the husband – who must now replace wife and mother – and for the doctor, who becomes his patient's lover. Even the daughter is split by taking over, to a certain degree at least, the role of the mother in relation to her father. The film lays the groundwork for these broad oppositions by dividing the story space into two different action spaces: the home and the sanatorium. Each space is ascribed to one of the men and juxtaposed via parallel editing used to depict different modes of communication between the two men (telephone, telegram).

This split on the level of the story is established spatially in two shots when the mother is left in the sanatorium by her family. Their particular spatial articulation can be regarded as the center of the film on several formal levels. Both shots, by using a diegetically impossible camera view, show two rooms at once by panning 'through' a wall which appears as a visible marker of the compositional pattern in the middle of the frame.[18] At first glance, the two shots have the same spatial structure, but closer inspection reveals that all characters – with the exception of the female protagonist – are substituted in their placement within this structure *after* the cut: the doctor is substituted by his assistant at the side of the patient's couch; in the place of the assistant now stands the nurse and instead of a third man in the frame, it is the father who holds the child; in the center, exactly where the father was just about to reappear from behind the wall, the doctor now emerges in his stead.

---

17 This spectacular variation of the suicide to end a melodramatic narrative was common in German cinema of the early 1910s. Apart from examples in numerous surviving films and/or plot synopses in the contemporary trade press, this is also illustrated by the fact that in 1912 a newly established site for location shooting meant to attract production companies by hinting at the fact that it included a bridge that would be "wonderfully suited for depictions of suicide." Adolf Sellmann: *Der Kinematograph als Volkserzieher?* Langensalza 1912, 19.

18 Edward Branigan has described such a gap between screen space and story space as a visible marker of the narrational process that "leads to degrees and kinds of 'impossible' space; that is, to space which cannot be justified as existing wholly within the diegesis." According to Branigan, "impossible spaces" in turn lead to "perceptual problems of a new kind that force the spectator to reconsider prior hypotheses about time and causality." Edward Branigan: *Narrative Comprehension and Film.* London 1992, 44. For a similar terminological distinction between "story space" and "discourse space," cf. Seymour Chatman: *Story and Discourse. Narrative Structure and Film.* Ithaca 1978, 97–98.

Although this particular pattern of substitution might conceivably be the result of a continuity error during filming, it also instantiates a structural strategy of character substitution that fulfils a narrative function throughout the film. The wall renders visible a spatial narrative code of left/right screen division, which has been at work from the outset and which throughout the narrative continues to constitute the film's key area of formal articulation (Fig. 2.3). This division ascribes the right side of the screen to the mother, while the left side is associated with the two men, respectively. It is through this spatial organization that desire and loss, as the two foremost narrative concerns, are codified within the visual field.

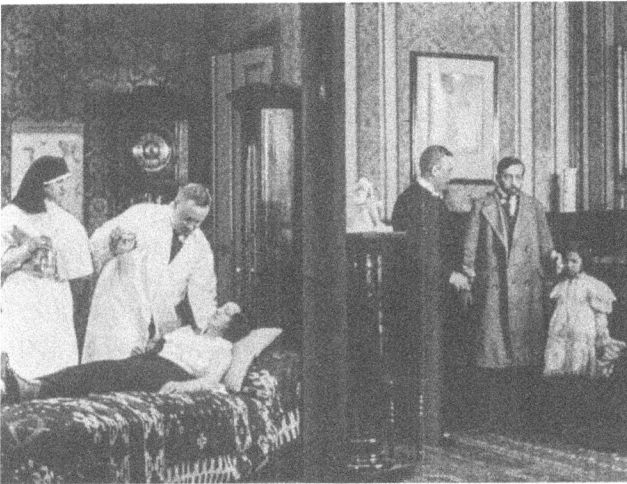

Fig. 2.3: Visibly marking the left/right screen division.

2.3 Spaces of desire

The female protagonist appears almost exclusively on the right half of the screen, whether as the loving wife and mother of the opening shot (Fig. 2.4), the three shots where we see her as a patient in the sanatorium, or in another three shots as the apparent corpse in the chapel.

The left half of the screen space is in a first instance alternatively shared by the two men, and the visualization of their desire leaves the right 'empty' in terms of one character density, most visibly in the sequence after the doctor's love for the patient is revealed, and in the scene where he informs the husband via telephone about the necessity of her extended stay in the sanatorium.

Fig. 2.4: Loving wife and mother.

Compared to the opening shot of the film, the first shot of this scene (and the first to return to the family living room) sets up a strong pattern of repetition, variation and substitution in terms of which one character occupies another character's initial space. This time, we find the daughter in the right half of the screen, a space that was exclusively occupied by her mother in the film's very first shot. After a few seconds, the father enters the shot through the door in the background center (as did the mother in the opening shot), whereupon the daughter stands up and runs towards him. Both sit down on the chair in the foreground left, exactly where they were when the film began, except that now the mother's absence is doubly marked by the empty armchair on the right half of the screen. Next, the father picks up the phone and dials. The following shot cuts back to the mother's hospital room, where the doctor is told by a nurse to answer the call. In the shot that follows, we see the doctor in his office on the phone on the left side of the screen. Parallel to the spatial organization of the domestic scene in the first shot of this sequence, the right half of the frame is marked as that of the absent love object signified by the now empty couch, where the doctor first encountered the mother when she was brought in as a patient. This parallelism is further pronounced by a cut back to the disappointed father and daughter who remain in the same position on screen (Fig. 2.5). The father then kisses his daughter with a vehemence hovering between displaced desire and utter despair, in the very space in the frame where he had kissed his wife in the film's opening shot. Finally, both father and daughter – now aware that the wife/mother will

Fig. 2.5: The absent love object.

stay away a longer period – move over to the sofa on the right side of the screen, thus invading and occupying 'her' diegetic action space for the first time.

It would seem, therefore, that the spatial codification of desire works on a specific division of the screen space, which runs the emotional states of the two male protagonists in tandem, thanks to a strong 'visual rhyme' created via the interaction of story space (location), shot space (left/right division) and continuity/contiguity space (parallel editing).

The use of parallel editing for character psychology has been explored in American film since 1908/09, most notably perhaps in melodramas by D.W. Griffith,[19] familiar to German audiences from at least 1910 onwards.[20] In ZWEI-MAL GELEBT, however, the editing pattern deviates from Griffith's psychological editing in its much more elaborated visual composition of the non-centered shot space. It is on this level that the narration articulates the sequence's psychological substance most visibly, creating significant analogies and variations in relation to earlier shots in both the doctor's and the father's spheres.

The organization of the shot space moreover reveals several important substructures connected to the characters' psychology. The opening shot of the

---

19 See Tom Gunning: Weaving a Narrative. Style and Economic Background in Griffith's Biograph Films. In: Thomas Elsaesser with Adam Barker (eds.): *Early Cinema. Space, Frame, Narrative*. London 1990, 336–347, here 343–344. For an extensive discussion of early examples, cf. Tom Gunning: *D.W. Griffith and the Origins of American Narrative Film. The Early Years at Biograph*. Urbana and Chicago 1991, 85–129.

20 According to Herbert Birett, between 1908 and 1911, 109 Griffith films were released (or at least submitted to censorship boards) in Germany, including Gunning's prime examples for "psychological editing," SUNSHINE SUE (1910) and ENOCH ARDEN (1911). Cf. Birett: *Das Filmangebot in Deutschland 1895–1911*. Munich 1991, 161 and 595 (for the two mentioned titles).

analyzed sequence reveals the father's tendency to replace his wife by occupying the spaces she had previously filled and to displace his (sexual) desire onto his daughter. The doctor's desire, on the other hand, causes no such displacing activity, since it is he who is now 'in possession' of the desired woman. In his sphere, the right screen space remains reserved for her, her absence being only temporary – a hypothesis underlined by the metaphorical placement of a huge wall clock in the background right. Whereas the father's desire is thus already infiltrated with negative signs of loss and substitution, the doctor's desire as it is visually represented can still hope for fulfilment.

2.4 Ciphers of loss

Analogous to the sequence just described, the characters' experiences of what they assume to be the definite loss of the desired woman – the reaction of the two men faced with the heroine's death – is expressed via parallel editing and the symmetrical lateral division of the screen space, whereby several patterns are reverted, confirmed and strengthened. In the longest shot of the whole film,[21] we see the daughter being put to bed in her room by a maid who is introduced here for the first time, thus reinforcing the notion of replacement of the mother. Once more, the father, who enters the shot through a door on the right, and the maid, who then exits by the same door, pass through the right space and create a spatial balance which clearly contrasts with the earlier shot composition articulated in order to create a sense of desire. The maid briefly reappears again from the right to deliver the telegram with the news of his wife's death. The film communicates the news to the spectator with a written insert: "We hereby comply with our sad duty to inform you about the demise of your wife. The sanatorium." The father, who reads the telegram while standing center frame, now sinks into a chair placed foreground left in front of the daughter's bed, re-establishing the familiar spatial division of the previous shot. As

---

21 This shot lasts for 96 seconds. It is interesting to note the tendency of ZWEIMAL GELEBT to retain a coherent shot space in key moments of the narrative. This is reflected, for instance, in the extreme duration of the opening shot (70 seconds); the shot depicting the mother's relapse (83 seconds); and the shot in which the female protagonist and her former family nearly meet while taking a boat trip (69 seconds). The extreme shot duration is always paired with medium long, long, or very long framing. The fact that the film's narration makes no use of closer framing to manipulate the spectator's attention for relevant actions and create the sense of suspense and character psychology once more reinforces the impression of an 'alternative' stylistic paradigm. On this paradigm, cf. David Bordwell: *On the History of Film Style*. Cambridge, Mass. and London 1997, 158–198.

before, he takes his daughter in his arms and hugs her intensely (Fig. 2.6). Though the right shot space is empty again, the connotation with the mother is much weaker since the space has been occupied by the maid and the father just before. The loss of the mother and wife seems to have been accepted, her maternal and sexual roles filled by other female characters.

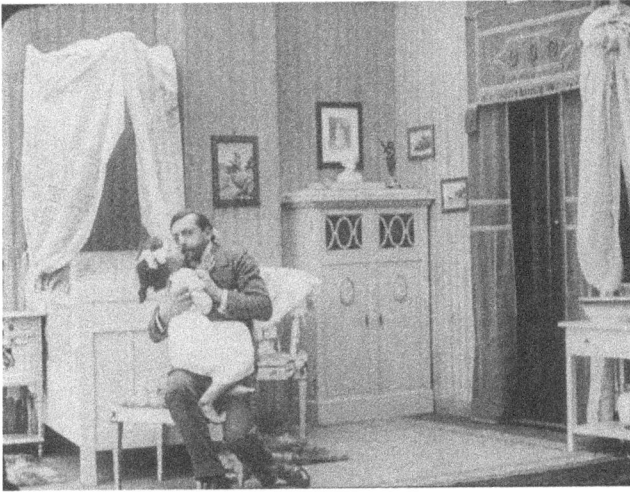

Fig. 2.6: Re-established spatial division.

The visual composition of the shots in which the doctor assimilates the feeling of loss reveals a variation of this pattern that is most crucial for the psychological motivation of the further narrative outcome. Although the doctor is present at the moment of her relapse, the film delays showing his psychological reaction, showing us instead the father's reaction. But following the sequence in the daughter's bedroom and, as we are told by an intertitle, two days later in diegetic time, a shot visualizes the doctor's desire: he sits at his desk in his office in the left half of the shot, with the wall clock and the couch on the right. Immediately, a strong sense of contrast is established with the spatial organization of the shots of the daughter's bedroom, where this visual imbalance was constantly transformed. The film then cuts to the mother lying in the chapel, before an intertitle describes the doctor's feelings ("His thoughts are still with the beloved dead woman") and we are returned to the doctor's office. Still in the same position, his look is kept off-screen, while the image of the mother is superimposed on the right half of the screen between the couch in the foreground and the wall clock at the rear (Fig. 2.7). Only after her image has disappeared does the doctor move over to the couch on the right.

Fig. 2.7: Superimposition of the beloved woman's image.

Fig. 2.8: The woman's resurrection.

In both cases, then, the space of the mother does not remain empty in order to articulate the desires of the two male protagonists as it did – almost without exception – throughout the previous part of the film. Now, as she is assumed to be irretrievably lost to both, the space attributed to her is filled, but in different ways for each of the men. Against the mobility and interchangeability of roles in the domestic space, the compositions expressing the doctor's psychological state 'recreate' the woman in her space with no trace of replacement, connoting the constancy and duration of grief through the repetition of the spatial structure. When, in the next series of shots, the woman re-awakens in his presence, the same logic of visual structure and narrative psychology is at work, once more 'resurrecting' her in her space (Fig. 2.8). In this sense, the visual codification of the shot functions to clarify the narrative's psychological motivation, to bolster the intelligibility of the narrative development and to provide a rationale by which the audience can accept as justified an action otherwise morally reprehensible and professionally criminal.

2.5 Narrative under erasure

The narrative's outcome – the heroine's suicide – results from the ultimate conversion of the respective narrative spheres of the doctor and the father. In the film's final sequence, we encounter the heroine by the seaside, still unaware of her daughter and former husband's presence, appearing diagonally from behind a tree and moving from background right to foreground center. After a cut, we see her daughter at another point on the shoreline, occupying the same shot space foreground center, a visual 'substitution' underscored by the fact that behind her to the right is a small tree whose branches frame the upper space of the shot, just as those of the large tree did in the previous shot with the mother (Fig. 2.9).

Cut back to the shot of the mother, in which the daughter appears from behind the tree in the right background and moves diagonally to foreground left, now face to face with her mother, who stands up and looks alternately at her and off-screen right (Fig. 2.10). As the next intertitle reveals, this is the very moment she regains her memory.[22]

---

22 This form of activating off-screen space via the ostentatious look of a character here, as well as throughout the film, differs from 'classical' modes of visual representation in the cinema in which an imaginary activity constantly refers the off-screen back to the on-screen in the process of creating the illusion of a coherent diegetic world. By contrast, and as an important element of the alternative use of space in ZWEIMAL GELEBT, off-screen space here remains invisible; its activation via the characters' gaze signifies mental activity, memories of an absent object or experience.

Fig. 2.9: Visual substitution.

Fig. 2.10: The mother regains her memory through the shock of recognition.

The daughter rushes off-screen right, with the mother following her to the tree. The mother hides behind the tree when the daughter reappears with her father, crossing the space to the foreground of the shot as the mother glides around the tree to remain hidden from the view of her husband, but visible for the audience. Not finding her, father and daughter leave the shot foreground left, allowing the mother to regain her initial position foreground center, as she gives way to despair.

While indebted to the proscenium space of the theater, with its entrances and exits, and with the tree standing in for stage props, the sequence also works through the very codes – lateral screen division, spatial substitution and visual rhymes, diagonal character movement, camera movement, framing – by which the characters have been profiled psychologically throughout the different stages of the film's action. At the end of the sequence, the woman is positioned center frame, not only by general consent the weakest position on screen for a character, but also, through the film's specific codification of space, a position that does not correlate to any of her former roles as mother, wife, patient, or lover.

The final sequence keeps her in the center of the frame, while a line of trees distinctly segments the space around her (Fig. 2.11). Just as the wall signified the split between the two spheres of the male protagonists, the two men are now superimposed next to the nearest trees on either side of her. In the following shot, she climbs over the railings of the bridge visible in the background of the previous shots and jumps. The line of her fall symmetrically splits the film's final image in in two, at once closing the narrative and literally 'erasing' its mode of visual articulation.

Fig. 2.11: Segmented space.

2.6 Reframing Max Mack

In devising critical paradigms for cinematic narration, subjectivity and character psychology, most of film theory has been conceived around the visual system of classical continuity cinema. Film theorists generally agree that filmic narration works primarily through a set of textual operations by means of interlocking shots that are sometimes seen as equivalent of syntactic relationships in linguistic discourse. Classical devices of continuity editing and cinematic suture – such as scene dissection, shot reverse shot patterns and point-of-view editing – have traditionally been privileged over the composition of the individual shot, which has until recently rarely been explored for its function and value in conveying narrative information and character psychology.[23] In turn, early cinema's different articulation of time, space and causality – often based on the internal organization of the single shot – was long regarded as "ab-psychological [sic] at its most characteristic."[24]

The example of ZWEIMAL GELEBT, however, clearly suggests that the advent of the industrial mode of the *Monopolfilm* and the transition to longer films with more narrative complexity did not also mean the unilinear 'literarization' of film.[25] It existed instead as a dialectical process whereby narrative codes were transposed into the visual space of the cinema. Max Mack's coherent deployment of visual rhymes and spatial codes in ZWEIMAL GELEBT further problematizes the assumption that the internationally uneven transitions and wildly differing approaches to narrative filmmaking can be measured solely by the yardstick of a historical master narrative told from the retro-perspective of the

---

23 The exception being Bordwell's *On the History of Film Style*. Cf. also, more recently, Bordwell: *Figures Traced in Light. On Cinematic Staging*. Berkeley, Los Angeles and New York 2005.
24 For Noël Burch "the *autarky* and *unity* of each frame" and "the *non-centered quality* of the image" are the primary reasons for his conclusion that the "Primitive Cinema at its most characteristic is ab-psychological." (Emphasis in original.) Burch: Primitivism and the Avant-Gardes. A Dialectical Approach. In: Philip Rosen (ed.): *Narrative, Apparatus, Ideology. A Film Theory Reader*. New York 1986, 483–506, here 487.
25 Early German cinema's transition to the long narrative film has traditionally been described in terms of 'literarization.' Apart from the large amount of literature on the phenomenon of the *Autorenfilm*, cf. e.g. Anton Kaes: The Debate about Cinema. Charting a Controversy (1909–1929). In: *New German Critique* 40 (Winter 1987), 7–34, here 9; Joachim Paech: *Literatur und Film*. 2nd ed., Stuttgart 1997; Sabine Hake: *The Cinema's Third Machine. Writing on Film in Germany, 1907–1933*. Lincoln and London 1993, 61–88. Cf. also the extensive collection of contemporary sources in Anton Kaes, Nicholas Baer and Michael Cowan (eds.): *The Promise of Cinema. German Film Theory, 1907–1933*. Oakland 2016.

'dominant' industrial mode of continuity cinema that became the norm for American filmmaking since the mid-1910s.[26]

As the comparison to Griffith's early melodramas suggests, international influences are all too often subject to culturally specific redefinitions and re-appropriations. Such reconfigurations, as can be observed in ZWEIMAL GELEBT, point to the larger cultural force field within which early German cinema in particular sought legitimacy and the appreciation of its public, for whom the theater experience, for instance, constituted a significant intermediary reference point. In this sense, the triangularity of emblematic openings in later films, showing author, star and director, only seems to epitomize the different spaces folded into this process: the story space of the narrative, the filmic space of the screen, the performative space of the acting and the experiential space that results for the audience in the cinema.[27]

This double- and triple-coding inherent in the articulations of cinematic space should make us wary of any direct reading of filmic patterns or motifs in the essentially literary terms of 'influence' or 'authorship.' Mack's simultaneous presence in and absence from the films he directed is thus symptomatic: given the many references in his writings to contemporary stage practices, painting, landscape photography and music hall variety culture, the very stylistic sim-plicity or alleged backwardness of a film like ZWEIMAL GELEBT could well reveal itself as a palimpsest whose code is no longer in our hands. Mack's ability to bind together different textual authorities and cultural frames within one cine-matic space while remaining in tune with the sensibilities of contemporary audiences, spells out the logic that made him one of the German cinema's most popular directors of the 1910s.

---

26 Cf. the extremely instructive comparative analysis in Barry Salt: Early German Film. The Stylistics in Comparative Context. In: Elsaesser with Wedel (eds.): *A Second Life*, 225–236.

27 "The opening sequence is the visiting card of the film director. Before the colorful play be-gins, a gentleman bows and takes a call, smiling at the audience with friendly reservation, stroking his dog with Napoleonic seriousness or agonizingly browsing through the manu-script. This is the film director who in this unobstrusive manner hammers into the brains of the audience that he is the maker of this world. Usually, the actors, too, follow with a sweet smile and sometimes, in the big hits, also the film author, deeply absorbed in his thoughts, bent over his writing desk. The opening sequence deals with everything in the film. Presenta-tion, taking a call, making a bow: in short, all those captivating vanities of the stage. And the audience is by now so used to it that popular directors are made welcome by a warm round of applause the very moment their faces appear on the screen." Max Mack: Die Toilette des Films. In: Max Mack (ed.): *Die zappelnde Leinwand*. Berlin 1916, 124–125.

3 Frames of desire: Franz Hofer, melodrama and narrative space

> Every typical space is produced by typical social relations which it expresses without the distorting intervention of consciousness. Everything denied by consciousness, everything studiously ignored participates in the construction of such a space. The images of space [*Raumbilder*] are the dreams of society. Wherever the hieroglyph of a spatial image is deciphered, it displays the foundation of social reality. Siegfried Kracauer, 1930[1]

One dimension that the methodological distinction between a "cinema of attractions" and a "cinema of narrative integration"[2] has contributed to the understanding of early cinema is to have sharpened our sensibility for the manifold ways in which the individual style of a film mediates transitions and inaugurates differentiations between cinema's 'discursive reality' and other contemporary forms of cultural production and popular entertainment. The abstraction inherent in trying to chart these two modes of cinematic practice in the form of a set of parameters – frontality and direct audience address on the one hand, continuity editing and the creation of an imaginary diegetic universe on the other – implies a radical 'openness' as to the articulation of cinematic space. Its 'ideal type' or paradigmatic 'virtuality' requires historically grounded re-definitions and specifications, due to its openness to different kinds of variables: internationally-uneven industrial developments, national audience compositions, genre formations and pertinent media intertexts.

Confronted with – and responding to – some of the striking stylistic 'non-synchronicities' in international film heritage of the 1910s, historians have called upon a number of readily available explanations for the visible 'delay' of the German cinema. The relatively late establishment of domestic film production and the conservative pressures exerted by the reformist writings of the cultural elite

---

1 Siegfried Kracauer: Über Arbeitsnachweise. Konstruktion eines Raumes [1930]. In: *Schriften*, vol. 5.3: *Essays, Feuilletons, Rezensionen*, ed. by Inka Mülder-Bach. Berlin 2011, 249–257, here 250; transl. quoted from Miriam Hansen: Mass Culture as Hieroglyphic Writing. Adomo, Derrida, Kracauer. In: *New German Critique* 56 (Spring/Summer 1992), 43–73, here 66.
2 Tom Gunning: The Cinema of Attraction. Early Film, Its Spectator and the Avant-garde. In: *Wide Angle* 3–4 (1986), 63–70. Cf. also Tom Gunning: Non-Continuity, Continuity, Discontinuity. A Theory of Genres in Early Film. In: *Iris* 2:1 (1984), 100–112. On the influence of Gunning's concept, cf. the essays collected in Wanda Strauven (ed.): *The Cinema of Attractions Reloaded*. Amsterdam 2006.

https://doi.org/10.1515/9783110613551-004

have been seen as primarily responsible for the phenomenon of stylistic 'backwardness' visible in the *Autorenfilm*, a genre that seemed to epitomize German cinema's *Sonderweg* (separate development) well into the 1920s. Slow cutting rates, the lack of scene dissection and continuity editing, tableau-like framings and frontal acting, combined with complicated and often contradictory plots, seemed to reconstruct a 19th-century theatrical narrative space devoid of spectacle and visual pleasure.

But the (methodo-)logical gaps and improbabilities of this historical narrative have become ever more evident as archive restorations have obliged scholars to revise their preconceptions of early German cinema in the face of the stylistic multiplicity that has come to light across the popular genre films and in light of the versatility of directors like Mime Misu and Max Mack. With the rediscovery of the films by Franz Hofer in particular, German cinema's "backwardness" has had to be rethought.

Franz Hofer started out as a stage actor and playwright in 1909. A year later, he began working as a screenwriter for Oskar Messter's Henny Porten series and for directors such as Viggo Larsen (DIE SCHWARZE KATZE/THE BLACK CAT, 1910) and Walter Schmidthässler (DAS WEIB OHNE HERZ/THE WOMAN WITHOUT A HEART and DER ZUG DES HERZENS/THE PULL OF THE HEART, both 1912). After directing his first film DES ALTERS ERSTE SPUREN (FIRST TRACES OF AGE, 1913) for the newly founded Luna-Film, Hofer directed a total of 25 films for the company over a three-year period, the most productive and commercially successful phase of his career.[3] Combining the roles of scriptwriter and director, Hofer exercised almost complete control over the style and content of his films, whose generic provenance ranged from early sophisticated comedies (e.g., HURRAH! EINQUARTIERUNG!/HURRAH! QUARTERING and DAS ROSA PANTÖFFELCHEN/THE PINK SLIPPER, both 1913) and detective films (e.g. DER STECKBRIEF/THE 'WANTED' POSTER, 1913, and VAMPYRE DER GROSSSTADT/VAMPIRES OF THE CITY, 1914) to melodramas (KAMMERMUSIK/CHAMBER MUSIC, 1915). His films were often set against the background of World War I, as in WEIHNACHTSGLOCKEN 1914 (CHRISTMAS BELLS 1914, 1914). Although his films were exposed to radical censorship measures from early on, DIE SCHWARZE NATTER (THE BLACK VIPER, 1913) and DIE SCHWARZE KUGEL ODER DIE GEHEIMNISVOLLEN SCHWESTERN (THE BLACK BOWL, OR, THE MYSTERIOUS SISTERS, 1913) greatly contributed to the development of the *Sensationsfilm*, a genre based on fast-paced physical action, heavy eroticism and explicit

---

3 For more filmographical information about Hofer, cf. Andrea Dittgen: *Franz Hofer*. Saarbrücken 1999.

violence. The *Sensationsfilm* became the primary target of the conservative cinema reform movement in Germany.

Because Hofer wrote his own scripts, the trade press, however, honored his films as *Autorenfilme* and thereby acknowledged an unmistakable stylistic signature marking his work from at least 1913 on.[4] Judging from eleven surviving films from the years 1913 to 1916, Hofer's films' main formal qualities consisted of bizarre twists of plot; extravagant decors and lighting patterns, often emphasizing ornamental shadows and picturesque silhouettes; a complex use of symmetrical compositions, masked shots and internal montage through superimposed views; and, finally, a strong emotional charge produced by keyhole shots and point-of-view editing, frontal staging and direct address. Navigating his protagonists through such intricate cinematic terrain, Hofer also drew memorable performances from (predominantly female) actors whose names are today long forgotten. The most notable was the young Dorrit Weixler, who rose to stardom with Das Rosa Pantöffelchen. Weixler appeared in ten more of his films before she split from Hofer and committed suicide in December 1916 at the age of 24.

Hofer's idiosyncratic use of cinematic space in a series of popular genre films produced in 1913/14 and thus during the heyday of the *Autorenfilm* proved that German directors were indeed capable of matching international standards of narrative filmmaking. On the other hand, Hofer's ambiguous construction of narrative space via the use of masking and silhouettes, close-ups and point-of-view shots, frontality and direct address, internal montage and shot composition reveal a stylistic paradigm radically different from both American standards of continuous narration and from the immobile 'theatricality' of national productions, whether French or German.

Indeed, the elegance and originality with which Hofer's visual space of 'attractionist' devices is integrated into the narrative process point to the lasting relevance of a number of 'popular' intertexts such as the variety theater and the shadow play, the stereoscope and the Magic Lantern. In the first place, then, Hofer's films remind us once more that the distinction between attractionist and narratively integrated modes of cinematic space was never meant to be a self-explanatory analytical tool according to which individual films could be lined up within a linear transition to narrative cinema. They instead provide us with a set of traits whose variable configurations constitute the historically unique discursive space of the individual film: the hieroglyph of its historicity.

---

4 Cf. the article on Hofer in *Die Lichtbild-Bühne*'s 1913 special issue on the "Kino-Regisseur," no. 23 (7 June 1913).

3.1 Melodrama/social drama: Training for marriage?

The last point bears especially on the image of women's films in early German cinema, which, in the wake of Gunning's distinction, has been defined by a number of bi-polar models and oppositional pairs. A first opposition emerged around the two major female stars: Henny Porten and Asta Nielsen. While Porten has been characterized as "a star who fits in well with the conventions of the melodramatic scene," Nielsen has gained exemplary status as the one actress who gave "a voice to a female presence in early cinema narratives, a voice notably absent in those adaptations of melodrama that perpetuated the stage image of women as prescribed by the dramatic sources."[5]

Along the lines of the distinction between a 'cinema of attractions' and a 'cinema of narrative integration,' Heide Schlüpmann has principally argued that the transition from the attractionist-exhibitionist form to the voyeuristic cinema of continuity in Germany meant not only a rise in cultural respectability through the co-option of famous writers and actors into the film business, but also a compliance to patriarchal power structures in the narratives themselves:

> [W]ith the establishment of narrative cinema, there was a tendency to degrade woman's history to the status of mere content for which male bourgeois culture provided the form of representation. To the extent that there remained, however, a tension between the represented story and the dramatic framework [...], there was always a chance for the actress in the film to express an oppositional standpoint. This tension can be attributed to the collision between two media (literature and film) which also implied a collision between two cultures – classical bourgeois and modern mass culture.[6]

---

5 Heide Schlüpmann: Cinema as Anti-Theater. Actresses and Female Audiences in Wilhelminian Germany. In: *Iris* 11 (Summer 1990), 77–93, here 90. With similar implications, Janet Bergstrom has described Asta Nielsen's characters: "If one looks at the story structure, Nielsen's female characters are punished for their transgressive behavior, or punish themselves, or move back within social norms in the final scenes. In many of her melodramatic parts, she is a victim at the end. Yet, she is never a conventional victim. The very naturalness with which she endows so many actions deemed unusual for women, her integrity, her depth of feeling, her active sense of intelligence, her particular kind of sensuality, mark her female roles with an individuality that resists the reduction to types that will become common during the 1920s in Germany. In Asta Nielsen's films of the pre-Weimar period, she creates characters based on familiar melodramatic types, but who are nevertheless individualized by a strong sense of self-identity and self-definition through their expression of interiority and the way they assert their presence within the environment." Janet Bergstrom: Asta Nielsen's Early German Films. In: Paolo Cherchi Usai and Lorenzo Codelli (eds.): *Before Caligari. German Cinema, 1895–1920.* Pordenone 1990, 162–185, here 178–180.

6 Heide Schlüpmann: Melodrama and Social Drama in Early German Cinema. In: *Camera Obscura* 22 (January 1990), 73–89, here 75–76.

In order to investigate the ideological reverberations of this tension in the films, Schlüpmann distinguishes between "melodrama" and "social drama" in Wilhelmine cinema. According to this logic, melodramas represented social problems of women in a stylized tragic structure, by which the suffering of the heroine in a male-dominated society is transfigured into an image of sacrifice. This sacrifice serves only to domesticate the female narrative perspective, which in turn serves to confirm an always already defined femininity: "The actress, representative of femininity, i.e. of male projection rather than articulation of female experience, no longer represents her own narrative perspective, but enforces the dominant order."[7]

In contrast to the melodrama, the social drama did not force the female narrative perspective in favor of a stereotypical representation of femininity within a dramatized story. Instead, by appealing to the curiosity of female spectators, gave the subjectivity of the actress a "spatial framework" in the text that derives its strength from the foundation in the mode of the cinema of attractions.[8] In conclusion, Schlüpmann states:

> The appropriation of German cinema through the melodrama developed a repressive distraction in the sublimation of the female gaze and its power. By contrast, the dramatization of the female gaze through the social drama tended towards a representation of male sexuality, of the man as sexual object. This tendency obviously collided with the influence of the guardians of bourgeois culture; social drama, unlike melodrama, disappeared from narrative cinema after World War I.[9]

Despite the strong dialectical formulation that concludes her article, Schlüpmann sees constitutive elements of the social drama shifting 'underground' into a variety of genres during and after World War I. Accordingly, the main indicator of this transition is the formation of the couple, represented within the institution of marriage, itself mediated by a particularly fetishistic articulation of female sexuality:

> In this mediation lay the real significance of the objects. On the one hand, they are everyday objects that play a role as props in the course of the narrative. On the other, they possess a fetish character insofar as they appear in the place of the openly erotic attraction in the "mistress films." They substitute for the sexual element repressed in the representation of marriage.[10]

---

7 Schlüpmann: Melodrama and Social Drama in Early German Cinema, 76.
8 Schlüpmann: Melodrama and Social Drama in Early German Cinema, 78.
9 Schlüpmann: Melodrama and Social Drama in Early German Cinema, 86–87.
10 Schlüpmann: Melodrama and Social Drama in Early German Cinema, 85.

Although Franz Hofer's Heidenröslein (1916) may serve as an example of this historical mediation between the traditional dramatic formula of the melodrama and the explosive subversive potential of the social drama in German filmmaking of the late 1910s, it should be noted that Schlüpmann's argument shifts onto the content level at this point, presupposing as given and solidly established a representational logic (classical continuity cinema as the norm) which makes this displacement necessary in the first place.

The following analysis of Heidenröslein seeks to conceive of the genre's 'social' potential without relying on the film's content level or on diametrically-opposed star images or acting styles. Instead, the film suggests a mediation of another kind, one that uses the visual capacity of cinematic discourse to externalize individual emotion and desire while at the same time internalizes historical processes by rendering social conflicts in spatial terms. My analysis does not assume a linear transition from an attractionist to a narratively integrated cinema. Given that the film reveals only three instances of closer framing than medium shot and only two moving shots, its formal articulation emerges from the 'primitive' tableau.

We can here take Peter Brooks at his word when he claimed that the melodramatic tableau gives the "spectator the opportunity to see meanings represented, emotions and moral states rendered in clear visible signs."[11] What follows is thus less a symptomatic reading of the narrative itself than a deciphering of the concrete spatial condensations of social and moral codes that fill the melodramatic formula.

3.2 Deep space and frontal space: Condensations of a social code

The historical evidence for Schlüpmann's argument goes back to the sociological data assembled in Emilie Altenloh's pioneering study *Zur Soziologie des Kino* from 1914.[12] Based on a close analysis of movie theater statistics and over 2,000 questionnaires conducted in Mannheim, Altenloh's *Sociology of the Cinema* has to be considered one of the most sophisticated sources on spectator preferences and attitudes in the context of an industrial city before World War I. The study has generally remained of special interest for its emphasis on

---

11 Peter Brooks: *The Melodramatic Imagination. Balzac, Henry James, Melodrama and the Mode of Excess*. New York 1985, 62.
12 Emilie Altenloh: *Zur Soziologie des Kino. Die Kinounternehmung und die sozialen Schichten ihrer Besucher*. Jena 1914. The survey was undertaken in 1913.

women making up a significant part of early cinema's audience – a phenomenon that, according to Altenloh, is the result of a complex interplay between capitalist marketing via genres on the side of the industry and a socially as well as sexually determined popular taste on the side of the audience. Altenloh herself explains the transformation that occurred around 1910 as being the result of a combination of factors, not least of which were the rise of melodramatic narratives and the establishment of larger, more comfortable theaters in city centers.

Being especially interested in why women liked watching films, Altenloh found that women had marked preferences for melodramas and social dramas. In both genres, according to Altenloh, the central narrative conflict is set up by "a woman's battle between her natural, feminine instincts and the opposing social conditions."[13] For the female protagonists of these dramas, Altenloh further notes, the choice is between "on the one hand prostitution, on the other the possibility of marriage at the side of a man, who mostly belongs either to a considerably higher or lower social grade."[14]

Despite the common view that Hofer "was apparently not a director of melodramas or social dramas,"[15] a conclusion drawn almost exclusively from a fixed perspective on his pre-war productions, Hofer in fact directed a number of melodramas with strong social undercurrents in the mid- and late 1910s, including a series of films for Apollo-Film starring Lya Ley in 1916, as well as another series in 1918/19, starring Werner Krauss, who would later that year play Dr. Caligari in Robert Wiene's seminal expressionist film DAS CABINET DES DR. CALIGARI (THE CABINET OF DR. CALIGARI).[16] As a first run through the plot may indicate, Hofer's 1916 film HEIDENRÖSLEIN, based on Goethe's famous poem of the same name and accordingly advertised by its production company as a *"Kunstfilm"* (art film),[17] offers a clear example of a melodramatic narrative: Little Rose (Lya Ley) has come to visit her grandparents for the summer holidays. She chances upon the young Count von Brödersdorff (Fritz Achterberg) on one of the walks both are taking in the nearby forest. Soon after, Rose is asked to tend to the count's mother, the local Baroness, who is suffering from rheumatic pains. On this

---

13 Altenloh: *Zur Soziologie des Kino*, 58.
14 Altenloh: *Zur Soziologie des Kino*, 58.
15 Heide Schlüpmann: The Sinister Gaze. Three Films by Franz Hofer from 1913. In: Cherchi Usai and Codelli (eds.): *Before Caligari*, 452–472, here 452.
16 For the latter series, cf. Fritz Güttinger: Franz Hofer: Ausgrabung des Jahres? In: Fritz Güttinger: *Köpfen Sie mal ein Ei in Zeitlupe. Streifzüge durch die Welt des Stummfilms.* Zurich 1992, 15–22; Dittgen: *Franz Hofer*, 63–68.
17 Cf. *Die Lichtbild-Bühne* 38 (23 September 1916), 41.

occasion she once more meets the Count and at this point they both realize they are in love with each other. From then on, they continue to meet, though not only when Rose visits the Baroness. Their love makes them bold: they have secret dates in the forest or in a small apartment the Count owns down in the village. When Rose's grandfather eventually finds out, he is furious because of the shame her action has brought on him and his family. Because Rose entirely disappears from the public eye, the Count begins to believe the rumours of her having died of shame. Haunted by memories of their mutual past as lovers, he returns to the little room to imagine her funeral service. Unwilling to stay in the dark about her fate any longer, he decides to go to visit her grandparents' house, where he finds Rose alive and well and assures her grandfather of his intentions to marry her.

If, for the purposes of analysis, we adopt Altenloh's definition of the central melodramatic narrative conflict and focus on how the opposition between female desires and social restrictions is visually concretized in HEIDENRÖSLEIN, we find a pattern of spatial character movement according to a division between deep space and frontal shot composition. Established in the opening sequence, this pattern becomes the basis for an ingenious visual structure centered on the generic conflict identified by Altenloh that echoes the stages of the narrative development. Framed by two intertitles announcing the imminence of Rose's annual visit and her actual arrival, the film's first image shows the grandparents in a medium long shot in the foreground of their living room. The first use of deep staging occurs with Rose's anticipated appearance in the film as she enters the front garden from the background and moves on a long diagonal axis toward the open entrance door behind which the camera is placed in the dark foreground. In this sequence, she enters the dark interior and leaves the shot past the camera.

The film's principal character Rose creates a dynamic three-dimensional action-space that is here, as in later shots, paired with frontal staging and the character's direct eye contact with the camera, something that connects strongly to elements of cinematic exhibitionism and spectacle. The shot's particular organization of character movement, camera position and lighting could even be read as a mediation between the filmic space and the imaginary space of the darkened cinema. Rose meets her grandmother and grandfather in the next two scenes. In one scene she enters into their frontal space, and in the other, she remains immobile in the background. She regains her initial spatial mobility only in situations in which she is either alone in the shot and/or just about to leave the sphere of her grandparents.

While this division between deep space and frontal staging in the first part of the film remains on the level of character movement and character position, there is a considerable change once Rose encounters Count Brödersdorff. Once again, it is Rose who moves from background to foreground, stopping to pick some roses from a bush. In the meantime, Brödersdorff has entered in the background and observes Rose while leaning on a fence. The fence visibly marks, for the first time in the film, a near/far distinction, which previously had to be traversed by Rose in order to be marked as such. Now it is bridged by the looks of the lovers-to-be, with the pleasure of the male look accentuated for the audience by the metaphorical pairing of young Rose with real roses in the foreground. Although the shot's visually adroit near/far division of space undoubtedly alludes to their social difference, the full significance of this particular shot composition for the overall narrative conflict between an unrestricted articulation of female activity and desire, and the surrounding constraints of the social and family hierarchies emerges only when, in subsequent shots, this division increasingly acts as a barrier and disruption of the action space identified with Rose. Along the lines of a similar spatial division, a later shot completely suppresses her diagonal movement as she leaves her grandparents' living room. In order to leave the family group situated in the foreground, she first has to move to foreground right and then exit the frame altogether, before reappearing in the background behind a window at the rear wall. The spatial configuration of this shot thus metaphorically condenses the entirety of her narrative trajectory in the film.

3.3 Looks and mental spaces

Even more instructively, the organization of the subsequent shots indicates the scale of the multiple spatial codifications, in particular the gradual destruction of Rose's initial mobility. Rose enters the background of first shot of the sequence, visible inside the house through the window where she stops to look outside to the foreground terrace. In the following shot, the door is open and Rose is on her way to the bushes in the foreground, overgrown with white roses, obliging her to stop. While her look is directed off-screen, the image of Count Brödersdorff becomes superimposed to her left, fading at the very moment she seems to turn her eyes towards it.

Once more, her diagonal movement has been partially blocked by a door, which here is further pronounced by a cut. Her movement to the foreground is now strongly associated with the desire to recreate herself in the place where she was seen by Brödersdorff, which is indicated not only by the superimposition of the object of her thoughts but also by the repetitive metaphorical use of the roses. The frontal space is, in the end, established as the place of the romance and thus the second socially defined sphere: even in the female protagonist's imagination it is determined by the objectifying male look. At the same time that her desire is granted visual expression, Rose's immobility exposes her to the voyeuristic gaze of the male spectator, split – as before – between the male mirror image on screen and the pleasure of the visual metaphor aligning Rose with roses. If she were to return the look as she had previously done, the pleasure of the voyeur would vanish just as the Count's image vanishes.

Whereas this new social dimension of the near camera space constitutes an opposition to the social space shared with the grandparents, both of these social spaces stand in opposition to Rose's initial action space in that they suppress diagonal movement and are instead marked by a seeing/seen pattern within the single shot that exposes her to the controlling look of either the Count or the grandfather. That this basic opposition is again predominantly constructed around the division of deep and frontal space is made clear several times during the film. Once, during one of their secret meetings, Rose enters from the far background on the familiar diagonal axis and meets the Count in the foreground, before both leave the subsequent medium shot, foreground left. Another time, when Rose is about to leave her grandparents' house through the front garden – inverting the axis of her entering the film in the first scene – and the grandfather forces her to step back into the house and thus to remain in the foreground.

The most striking example of this pattern is to be found, however, when Rose and her grandfather visit the baronial estate. Framed in a very long high angle shot, Rose approaches diagonally the (once more darkened) foreground. The next shot finds her exposed to a whole assembly of socially controlling looks, most notably that of the Count, the grandfather and the Baroness, the Count's mother.

Heidenröslein thus relies on two visual systems, deployed systematically and within a determinate narrative and poetic logic. The development on the level of shot space from forms of female spectacle-display to patterns of social, predominantly male control through the agency of the look is paralleled by transitions in the seeing/seen pattern on the level of the imaginary space constructed by the editing. While in the first part of the film the editing was dominated by the female protagonist's active look or movement, in the course of the action this agency is increasingly taken over by the two male protagonists, the Count and the grandfather, acting as patriarchal figures par excellence. For example, whereas Rose initiated the first of her morally and socially transgressive romantic meetings with Brödersdorff through a point-of-view construction relying on the near/far division, it is Brödersdorff's look and continuity editing of left/right screen direction that drive their last meeting, during which they are temporarily separated by the grandfather. Likewise, the film initially depicts the psychological motivation for their secret meetings as belonging to Rose's subjectivity. The long flashback and funeral dream sequence, however, focalize Brödersdorff's subjectivity and lead to his decision to finally marry Rose. Concomitantly, the active agency of the look is taken over fully by the grandfather who observes Rose in a number of point-of-view constructions. The two key constituents of narrative agency, character movement and the active gaze, are split between the two male protagonists, propelling the action towards the generic outcome of 'melodrama' (marriage), which either of these elements alone would not have succeeded in bringing about.

A male perspective replaces and undermines Rose's once dominant narrative agency in the film, one that tries to prevent the formal elements that gave cinematic 'voice' to her desires. When, for instance, her gaze and movement still seem to initiate a cut on action during a visit to the Baroness, the next shot reveals both had been provoked by the 'off-screen' sound of the Count playing the piano: Most likely, a musical version of Goethe's *Lied* from which the film borrows its title. Consequently, Rose's movement remains within the foreground of the two shots, the place of social interaction and control. In a similar vein, the grandfather does not succeed in his disciplinary efforts until he can literally remove Rose from her diagonal action space, carrying her from the foreground to off-screen left after catching her on her way to another secret rendezvous.

The extent to which the film relates frontal acting and lateral character movement to oppressive patriarchal conditions towards female identity emerges for a last time in the structural relation between the only two moving shots. The camera pans to the left when Brödersdorff's 'off-screen' piano music motivates Rose's change of action space from the diagonal to the lateral axis. And in the dream sequence towards the end of the film, in which the Count imagines Rose's funeral service in the local church, the camera pans slowly to the right, away from the organ-playing priest to the grandfather whose pupils intone what is supposed to be a requiem. Not only does the second pan shot to the right close the space opened up by the earlier camera pan to the left; by substituting for the piano-playing Brödersdorff a priest playing a requiem, it also establishes a strong connection between the oppressive redefinition of Rose's female narrative perspective and her imaginary misery.

3.4 Silhouettes and hieroglyphics: Training for effect

At the end of HEIDENRÖSLEIN there is the anticipation of marriage. In this respect, 'Training for Marriage' might have been a more appropriate title for this film, one that would have made explicit much of German family melodrama's most common dramatic feature from the 1910s to the 1960s. In fact, DRESSUR ZUR EHE (TRAINING FOR MARRIAGE) was the title of a film, now presumed lost, directed by Hofer in close temporal proximity to HEIDENRÖSLEIN, also starring Lya Ley as Rose and Fritz Achterberg as her male counterpart: DRESSUR ZUR EHE, however, was a light, comic melodrama that casts the husband as the figure who has to be trained for marriage on his honeymoon by his wife and mother-in-law,[18] re-inforcing once more that this genre's social dimension unveils itself more easily under the disguise of comedy.[19]

In HEIDENRÖSLEIN, by the time Rose's trajectory has turned toward marriage, she has passed along the razor's edge between kept mistress and victimized wife. Despite its gradual erasure of the female narrative perspective, however, the film does not arrive at anything comparable to classical 'voyeuristic' cinema's sense of narrative closure. Instead, it leaves traces of alterity as the visible markers of the melodramatic genre: the film's studied visual elaboration gives an over-determined – even ironic – status to the role of Rose as mistress, rendering the secret love scenes as pure shadow plays of silhouettes, while depicting female victimization as the 'dream' of male subjectivity.

The tableau of the last shot, which seals the promise of marriage, is again composed as an echo of the cinematic situation itself: the grandfather, re-framed in a rectangle formed by the wooden trellis entwined with white roses, observes the couple in the foreground. The phantasmagoric quality of such visual compositions seems to suggest that the social reality to be read from these hieroglyphs of happy endings necessarily takes the form of an illusion. Such a closing scene suggests that in Wilhelmine Germany, as in other cultural contexts undergoing the transition to modernity, the melodramatic mode can function as a form of narrative ambiguously poised between conformism and subversion, for which, in the wake of Peter Brooks, film scholars have appropriated the term 'excess.'[20] This suggests to me, as it did to one unknown contemporary reviewer, a different title altogether: not 'Training for Marriage' (*Dressur zur Ehe*) but 'Training for Effect' (*Dressur zur Wirkung*).[21]

---

18 Cf. *Die Lichtbild-Bühne* 35 (2 September 1916), 34.

19 Cf., for example, Jürgen Kasten: Dramatik und Leidenschaft – Das Melodram der frühen zehner Jahre. Von ABGRÜNDE (1910) bis VORDERTREPPE UND HINTERTREPPE (1915). In: Werner Faulstich and Helmut Korte (eds.): *Fischer Filmgeschichte*, vol. 1: *Von den Anfängen bis zum etablierten Medium 1895–1924*. Frankfurt a. M. 1994, 233–247, here 243–244.

20 Cf., for example, the contributions to Frank Kelleter, Barbara Krah and Ruth Mayer (eds.): *Melodrama! The Mode of Excess from Early America to Hollywood*. Heidelberg 2007.

21 *Die Lichtbild-Bühne* 35 (2 September 1916), 28: "What Franz Hofer actually delivers here is proof of the training for effect [*Dressur zur Wirkung*]."

4 Phantasmatic intimacy: The tears of Asta Nielsen

> There must be [...] an organic connection between the independence of the actor's nature and his specific artistry, on one side, and the rights and the meaning of the play, on the other; there must be an ideal sketch to set forth how the role should be made sensual, in which the charm and appeal of the actor's personality and the objective demands of the play are woven together, without offering a mechanical mixture, which is truly unthinkable.
>
> Georg Simmel, 1920/21[1]

On October 15, 1920, director Ernst Lubitsch addressed an open letter to actress Asta Nielsen.[2] Lubitsch was responding to an interview given by the actress the week before, published only a few days earlier, in which Nielsen criticized a certain "foregrounding of the technical" (*Hervordrängung des Technischen*) that would increasingly limit the "broadening of the artistic" (*Ausbreitung des Künstlerischen*) and thus considerably reduce the quality of German cinema.[3] Their public dispute would polarize into two axiomatic positions, bringing into the open a fundamental tension between acting and directing and highlighting larger shifts in film form and cinematic performance styles.

In the interview, Nielsen spoke of her painful experience with the tendency to privilege directing in the course of Lubitsch's adaptation of August Strindberg's stage play RAUSCH (INTOXICATION, 1919) in which she played the main protagonist Henriette. Arguing that in Strindberg's play, the "meaning and emotional content [*der seelische Gehalt*] [...] are not to be found outside the narrative" but reside directly in "the events and sensations" themselves, Nielsen contended that a successful interpretation, one that did justice to the exceptional quality of the literary source material, was only possible if the external dramatic action and the internal emotional content of the drama were shaped into a single expressive form by the actress's performance. According to Nielsen, it is only through the unique artistic virtuosity of the performative act itself that the

---

1 Georg Simmel: Zur Philosophie des Schauspielers [1920/21]. In: Georg Simmel: *Das individuelle Gesetz. Philosophische Exkurse*, ed. Michael Landmann. Frankfurt a. M. 1987, 75–95, here 85. English translation of Simmel's posthumously published text by Philip Lawton from Georg Simmel: Towards the Philosophy of the Actor, 9. Available at https://papers.ssrn.com/sol3/papers.cfm?abstract_id=2897044 (accessed 15 April 2018).

2 Asta Nielsen und Ernst Lubitsch. Ein offener Brief an Asta Nielsen. In: *Lichtbild-Bühne* 43 (16 October 1920), 31–32.

3 Walter Steinthal: Bei Asta Nielsen. In: *Die Lichtbild-Bühne* 41 (9 October 1920), 42.

https://doi.org/10.1515/9783110613551-005

dramatic action and its inherent emotional content can be brought together and transmitted to the audience via the immediate experience of sensual perception.[4]

This particular configuration of dramatic action and its inherent emotional content, of performative expressivity and aesthetic sensibility on the part of the audience, seems to have been what Nielsen perceived as the challenge that was put before her when she was playing Henriette. It was a challenge that would require the actress to claim an autonomous dimension of time and space for her individual interpretation of the character within the process of adaptation. But, as Nielsen further points out, current audience taste demanded nothing more than "pure narrative action, sensation after sensation": "The artist isn't given any time anymore to fully develop her acting skills [in front of the camera]. Or, if the time is granted to her during shooting, the scissors of the director are taking it away again after the fact: as superfluous."[5] In a very concrete sense, Nielsen here alludes to a scene in RAUSCH where she brought to the fore one of her most succinct expressive gestures as an actress: a close-up shot in which she weeps, communicating to her audience an inner emotion authenticated by the physical act of shedding 'real' tears.

Lubitsch understood immediately what Nielsen was getting at and he knew exactly which shot she meant, not least because it was very likely Lubitsch himself who (in a characteristic play on words) had called Nielsen's extended crying "*über-flüssig*" – meaning "superfluous" and "dispensable" and a pun on "overly fluid." Responding to Nielsen's half-disguised protest, his open letter sought to save the situation, in a move only too typical for the director, by turning his abridgement of the scene into a coded compliment: "You still cannot forgive me that I let you cry in close-up for only two meters instead of five. But believe me, your tears were running down from your eyes over your cheeks onto your blouse so realistically that the audience was completely captivated and moved by it already after two meters of film."[6] Lubitsch could invoke a critical reaction that had celebrated his film – today presumed lost – as a "masterpiece" and had been full of praise for his innovative use of close-up framing and fast editing. Rapid changes from shot to shot likely bookended the contested close-up, and perhaps it belonged to those rare moments in the film that even benevolent critics felt that a little more patience in the editing would have been more appropriate.[7]

---

4 Steinthal: Bei Asta Nielsen, 42.
5 Steinthal: Bei Asta Nielsen, 42.
6 Asta Nielsen und Ernst Lubitsch, 31.
7 As one of the critics put it: "Notwithstanding the film's dominant principle of cutting into a shot at a moment when it is still most fascinating, some shots could have lasted a little longer,

In the ensuing public debate, an anonymous actor supposedly familiar with Nielsen and eager to disclose some insider knowledge, claimed that the tears she shed on the set of RAUSCH were nothing more than the artificial products of a standard acting routine, equal in status to all the other techniques at the medium's disposal – editing, framing, *mise en scène* etc. He asserted that Nielsen's tears weren't real at all, but in fact drops of glycerin applied before the filming – and thus far more effective than the genuine article because of the visible trace the chemical substance left on the make-up, shimmering under bright studio floodlights.[8]

This position, which neatly subsumed Nielsen's tears under cinema's efficient "power of the false,"[9] was countered by a diametrically opposed second opinion, voiced by the celebrated stage and screen actor Paul Wegener. Wegener emphasized the genuinely artistic nature of Nielsen's performance, arguing that it infused an otherwise technical process of representation with subjectivity and originality of expression. In late 1920, Wegener had been Nielsen's co-star in STEUERMANN HOLK (HELMSMAN HOLK). Invoking this recent experience, he disputed the claim that Nielsen's tears were fake, declaring that the tears he kissed from Nielsen's cheeks had not had the "greasy and sweet" taste of glycerin, but rather were "watery and salty."[10]

4.1 Phantasmatic intimacy

It is easy to see how the debate around 'false' and 'real' tears echoes Nielsen's principal distinction between acting as the art of individual performative expressivity and acting as merely one among many external techniques of cinematic simulation. What Nielsen refers to as an actor's freedom of creative expression implies at the same time a specific mode of audience address that was closely associated with her acting. What emerges from the debate around the reality status and affective potential of Nielsen's tears in an almost symptomatic fashion is the fact that it was exactly this relationship between the actress and her audience that had entered into a state of crisis. Around 1920, as filmmaking standards

---

mind you, just at some rare points, and just a little." Bobby E Lüthge: Rausch. In: *Film-Kurier* (3 August 1919); quoted from Hans Helmut Prinzler and Enno Patalas (eds.): *Lubitsch*. Munich and Lucerne 1987, 132.

8 Die Tränen der Asta Nielsen. In: *Die Lichtbild-Bühne* 49 (4 December 1920), 49.

9 The idea of the "power of the false" substituting for the "form of the true" in cinema is discussed in Gilles Deleuze: *Cinema 2. The Time-Image*. London 1989, 126–137.

10 Paul Wegener und Asta Nielsen. In: *Die Lichtbild-Bühne* 3 (15 January 1921), 48.

changed, films were generally dominated by fast, analytical and narrative-driven editing, thoroughly transforming the very conditions of Nielsen's relationship with the audience. This transformation would prove to have decisive consequences for her career as a film actress, including her gradual withdrawal from the film business during the mid-1920s.

Lubitsch's intervention into Nielsen's interpretation of the tragic scene in RAUSCH likely reminded the actress of previous encroachments executed by various official censorship boards, as she reports in her autobiography. Already at the very start of her film acting career, she writes in retrospect, "all scenes where I was crying were banned from exhibition, and this ban was justified by the claim that real tears could have too strong an impact on nervous people."[11] The gestures of sorrow and mourning, as they are to be found in rich variation in Nielsen's tragic or melodramatic roles, articulate a mode of emotional address to her audience that probed the limits of cinematic affect. The tendency to contain this affective potential, either by means of technical rationalization or via strategies of filmic sublimation, or through censorship, can thus be understood as attempts at controlling and confining the particular mode of immediate physical affect that Nielsen's acting unleashed upon her audience.

In the early 1910s, when Nielsen rose to stardom as Germany's first genuine film actress, her broad popularity and artistic reputation were built on the special physical quality of her acting style and its unique affective potential. The public debate around the authenticity of her tears in 1920/21 indicates a more general and far-reaching stylistic change in German film history, in the context of which this particular signature – at odds with a new order of cinematic discourse – grew increasingly problematic. Hence, what is so illuminating here is not so much the focus on the real or fabricated quality of the actress's tears, but rather the question that it raises: How, if at all, could the particular sensation of immediate emotional intimacy that Nielsen's tears were able to evoke in audiences be integrated into the emergent discourse of the art film of the early Weimar period?

In a different context, philosopher Slavoj Žižek once described the "fright of real tears" in the cinema as the anxiety of entering into a realm of phantasmatic intimacy that one should access only via a "move into fiction" in order to avoid the "pornographic trespass into intimacy."[12] This transition into an intermediate space of de-sublimated perceptual empathy, characterized by Žižek as a fundamental violation of the symbolic order, has been qualified by Heide Schlüpmann

---

11 Asta Nielsen: *Die schweigende Muse. Lebenserinnerungen*. Berlin 1977, 111 and 164.
12 Slavoj Zizek: *The Fright of Real Tears. Krzysztof Kieslowski Between Theory and Post-Theory*. London 2001, 75.

as a central feature of the perceptual culture of early cinema where "the movie theater still constituted a sphere where the individual spectator could let go of his or her habitual defense shields and forget their bourgeois personalities, where the bodies could extend and reach out without being hurt."[13]

This phenomenon of phantasmatic intimacy between star and audience has left numerous traces in the early reception of Nielsen's films. In her study of early cinema audiences, Emilie Altenloh noted that the films of Asta Nielsen were not only most popular with the audience, but also creating empathy and compassion between spectator and screen: "Indeed emotional identification is the crucial factor here, for film representations have a very direct effect, sweeping spectators along with the action and enabling them to experience the hero's predicaments."[14]

4.2 The explosion of the individual

Wherever Nielsen's films were shown, people testified to the unique affective potential of her acting. The impact of her tears and tragic gestures are well documented in both domestic and international accounts.[15] Many sources seem to confirm what Rudolf Kurtz in retrospect identified as the key feature of Asta Nielsen's historical significance for German cinema:

> Perhaps Asta Nielsen is the personality with whose emergence something like film art became visible. If what had been achieved up until then was meant to amuse the audience or to keep it in suspense – only her films succeeded in stirring feelings and shaking the audience emotionally. If one browses through the newspapers of those early days, one is struck by the intensity with which people expressed their admiration for her, and this despite the fact that something like "film criticism proper" was at the time still an absurd idea.[16]

---

13 Heide Schlüpmann: *Abendröthe der Subjektphilosophie. Eine Ästhetik des Kinos.* Frankfurt a. M. 1998, 61.
14 Emilie Altenloh: A Sociology of the Cinema. The Audience [1914]. In: *Screen* 42:3 (Autumn 2001), 249–293, here 259.
15 For an extensive account of Asta Nielsen's early career, cf. Martin Loiperdinger and Uli Jung (eds.): *Importing Asta Nielsen. The International Film Star in the Making, 1910–1914.* New Barnet 2013. Also cf. the essays on Nielsen's international reception in Heide Schlüpmann et al. (ed.): *Unmögliche Liebe. Asta Nielsen, ihr Kino.* Vienna 2009.
16 Rudolf Kurtz: Die Geschichte des Filmmanuskripts. Die seelische Vertiefung. In: *Der Kinematograph* 71 (6 April 1934).

With the emergence of an institutionalized, professional film criticism in the early 1920s, forms of admiration changed, and with them, stylistic parameters.[17] Two critical models illustrate this shift in perception. The first, derived from the early writings of Béla Balázs, is well known and continues to be influential in shaping our view of Nielsen. The second critical model, contemporaneous with that of Balázs, was put forward with no less consistency and poetic elegance by the film critic and screenwriter Willy Haas. My account of both critical models of Asta Nielsen reception is guided by the two cinematic techniques that were central in the debate between Nielsen and Lubitsch in 1920: the spatial dimension of the close-up (as discussed in connection to Nielsen by Balázs) and the temporal dimension of editing (as discussed by Willy Haas).

Balázs's early writings on film understand cinema not primarily as a mimetic medium for the reproduction of the external world, but rather as a means of expression to render visible interior states and emotions. For Balázs, cinema is the agent of a purely sensual, non-alienated language without words, an "image-language" of movements and gestures with a direct expressive impact on the perception of the audience. At the center of what he calls the illusion of life-like emotional expressivity is the "tacit understanding" between the audience and a human face in close-up. Nielsen's extremely reduced mimic vocabulary came to stand as the very epitome of this encounter:

> The extraordinary artistic standard of Asta Nielsen's eroticism stems from its absolute intellectual quality. It is the eyes, not the flesh, that are of most importance. As a matter of fact, she has no flesh at all. The dressed Asta Nielsen can show obscene nakedness *in her eyes*, and she can smile in a way that is liable to make police feel the film ought to be seized on account of pornography.[18]

According to Balázs, the secret behind this particular effect was in the subdued and spiritual – almost reflexive – quality of Asta Nielsen's face in close-up:

> There is a film in which Asta Nielsen is looking out of the window and sees someone coming. A mortal fear, a petrified horror, appears on her face. But she gradually realizes that she is mistaken and that the man who is approaching, far from spelling disaster, is the answer to her prayers. The expression of horror on her face is gradually modulated through the entire scale of feelings from hesitant doubt, anxious hope and cautious joy, right

---

17 For a general account of this transition in German film criticism, see Sabine Hake: *The Cinema`s Third Machine. Writing on Film in Germany, 1907–1933*. Lincoln and London 1993, 107–129.
18 Béla Balázs: Die Erotik der Asta Nielsen [1923]. In: Béla Balázs: *Schriften zum Film*, vol. 1: *Der sichtbare Mensch / Kritiken und Aufsätze zum Film 1922–1926*, ed. Helmut H. Diederichs et al. Berlin 1982, 185–186 (emphasis in the original).

through to exultant happiness. We watch her face in close up for some twenty meters of film. We see every hint of expression around her eyes and mouth and watch them relax one by one and slowly change. For minutes on end we witness the organic *development of her feelings*, and nothing beyond. [...] The close-up is the technical precondition for the art of facial expression and hence of the higher art of film in general. [...] In close-ups every wrinkle becomes a crucial element of character and every twitch of a muscle testifies to a pathos that signals great inner events. The close-up of a face is frequently used as the climax of an important scene; it must be the *lyrical essence* of the entire drama.[19]

Balázs ultimately denies Nielsen's acting its physicality by sublimating it into the cipher of pure intellectual spirituality. Moreover, his idea of Asta Nielsen is based on her films from the 1920s and lacks any reference to her earlier films. This is all the more evident if one considers that Balázs, in his early writings, tends to draw a rather straight line of film historical evolution and stylistic perfection that leads to the close-up as the ultimate point of culmination of the medium's expressive and affective potentials. By looking at Nielsen's acting from this particular vantage point, Balázs projects onto it an organic development and aesthetic coherence that tends to obscure the manifold breaks and transformations to which it was exposed in the transition from the 1910s into the 1920s. His account does not adequately reflect the many moments of crisis, contradiction and tension that would affect Nielsen's later career.

Willy Haas, too, called Nielsen's face the "creative center"[20] of her expressive powers, but he did so without insisting on the primacy of the close-up as their ultimate condition of possibility. Haas saw the specific quality of Nielsen's acting style to stand in direct opposition to – or in a fundamental tension with – the new formal standards of scene dissection, such as the emotionally intensifying close-up and fast, narrative-driven analytical editing. His reading thus retains a sense of a directly felt, immediate physicality that was so characteristic of her early films and the change in her films of the 1920s, which were being redefined along the lines of a completely different stylistic system and cinematic mode of audience address.

Within this new framework, Nielsen's unique talent for transmitting a direct physical and emotional impact to her audience was reduced to what Haas characterized as isolated "moments of genius" where one could witness the

---

19 Béla Balázs: Visible Man or The Culture of Film [1924]. In: Balázs: *Early Film Theory. Visible Man and The Spirit of Film*, ed. Erica Carter. Oxford 2010, 1–90, here 34, 37.
20 Willy Haas: HAMLET [1921]. In: Willy Haas: *Der Kritiker als Mitproduzent. Texte zum Film 1920–1933*, eds. Wolfgang Jacobsen, Karl Prümm and Benno Wenz. Berlin 1991, 45.

"emotional explosion of the individual."[21] Haas finds the last of such rare moments in DIRNENTRAGÖDIE (TRAGEDY OF A WHORE, 1927), preserved like a time capsule between two cuts. He takes director Bruno Rahn to task for his editing that – partly for reasons of dramatic pace, partly in order to achieve simple erotic effects – showed no respect for the unique qualities of Asta Nielsen's acting. "For heaven's sake," Haas writes at one point of his review of the film, "one mustn't interrupt any of her great scenes" but should "let her play on, let the music of her motions resonate, as far as I am concerned, for hours and hours."[22]

For the briefest moment, Haas has the pleasure of sensing the distinctive emotional pull of Nielsen's acting at the end of DIRNENTRAGÖDIE, before it is destroyed by the intrusion of an untimely cut. In the shot in question, Nielsen, playing an aging prostitute, "lies crying in front of a locked door, behind which some stupid chap with whom she had fallen in love amuses himself with a much younger prostitute and both act as if they weren't there, but the old lady feels exactly what goes on behind this door" – in Haas's words, "a well thought-out scene, indeed."[23] And yet, as the result of unfortunate cuts, Haas contends, the whole scene ultimately fails to unleash its complete emotional effect on the audience; here, as throughout the whole film, "it is not the light touch of a fingertip that commands the editing."[24]

4.3 Pictorial affects

What is so instructive about Haas' ambivalent perception of this climactic scene from DIRNENTRAGÖDIE is that it highlights a trademark element of Nielsen's acting: the motion of breaking down onto the floor in an emotional mixture of love and desire, grief and despair (Fig. 4.1). Nielsen concluded many of her tragic or melodramatic films in this way, crying with the whole of her body. In these moments, she offers an alternative modulation of performative expressivity and emotional affect that is clearly distinct from shots that reduce her expressive register to close-ups of her weeping. Haas here lights upon a marked formal difference that characterizes her films of the 1920s, even in those moments that leave intact the stable performative space of the long, tableau shot that recall her films from the 1910s.

---

21 Willy Haas: Genialität in der Filmdarstellung [1920]. In: Haas: *Der Kritiker als Mitproduzent*, 45.
22 Willy Haas: DIRNENTRAGÖDIE [1927]. In: Haas: *Der Kritiker als Mitproduzent*, 203.
23 Haas: DIRNENTRAGÖDIE, 204.
24 Haas: DIRNENTRAGÖDIE, 204.

Fig. 4.1: Emotional breakdown in DIRNENTRAGÖDIE.

The shift in the way Nielsen is presented to her audience before and after 1920 comes to the fore if one compares examples of her early and later films. In the penultimate shot of Nielsen's film debut AFGRUNDEN (THE ABYSS, 1910), her character suddenly breaks down in tears over the body of the man she has just killed (Fig. 4.2). Carefully calculated in all its seeming spontaneity and unprompted by any cut to a closer framing, what erupts in the sudden vertical

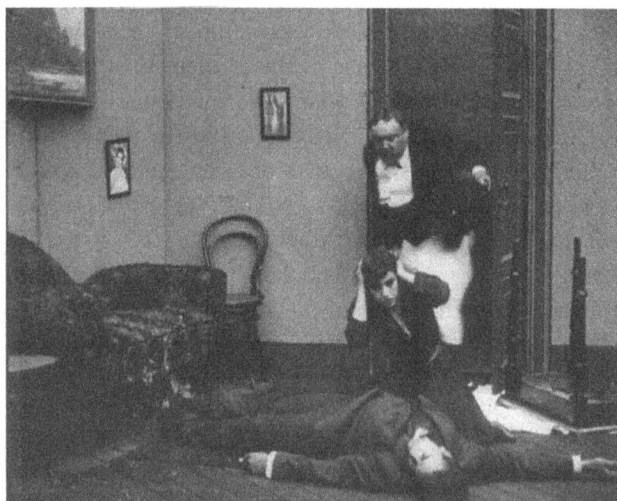

Fig. 4.2: Untamed physical energy in AFGRUNDEN.

trajectory of her entire body across the stable action space of the long tableau shot is a performative, physical energy untamed by cinematic discourse.[25] It is a moment of perceptual shock, but also of recognition and insight: it is only in the very instant of the body collapsing that the depth of her feeling of love and sexual bondage becomes clear, and the extent to which the killing of her ex-lover is less an act of liberating violence than the climax of a physical passion.

The shot thus represents not so much the dramatic endpoint of a narrative conflict, but rather resonates as a performative echo that closes the circuit of energy flowing between the two characters (and their bodies) ever since the film's famous Gaucho-dance scene (Fig. 4.3).[26]

Fig. 4.3: The Gaucho-dance scene in AFGRUNDEN.

A comparable, yet far from equivalent "tragic explosion," can be found in the closing shot of VANINA (1922). Nielsen, playing the title character of Arthur von Gerlach's historical *Kammerspielfilm* (chamber play film) based on Stendhal's novella, breaks down in front of a heavy wooden door behind which her lover has just gone to the gallows – a lover whom she believed she had saved but who now faces certain death. The motion of her despair – the drawn-out glide down the hard surface of the door, her arms slowly following the trajectory of

---

25 On Nielsen's vertical acting, cf. Angela Dalle Vacche: Asta Nielsen's Acting. Motion, Emotion, and the Camera-Eye. In: *Framework* 43:1 (Spring 2002), 76–94.

26 The huge success of AFGRUNDEN and Nielsen's other early Danish films in Germany was decisive for her ensuing German career and was instrumental in the foundation of Babelsberg as a film production site. For a short overview of this period, cf. Michael Wedel: The Beginnings/ Die Anfänge (1912–1921). In: Michael Wedel, Chris Wahl and Ralf Schenk: *100 Years Studio Babelsberg. The Art of Filmmaking.* Kempen 2012, 234–251.

her body – reflects the lines of the historically stylized set (Fig. 4.4). Perfectly in tune with the stylistic conventions of the *Kammerspielfilm* – a genre that was all about the symbolic inscription of hidden emotional energies into the topographical space of the action[27] – Nielsen's performative gesture is here safely contained by the fact that it does nothing more than redraw the pattern of an architectural space to which her movement symbolically assimilates itself within the pictorial composition of the shot. There is no cut to interrupt the execution of the gesture or a close-up to highlight its emotional intensity. What is revealed in this shot might be understood as the "emotional content" of the drama, making visible through a performative act the source of the character's downfall. The court's rules and power struggles define her familial and social position, regardless of the turns she takes, in the same manner as the architectural and ornamental design of the castle frame, limit and pre-structure the space in which she finds herself trapped in the end. In a marked contrast to the shot from AFGRUNDEN, in VANINA the emotional charge that results from the friction between space and movement only contributes to the creation of an image that, in its perfect composition, forestalls any performative explosion. It is an image that is only brought into its appropriate pictorial form, as it were, by this hopeless expenditure of energy.

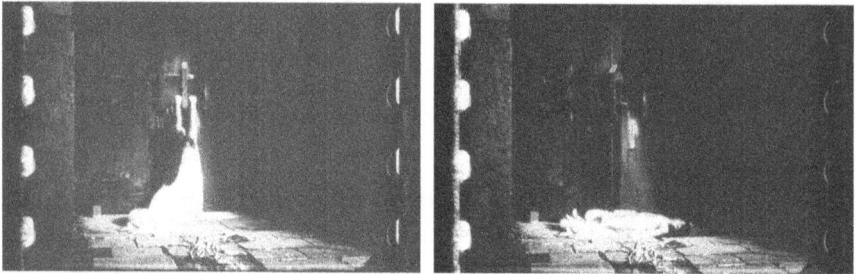

Fig. 4.4: The closing shot of VANINA.

Paul Wegener stars once more alongside Nielsen in VANINA, in the role of her despotic father, but his style of acting differs sharply from Nielsen's. Dependent on a pair of crutches and thus almost completely robbed of physical mobility, Wegener's character's political and patriarchal power assumes a spectral quality that turns the Turin castle into a haunted house and the Governor himself

---

27 On the aesthetics of the *Kammerspielfilm*, cf. chapter 5.

into its cyborg-like prosthetic extension. Wegener's inert interpretation stands as paradigmatic of an acting style gaining dominance in 1920s Weimar art cinema – one that Willy Haas aptly called "mask acting" (*Maskenschauspielerei*).[28] In Haas's understanding, this mode of performative expression constituted a radical move away from the task of establishing an intimate emotional contact between actor and spectator, instead creating the distance necessary to endow film with a higher degree of formal coherence and thus elevate the medium into the ranks of art. If one considers the trajectory of Wegener's own film career from DER STUDENT VON PRAG (THE STUDENT OF PRAGUE, 1913) via his interpretation of the Golem legend in DER GOLEM (THE GOLEM, 1914) and DER GOLEM, WIE ER IN DIE WELT KAM (THE GOLEM HOW HE CAME INTO THE WORLD, 1920) to the string of historical films he made in 1922 – VANINA, LUCREZIA BORGIA (dir. Richard Oswald), MONNA VANNA (dir. Richard Eichberg) – it becomes clear that he exemplified this second historical acting tradition of pictorial stylization into a "character mask," just as Nielsen's body language of unforeseen emotional eruption and extended melodramatic gesture exemplifies the first one. Wegener's style, carried over from the 1910s into the early 1920s, was bound to the artistic dominance of a "pictorial style" of early fantasy films, expressionist films and *Kammerspielfilme* that characterized German cinema between 1913 and 1924.[29] Both modes of acting, however, were soon to be surpassed by a third historical configuration between camera and character, cinematic space and performative gesture. Lubitsch pioneered this mode as early as 1920 but its arrival is perhaps most clearly signaled by Emil Jannings's performances in F.W. Murnau's DER LETZTE MANN (THE LAST LAUGH, 1924) and E.A. Dupont's VARIETÉ (1925): the turn to cinematographic virtuosity and a more subdued acting mode of psychological 'realism.'

---

28 Willy Haas: Gibt es eine Schauspielermaske im Film? Filmdramaturgische Notizen [1924]. In: Haas: *Der Kritiker als Mitproduzent*, 46–47.

29 Cf. Kristin Thompson: "*Im Anfang war...*" Some Links between German Fantasy Films of the Teens and the Twenties." In: Paolo Cherchi Usai and Lorenzo Codelli (eds.): *Before Caligari. German Cinema, 1895–1920*. Pordenone 1990, 138–161.

5 Metaphors and atmospheres: Murnau, fantasy and the *Kammerspielfilm*

> I like the reality of things, but not without fantasy; they must dovetail. Is that not so with life, with human reactions and emotions?   F.W. Murnau, 1928[1]

5.1 Weimar cinema as metaphorical cinema

At least since the publication of Michael Henry's *Le cinéma expressioniste alle-mande. Un langage métaphorique* in 1971,[2] Weimar art cinema, and German expressionist film in particular, has figured in film theory and film historiography as one of the key examples of a 'metaphorical' film style. A qualification that has acquired paradigmatic status, this notion has been based on the formal properties of such canonical films as DAS CABINET DES DR. CALIGARI (Robert Wiene, 1920) and METROPOLIS (Fritz Lang, 1927): the symbolic stylization of the sets, the complex organization of space and the deviation from principles of classical narration and continuity editing have been understood as producing an allegorical mode of cinematic representation and storytelling marked by the frequent use of subjective flashbacks, dream sequences and multiple narrative framings.

Trevor Whittock, in his book *Metaphor and Film*, argues along similar lines when he asserts: "Metaphors of the distortion type based on mise-en-scène range from the expressive sets of Robert Wiene's THE CABINET OF DR. CALIGARI [...] to the mood lighting effects of film noir."[3] With explicit reference to Henry, Thomas Elsaesser characterizes expressionist film as an "'excessively' metaphoric textual system, where the institution itself, i.e., the filmmaker, the audience, the screen appear as a *mise-en-abyme* and mirror images of each other, in infinite regress."[4] In Elsaesser's revisionist account of Weimar cinema, the implicit metaphorical logic of cinematic expressionism serves not only as a

---

1 F.W. Murnau: The Ideal Picture Needs No Titles. By Its Very Nature the Art of the Screen Should Tell a Complete Story Pictorially. In: *Theater Magazine* 47 (January 1928), 41 and 72; reprinted in Richard W. McCormick and Alison Guenther-Pal (eds.): *German Essays on Film.* New York and London 2004, 66–68, here 68. Murnau's text was originally published in German in 1927.

2 Michael Henry: *Le cinéma expressioniste allemand. Un langage métaphorique.* Fribourg 1971.

3 Trevor Whittock: *Metaphor and Film.* Cambridge 1990, 64.

4 Thomas Elsaesser: *Weimar Cinema and After. Germany's Historical Imaginary.* London and New York, 75–76.

https://doi.org/10.1515/9783110613551-006

methodological starting point, but also as a central template across which all kinds of films from the Weimar period – popular genre films as much as works aspiring to the ranks of art – can be re-read as belonging to a cultural formation resting on the unsteady grounds of allegorical "picture puzzles" that "refuse to be tied down to a single meaning."[5]

5.2 Shadows and shadowings: Metaphor/metonymy in film theory

Along with Soviet montage cinema of the 1920s,[6] French surrealist films of the 1920s and early 1930s,[7] and Hollywood's film noir of the 1940s and 1950s[8] – the latter often considered a continuation of the stylistic parameters of cinematic expressionism – Weimar cinema has come to stand as another *locus classicus* for conceptualizing and historicizing forms of cinematic metaphoricity. In the course of identifying these paradigmatic cases, the film theoretical appropriation of the concept of metaphor and the concomitant introduction of linguistic tropes and forms of literary figurativity into the field of film studies has been guided by Roman Jakobson's basic distinction between metaphor and metonymy and by Christian Metz's extensive elaboration on this distinction in *Psychoanalysis and Cinema. The Imaginary Signifier.*[9]

In his essay "Two Aspects of Language and Two Types of Aphasic Disturbances," Jakobson briefly addresses the question of how the metaphor/metonymy distinction could be related to the principal formal elements of film. Whereas he describes the close-up as a form based on the principle of synecdoche and film editing as a metonymic operation, he suggests that "superimposed dissolves"

---

5 Elsaesser: *Weimar Cinema and After*, 4.

6 Cf. Marie-Claire Ropars-Wuilleumier: The Function of Metaphor in Eisenstein's OCTOBER. In: *Film Criticism* 2:2 (1978), 109–127.

7 Cf. Linda Williams: The Prologue to UN CHIEN ANDALOU. A Surrealist Film Metaphor. In: *Screen* 17:4 (December 1976), 24–33; Linda Williams: *Figures of Desire. A Theory and Analysis of Surrealist Film.* Berkeley, Los Angeles, Oxford 1981; Linda Williams: Dream Rhetoric and Film Rhetoric. Metaphor and Metonymy in UN CHIEN ANDALOU. In: *Semiotica* 33 (1981): 87–103.

8 Cf. E. Ann Kaplan: The "Dark Continent" of Film Noir. Race, Displacement and Metaphor in Tourneur's CAT PEOPLE (1942) and Welles' THE LADY FROM SHANGHAI (1948). In: Kaplan (ed.): *Women in Film Noir.* Rev. ed. London 1998, 183–201; James Naremore: *More than Night. Film Noir in Its Contexts.* Rev. ed. Berkeley, Los Angeles and London 2008, 18–37.

9 Christian Metz: *Psychoanalysis and Cinema. The Imaginary Signifier.* Basingstoke and London 1982.

should be understood as "filmic similes" and thus cinematic equivalents of meta-phorical processes.[10]

Metz took up Jakobson's designations and criticized them for the simple one-to-one relationships they set up. Neither could "'superimposed dissolves' be attributed en bloc to the metaphorical principle" nor is "[e]diting, in itself, "[…] metonymical: it is syntagmatic."[11] Metz went on to show that distinctions between metonymy and metaphor cannot be made on the basis of formal film elements alone but should instead take into account the various levels on which similarity and contiguity operate in concrete configurations between the diegetic and the extra-diegetic, the referential and the discursive. As a consequence, in their actual distribution within a given film or group of films, metonymical and metaphorical operations rarely appear in pure forms but rather in figurations of intersection and mutual implication.[12]

A case in point for Metz is expressionist cinema's play with shadows. The particular film he mentions, without discussing it in any detail, is Arthur Robi-son's SCHATTEN (WARNING SHADOWS, 1923). On the one hand, as Metz points out, shadows – bound as they are to the contiguity of a body or object by which they are cast – are "metonymic by definition"; on the other hand, they are "impure" metonymies to the extent that they also establish a comparative relationship of similarity and transference.[13] One can infer from Metz's brief reference to the use of shadows in expressionist film (and in horror cinema) that the second dimen-sion to which he alludes is not reducible to a purely mimetic relationship but is instead dynamic, open to ambiguity and disruption of the semantic field. It can thus be understood as carrying the potential for metaphorical shifts in meaning.

5.3 The dream sequence in SCHLOSS VOGELÖD as figurative event

Even though Metz characterizes metaphor and metonymy as dynamic figures, overlapping and intersecting in changing patterns of dominance, his main interest is to provide a general classification for how the economy of cinematic discourse is structured by processes of selection and ordering, which he understands with reference to Freud and Lacan in analogy to the workings of the unconscious and

---

10 Roman Jakobson: Two Aspects of Language and Two Types of Aphasic Disturbances. In: Jakobson: *Language in Literature*. Cambridge, Mass. 1987, 95–114, here 111.
11 Christian Metz: *Psychoanalysis and Cinema*, 194.
12 Christian Metz: *Psychoanalysis and Cinema*, 200.
13 Christian Metz: *Psychoanalysis and Cinema*, 206.

the dream with its three levels of condensation, displacement and secondarization. As Dudley Andrew has observed, the model Metz provides for the analysis of cinematic figuration is not itself dynamic. Andrew argues instead that it is rather static in its structuralist view of film as a medium that generates meaning through narrative and that privileges metonymy: "All figuration for him is merely displaced narration."[14] From a Metzian perspective, metaphorical figurations in film – such as the excessive use of shadows in expressionist film – function as occasional irritations and calculated interruptions in the discursive and narrative economy of filmic signification, as overdetermined forms of expressivity shaped by the presence of 'unconscious' psychic energies.

A closer look at another example from the early Weimar period reveals the benefits but also the limits of such a view on the function of metaphor in film. Interpreted along the same lines as Metz's argument, the dream sequence in Friedrich Wilhelm Murnau's SCHLOSS VOGELÖD (1921) appears as a radical discursive intervention in and stylistic deviation from what otherwise seems to be a 'realist' *Kammerspielfilm* (chamber play film) painstakingly observing the rules of the unity of time, place and narrative. The extreme compression of time and space is indicated unambiguously at the beginning of each act of the film's five acts. Each act begins with a panoramic shot of the title's castle (or, more precisely, a miniature model of it, constructed by set designer Hermann Warm). Throughout the course of the film, intertitles register exactly how much time has passed: "The other day – a surprise: the sun is shining!" – "The day" – "The evening" – "At night" – "A quarter of an hour later" – "One hour later" – "The morning of the third day" – "Midday" – "Half an hour later" – "The evening."

The film's action takes place over three days at a country manor where a group of aristocrats have assembled for an annual autumn hunt. They are guests of the Lord of the Castle Vogelschrey and his wife Centa. Due to bad weather, the hunt is repeatedly postponed. After the unexpected appearance of Count Oetsch, an outcast of the local aristocracy ever since coming under suspicion for killing his own brother out of greed, the unresolved murder case becomes the main topic of the conversation among the group as they wait for the weather to change.[15] All the more so since the victim's widow, Baroness Safferstädt, is expected to join the hunting party soon with her new husband. Also expected at the manor is Father Faramund from Rome, a relative of the murder

---

14 Dudley Andrew: *Concepts in Film Theory*. Oxford et al. 1984, 170.

15 Much of the film's action takes place while the guests at the manor are waiting for the weather to change. Steve Choe has taken this narrative set-up as the basis for reading SCHLOSS VOGELÖD as an allegory of melancholy. Cf. Choe: *Afterlives. Allegories of Film and Mortality in Early Weimar Germany*. New York et al. 2014, 62–74.

victim. When the Baroness learns that Father Faramund is coming, she decides to confess to him that it was her current husband who killed her first one after misunderstanding her intentions. As the film develops in a slow succession of doublings and reversals and of absences and presences, it becomes clear that Count Oetsch appears on the scene disguised as Father Faramund in order to find out the truth from the Baroness and restore his honor. After the truth has come to light – in a number of slow-paced scenes, intensifying the atmosphere of doom and guilt rather than rushing to a dramatic climax – the film takes a tragic turn, as was characteristic of the German *Kammerspielfilm* of the early 1920s. The Baroness's husband commits suicide, while the Baroness, widowed for the second time, faces a wrecked life.

SCHLOSS VOGELÖD follows the main spatial logic of the early Weimar *Kammerspielfilm* genre, as it presents the deterioration of a community as motivated by an outside intrusion of something alien – in this case the double appearance of the outcast Count Oetsch / Father Faramund. In this respect, the film's dream sequence (one of two in the film) may indeed appear as a 'metaphor of distortion' in Whittock's sense and, along the Metzian paradigm, as an overdetermined expressive (and expressionist) figuration of the film's main poetic principle and generic formula, filtered through the unconscious fantasy of one of its characters – in this case one of the invited guests at the castle, tellingly introduced in the film's opening credits as "the anxious gentleman" ("Ängstlicher Herr").

The sequence is explicitly announced as a dream by an intertitle ("Dreams" [Träume]) and thus clearly marked as not belonging to the world of 'objective' reality represented in the film. A first shot, initiated by a widening iris mask, shows the character asleep in bed (the reality status of this image is somewhat uncertain: does it belong to 'objective' reality showing the character dreaming, or are we already within the dream reality in which the character dreams of himself sleeping?). In the next shot a monstrous, clawed hand appears outside the bedroom window. From this second medium shot, the film then cuts to a long shot, integrating the two previous partial views: the window has now been pushed open and the hand extends on a periscope-like outstretched arm across the room to grasp "the anxious gentleman" who wakes up in shock. The act of grasping itself is detailed in a medium close-up and divided into two phases: first, the shadow of the hand slowly approaching and finally falling on the body of "the anxious gentleman," then the hand itself dragging the man out of his bed and off-screen right. The dream sequence's final shot returns to the previous central position: a distanced view of the room with the now-empty bed on the left and the window through which we see the character disappearing under the steady grip of the monstrous hand on the right. The next shot, filmed from a similar but not identical camera position and starting with a widening iris mask (like the shot at the beginning of the sequence), shows "the anxious gentleman" back in bed, waking up and looking confused in the direction of the window, which is now kept off-screen through framing (Fig. 5.1).

A more traditional reading of the metaphorical operations at work in this sequence would consider it as a subjective representation of distorted reality based on the analogy of the dream work's processes of condensation and transference. In tune with what has been argued about the stylized reality of the frame narrative in DAS CABINET DES DR. CALIGARI,[16] the recourse to expressionist set and prop design, high contrast lighting and the use of cast shadows would be explained within this interpretive scenario as a moment of visual excess anchored in a character's (pathological) subjective fantasy. It is therefore not coincidental that the dream sequence from SCHLOSS VOGELÖD has been compared with the staging of the first murder scene in DAS CABINET DES DR. CALIGARI.[17]

But considering the function of metaphors in the context of narrative cinema as isolated instances of stylistic excess – or as disruptive avant-garde moments of deviation from an otherwise consistently ordered fictional world – excludes a number of crucial theoretical implications and analytical insights. It was, again, Dudley Andrew who voiced his discontent with the way figuration, and especially metaphor, is conceptualized within film studies, making a claim for a radical reversal in our thinking about metaphor and metonymy:

> The metaphor demands close description since by definition no rule or convention can determine or locate its utility and scope. As it is elaborated in detail it becomes a model for the redescription of reality as such. Only the manifold of experience can determine the extent of metaphor's power [...] For structuralism will not recognize the event of cinematic discourse. It will always and only provide a description of the system which is put into use in the event. If [...] the system was born and exists only as a residue of such events of figuration, then we need a broader vision of the creation of meaning in films.[18]

---

16 Cf., e.g., Siegfried Kracauer: *From Caligari to Hitler. A Psychological History of German Film.* Princeton 1947, 61–76; Mike Budd: Moments of CALIGARI. In: Budd (ed.): *THE CABINET OF DR. CALIGARI. Texts, Contexts, Histories.* New Brunswick and London 1990, 7–121, here 36–51; Dietrich Scheunemann: The Double, the Décor, and the Framing Device. Once More on Robert Wiene's THE CABINET OF DR. CALIGARI. In: Scheunemann (ed.): *Expressionist Film. New Perspectives.* Rochester 2003, 125–156.
17 Piotr Sadowski: *The Semiotics of Light and Shadows. Modern Visual Arts and Weimar Cinema.* London et al. 2018, 119.
18 Andrew: *Concepts in Film Theory*, 169–170.

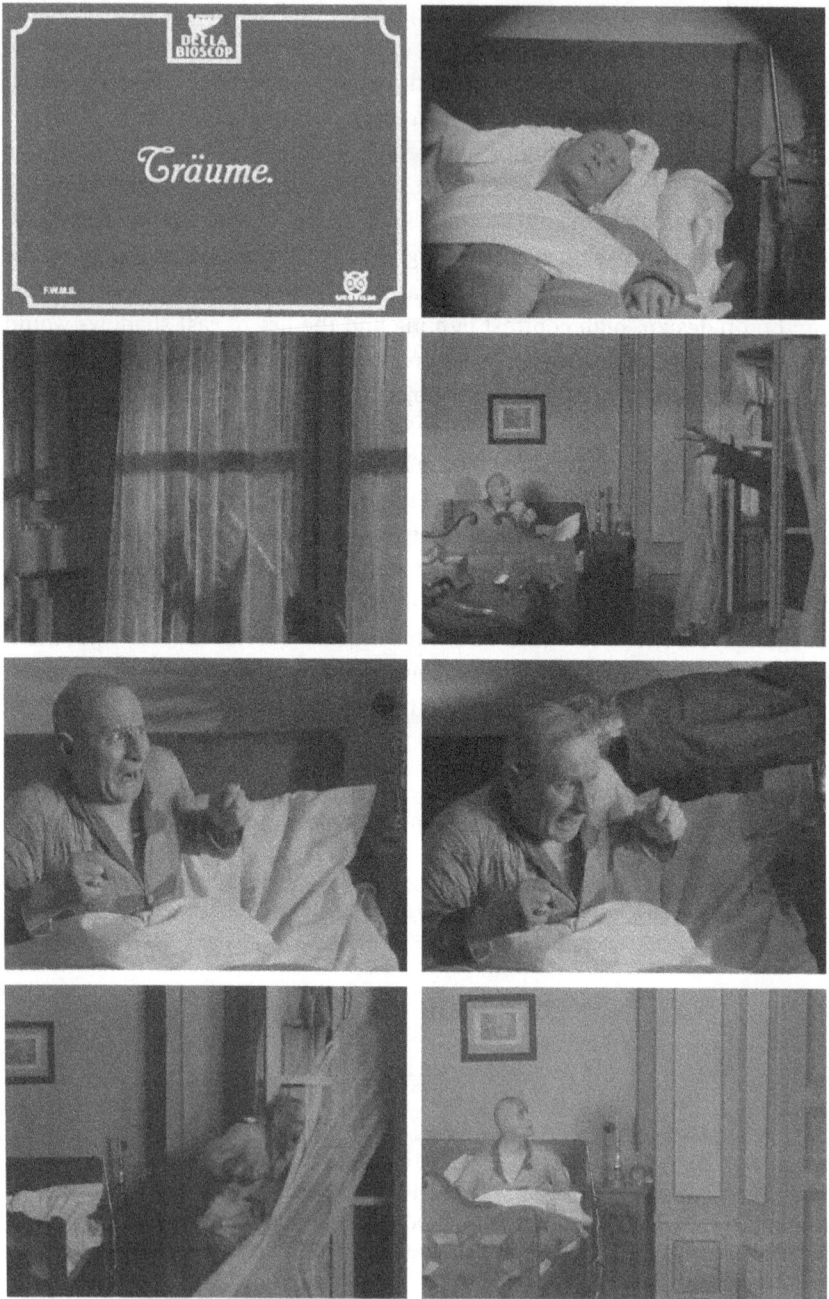

Fig. 5.1: The dream sequence in SCHLOSS VOGELÖD.

The model of cinematic metaphor proposed recently by Cornelia Müller, Hermann Kappelhoff and colleagues allows for such a broader, experience-based theoretical perspective. As Müller and Kappelhoff put it,

> only when metaphoricity is grounded in this media-specific perceptual experience, can we speak of cinematic metaphors. Cinematic metaphors emerge in a process of affective perception of cinematic expressive movements. They are emergent, dynamic, temporally structured and grounded in the rhythms, intensities and other affective qualities of cinematic expressivity.[19]

By introducing the heuristic category of *cinematic expressive movements* as "a form of cinematic composition that modulates affective experiences of film viewers"[20] and that offers access to the overall compositional *gestalt* which shapes the processes from which metaphorical meaning emerges in the temporal unfolding of a film, this model of cinematic metaphor provides the analytical instruments for the close description Andrew deems necessary to conceive of metaphor "not as a verbal substitution but as a process resulting in the redescription of a semantic field" and for the concept to become "useful to film theory" at all.[21]

5.4 Worlds, atmospheres and the poetics of affect

In contrast to structuralist film theory, which sees metaphorical constructions as punctuated occurrences within an otherwise metonymically stitched together diegetic universe, Müller and Kappelhoff consider the process of metaphorization as constitutive for creating a cinematic world, key to what Andrew calls the filmic "redescription of reality."[22] For,

> [...] what makes up a cinematic metaphor is that it unfolds over the course of the film in ever new variations, as a dynamic process, temporally divided into segments, of ever new metaphorical transferals and shifts. This process structures the process of understanding as an interplay of optical-acoustic expressive movement, of linguistic signification in the dialog, and of the action represented.[23]

---

19 Cornelia Müller and Hermann Kappelhoff (in collaboration with Sarah Greifenstein, Dorothea Horst, Thomas Scherer and Christina Schmitt): *Cinematic Metaphor. Experience – Affectivity – Temporality*. Berlin and Boston 2018, 179.
20 Müller and Kappelhoff: *Cinematic Metaphor*, 129.
21 Andrew: *Concepts in Film Theory*, 167.
22 Andrew: *Concepts in Film Theory*, 169.
23 Müller and Kappelhoff: *Cinematic Metaphor*, 170.

According to their view on the matter, the terms of cinema's representational systems truly exist only as "residue[s] of [...] events of [metaphorical] figuration."[24] Within this theoretical model, the constant interplay between affective embodiment and the construction of meaning, cinematic expressive movements and the activation of metaphoricity

> [...] structures the time in which the film, through alternating ways of perceiving and various perspectives, reveals itself as a world that follows a logic quite of its own, that is, *a poetic logic* – and not that of our everyday life. [...] For there is no action disclosed to the spectators in an objectively given world, rather there is a subjective world of experience, experienced in concrete ways of perception and forms of sensation. [...] It is a world that in every element is a thought-out and sensed reality. Cinematic metaphors emerge from the affective parcours that viewers go through, they emerge from experiencing the aesthetics of cinematic expressivity.[25]

If we apply this perspective to SCHLOSS VOGELÖD, the film's dream sequence no longer appears to be a singular figurative event or an erratic stylistic imprint left on the genre of the *Kammerspielfilm* by expressionism. Taken as one element within a larger process of poetic modulation, it instead forms part of the film's overall expressive movement centered around the film's structuring metaphor of the past returning as an alien intrusion from outside. This metaphor is itself a variation on the genre's characteristic spatial logic built around the inside-outside division: the notion that the stability of a given community is pressurized by external forces which in turn serve as catalysts for unleashing the destructive power of internal frictions and tensions. Understood as part of an affective course along which Murnau's film takes its spectator, the dream sequence closely corresponds to the rhythms of arrivals and departures; the many tableau-like framings of groups of people and their subtle spatial arrangements of centralization and marginalization; and the alternation of indoor views of the manor and outdoor shots revealing the bad weather coming down on the house to be another external force obstructing the 'normal' course of events.

Furthermore, understood as part of an ongoing modulation of expressive movements shaping the affective experience of a cinematic world unfolding before our eyes, the fact that the dream can be ascribed to a particular character becomes less relevant than the degree to which it contributes to the spectator's (no less sub-

---

24 Andrew: *Concepts in Film Theory*, 170.
25 Müller and Kappelhoff: *Cinematic Metaphor*, 172.

jective) embodied perception and experience of this world.[26] In a purely formalist narratological sense, the fantasy we witness in the dream sequence might appear doubly detached from the represented world, first via internal focalization[27] and second, by comical-ironical distanciation (i.e. it is the clearly pathologized character who is having the nightmare). Phenomenologically, however, it is an integral part of the atmosphere created in SCHLOSS VOGELÖD, or what Müller and Kappelhoff would call its "poetics of affect" when they point out that the "affective resonances" a film generates

> are not identical with the feelings being represented or those of the characters represented. Instead, we are dealing with a complex atmospheric network of mood, extended over time, which only matches up with representational emotions in exceptional cases. It is thus primarily a matter of broad-based affective operations and episodic structures, which are called up and shaped on the part of the spectator through the staging strategies and compositional patterns of audiovisual images. It is in this sense that we speak of a poetics of affect in the ways audiovisual images are presented.[28]

For Lotte Eisner, it was the creation of affective atmospheres ("Stimmungen") that was Weimar cinema's highest achievement: "In any German film" of the Weimar period, she contends,

> the preoccupation with rendering *Stimmung* ('mood') by suggesting the 'vibrations of the soul' is linked to the use of light. In fact this *Stimmung* hovers around objects as well as people: it is a 'metaphysical' accord, a mystical and singular harmony amid the chaos of things, a kind of sorrowful nostalgia which, for the German, is mixed with well-being, an imprecise nuance of nostalgia, languor colored with desire, lust of body and soul.[29]

In particular, Eisner saw *Stimmung* as emanating from the composition of the world presented by the films and from their arrangement and staging of the *Umwelt* of the narrative action – "vibrant with wild poetry, the intensity of which appears to vary proportionately with the ill-fortune falling upon the characters" – as *the* defining characteristic of the *Kammerspielfilm* genre. In

---

26 Cf. also Daniel Yacavone: *Film Worlds. A Philosophical Aesthetics of Cinema.* New York 2015, 161–226; Alberto Baracco: *Hermeneutics of a Film World. A Ricoerian Method for Film Interpretation.* Cham 2017, 65–73.
27 On internal focalization in film, cf. Edward Branigan: *Narrative Comprehension and Film.* London and New York 1992, 100–107.
28 Müller and Kappelhoff: *Cinematic Metaphor*, 156.
29 Lotte H. Eisner: *The Haunted Screen. Expressionism in the German Cinema and the Influence of Max Reinhardt.* Berkeley and Los Angeles 2008, 199. Eisner's seminal study was first published in French in 1952.

this sense, a film's atmosphere "participates 'symphonically' in the action" and, "imbued with a kind of magic, takes on a particular meaning."[30]

It was her keen eye for Murnau's subtle maneuverings of *Stimmung* in the visual composition of SCHLOSS VOGELÖD that made Eisner consider the possibility that this particular *Kammerspielfilm* might actually be a horror film in disguise.[31] Although she quickly abandons this possibility, she points to the film's atmospheric and affective "Janus faced-ness," which she argues is communicated less through close-ups of faces to show character emotions than it is "through attitude and gesture."[32]

Examined in the light of the previously quoted passage from Müller and Kappelhoff, Eisner's emphasis on the atmospheric dimension of the *Kammerspielfilm* can be re-read as a poetics of affect that reaches far beyond the levels of narrative construction and character emotion.[33] With respect to SCHLOSS VOGELÖD, such an emphasis makes us aware of the degree to which the compositional elements and affective values of the dream sequence are implicated in the overall expressive movement of the film and the spectator's experience of it. Whereas the dream sequence's spatial arrangement can itself be seen as a *pars pro toto* condensation of the larger inside/outside division staged around the Vogelöd manor, the compositions of other scenes inside the house incessantly echo the figurative articulation of the dream sequence by placing individual characters in front of windows through which the bare branches of trees are visible moving in the storm (Fig. 5.2). Their iconic resemblance (transference by similarity) to the slender fingers of the monstrous intruder from the dream sequence thus keeps the menace of a threat lurking on the outside – the film's structuring metaphor – continuously present.

5.5 Eloquent gestures, metaphors on the move

Another prominent and closely related compositional element (which Eisner also highlights) from the dream sequences that returns in later scenes is the gesture of raising an arm towards someone who is already affected – and metaphorically 'touched' – by the shadow it casts over his or her body before there

---

30 Eisner: *The Haunted Screen*, 186.

31 Lotte H. Eisner: *Murnau*. London 1973, 101.

32 Eisner: *Murnau*, 102.

33 For another theoretical revision of the concept of cinematic atmosphere pointing in a similar direction, cf. Robert Sinnerbrink: *Stimmung*. Exploring the Aesthetics of Mood. In: *Screen* 53:2 (Summer 2012), 148–163.

Fig. 5.2: Visual echoes of the dream sequence in SCHLOSS VOGELÖD.

is any physical contact. Although Müller and Kappelhoff are quite clear about the fact that "cinematic expressive movements are not depicted human gestures on the screen," but rather "units of moving audiovision," they do consider the "parallel between gestural and cinematic forms of expressivity [. . .] as paramount for the analysis and theorizing of cinematic metaphor."[34] In the context of their model of cinematic metaphor, the act of gestural expression, the body's movement in its concrete temporal articulation, is congruent with the course of the spectator's affective experience: "the specific way of performing a gesture *is* the expression of an affective stance."[35]

This approach to metaphor introduces to the debate a new sensibility for cinema's time-based performative quality, a sensibility that Eisner called for and that is especially valuable when dealing with silent film's 'gestural elo-

---

34 Müller and Kappelhoff: *Cinematic Metaphor*, 179.
35 Müller and Kappelhoff: *Cinematic Metaphor*, 148.

quence,'[36] so common in early German and Weimar cinema, not least, as the previous chapter argued, in the films of Asta Nielsen or, indeed, in the work of Murnau. In SCHLOSS VOGELÖD, it is the Baroness who raises her arm and points her finger twice at Count Oetsch, first when she accuses him in the presence of the assembled hunting party of murdering her first husband and later, at the end of her confession to Father Faramund (Fig. 5.3). Unaware that she is in fact talking to Count Oetsch, she then repeats, in a trance-like state, the same gesture with the words (related by an intertitle): "I accused him of fratricide!"

Fig. 5.3: The gesture and its shadow as metaphor.

The second time, her slowly-executed pointing gesture is directed away from Oetsch and outside the image; however, the shadow that slowly comes into view with the raising of her arm rips straight into the heart of the man whose true identity is thereby revealed. This calculated effect of the scene's staging and lighting through which the shadow seems to emancipate itself from its metonymical ties to the Baroness's limb – in the act of the movement itself – assumes a metaphorical existence, disrupting the scene's semantic field and radically shifting its meaning. It is the expressive movement of the outstretched arm and its shadow – both physically and cinematically – that establishes another metaphorical relationship between the guilty woman and the monstrous nocturnal intruder, between the dream sequence and the rest of the film.

---

36 Cf. Roberta E. Pearson: *Eloquent Gestures. The Transformation of Performance Style in the Griffith Biograph Films*. Berkeley, Los Angeles and London 1992.

In contrast to many of their predecessors who, in the wake of Christian Metz, formulated their theories of metaphoricity in film with reference to individual auteurs (such as Eisenstein or Buñuel) or the stylistic innovations of historical film movements such as German expressionism, Soviet montage cinema, or French surrealism, Müller and Kappelhoff's theory of cinematic metaphor is more comprehensive and unbiased when it comes to the analysis of popular genre cinema. As the example of Murnau's SCHLOSS VOGELÖD indicates, neither cinematic expressionism nor the *Kammerspielfilm* are clearly distinguishable categories but form instead flexible configurations within a specific historical constellation. Tracing the migration of cinematic expressive movements and the transformation of the metaphorical meanings they carry with them across generical and cultural contexts is another promising perspective this approach opens up.

Within the oeuvre of Murnau alone, this pattern of trans-generic migration and transformation can be shown in manifold ways. Charting these patterns breaks open the rather strict genre divisions along which Murnau's films have been categorized. With the notable exceptions of an early detective film (ABEND – NACHT – MORGEN / EVENING – NIGHT – MORNING, 1920) and an operetta-like comedy (DIE FINANZEN DES GROSSHERZOGS / THE FINANCES OF THE GRAND DUKE, 1923), Murnau's films from the German period are traditionally considered as variations on two genres. The first is the *Kammerspielfilm*, a designation that includes, along with SCHLOSS VOGELÖD, DER GANG IN DIE NACHT (JOURNEY INTO THE NIGHT, 1920), DER BRENNENDE ACKER (THE BURNING SOIL, 1923), DER LETZTE MANN (THE LAST LAUGH, 1924) and TARTÜFF (TARTUFFE, 1925). The second genre is the fantastic film, which encompasses his early Jekyll-and-Hyde adaptation DER JANUSKOPF (THE HEAD OF JANUS, 1920) and the psychological fantasy PHANTOM (1922), along with the canonical NOSFERATU (1922) and FAUST (1926).

In this respect, a comparative archaeology of the migrations of compositional elements, metaphorical constructions and affective analogies would provide a dynamic model of genre articulation that helps to dissolve any binary conception that arises from trying to separate the 'realism' of the *Kammerspielfilm* from the fantastic. Murnau himself evoked this idea when he stated that the cinematic representation of the concrete physical world is pointless without the infusion of fantasy. That both dimensions of cinema ought to "dovetail," as he calls it, is evident not only with regard to the invasion of the uncanny into the enclosed worlds of Murnau's *Kammerspielfilme*, but also for a consideration of his films with fantastic subjects whose metaphysical transgressions are built on the strict temporal and spatial orders of the *Kammerspielfilm* and operate on a number of related compositional, atmospheric and metaphorical constructions.

The analogies are most conspicuous on the micro-level of individual expressive movements. If we consider once again the dream sequence from

SCHLOSS VOGELÖD, we see immediately that it provides the compositional blue-print for the scene from NOSFERATU – the next film Murnau made after SCHLOSS VOGELÖD – in which the vampire Count Orlok aka Nosferatu approaches Hutter, a guest at his castle in Transylvania, at night, his mighty shadow falling on the young man in bed and causing him to flinch (Fig. 5.4).

Fig. 5.4: Shadow of the vampire.

A second scene from NOSFERATU, the dramatic climax of the film when Ellen invites Count Orlok to her bedroom in Wisborg, sends Hutter away and sacrifices herself to the vampire, echoes the first scene in Transylvania, as it is again the vampire's shadow that falls first on the surroundings and finally on the body of his victim. In that it is the shadow of the vampire's hand, closing his fist around the heart of Ellen who squirms with pain (Fig. 5.5), the expressive movement here adds to the composition the metaphorical logic of the shadow pointing in the opposite direction of the arm of the Baroness, hitting Count Oetsch straight in the heart.

Another example that develops this expressive movement pattern even further can be found in a key scene from Murnau's version of FAUST, made four years after NOSFERATU. Led by Mephisto, Faust pays Gretchen a surprise visit at night. Although this is the moment in the film which marks the climax of Faust's rise to bliss and happiness, the scene also carries signs of doom, for it is the child that is fathered that night that sets into motion the tragedy of Gretchen. A closer analysis of this scene results in a number of striking

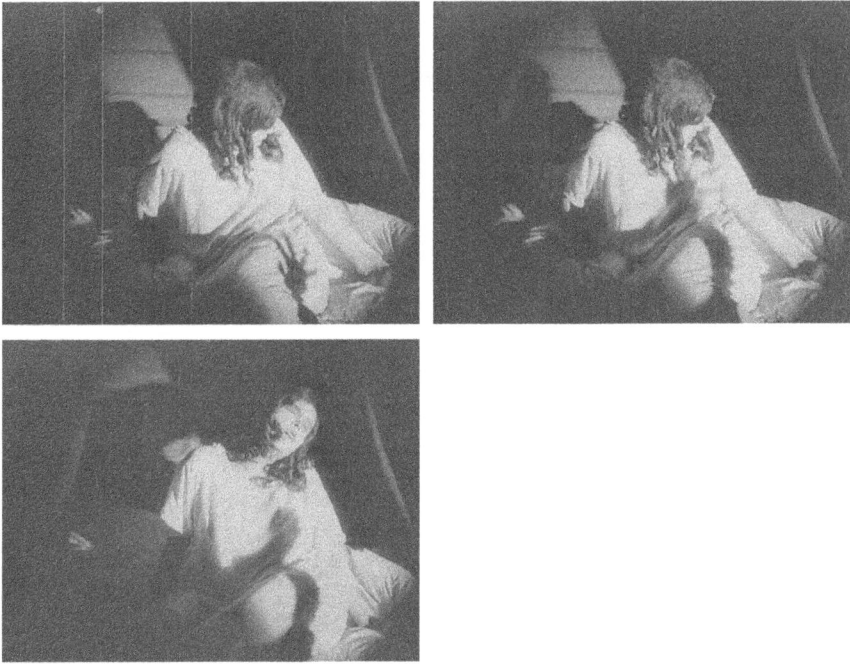

Fig. 5.5: Ellen sacrifices herself to the vampire.

Fig. 5.6: Shadows of Nosferatu and Mephisto.

analogies to the scene in which Ellen sacrifices herself to Nosferatu: Mephisto's huge shadow falling on the house in the beginning (Fig. 5.6); Gretchen's white nightgown and her opening and closing of the window (Fig. 5.7); Faust's forced entry into the room with his silhouetted hands pushing the

Fig. 5.7: Window shots in NOSFERATU and FAUST.

Fig. 5.8: Faust's forced entry.

window open (Fig. 5.8) and echoing the predatory gesture with which Nosferatu approaches both Hutter and Ellen.[37]

Such compositional resonances can, of course, simply be regarded as indicative of Murnau's consistency in directorial style. But, understood through Müller and Kappelhoff's theory of cinematic metaphor, the migration of cinematic expressive movements also allows us to see a basic similarity and gradual shift in the metaphorical organization and affective poetics underpinning the popular

---

[37] Similar visual configurations are to be found in Murnau's work up to SUNRISE – A SONG OF TWO HUMANS (USA 1927) – which appears almost as a remake of FAUST when judged on the basis of its compositional patterns – and his last film TABU (USA 1930), which is full of compositional allusions to NOSFERATU.

genres of the *Kammerspielfilm* and the Fantastic in Weimar cinema.[38] At any rate, Murnau's fantasy films of the Weimar period share with their *Kammerspielfilm* counterparts a world structured around inside/outside divisions, often marked by architectural elements such as walls, doors and windows; violent invasive movements of external forces into existing environments and communities (Vogelöd castle, Wisborg in NOSFERATU, Gretchen's village in FAUST); the unmistakably sexual connotation that comes with these penetrations of private spaces; and the transformative power of shadows and silhouettes turning the bodies of their carriers figuratively (and, at least in the case of Nosferatu, also literally) into something else altogether.

Reconstructing the signature of Weimar cinema's historicity from these figurations of cinematic metaphoricity and their affective resonances beyond the stylistic formula of expressionism and across individual oeuvres and genres provides a promising complement to Müller and Kappelhoff's theoretical template of cinematic metaphor. With a slight shift in perspective, focusing on the metaphor of film as a "plastic art in motion," the following chapter will take up this challenge of rethinking the history of German cinema's poetics of affect in terms of what Jussi Parikka, with reference to Thomas Elsaesser, once called a "Media Archaeology of the Senses."[39]

---

38 Both SCHLOSS VOGELÖD and PHANTOM belonged to a series of films that originated from a joint venture between the production company Decla Bioscop (in 1921 merged into Ufa) and the publishing house Ullstein. The five feature films produced in this context between 1920 and 1923, among them also Fritz Lang's DR. MABUSE – DER SPIELER (DR. MABUSE – THE GAMBLER 1921/22), were all based on recent popular bestsellers and aimed at a mass audience. Cf. Bernhard Schüler: *Der Ullstein Verlag und der Stummfilm. Die Uco-Film GmbH als Ausdruck einer innovativen Partnerschaft*. Wiesbaden 2013; Rebecca Kandler: *Phantom. Textgenese und Vermarktung*. Munich 1996.

39 Jussi Parikka: *What is Media Archaeology?* Cambridge, Mass. 2012, 19.

Part 2
Synchronizing the senses

6 Sculpting with light: Stereoscopic vision and the idea of Film as a "Plastic Art in Motion"

6.1 Film as a 'Plastic Art in Motion'

In early writings on the development of film style, the medium's artistic potential and the possibilities of unfolding cinematic space beyond the limits of the screen, film theoreticians, critics and practitioners frequently alluded to the metaphor of film as a "Plastic Art in Motion."[1] In his essay "The Birth of the Sixth Art" (1911), Ricciotto Canudo saw in cinema a "superb conciliation of the Rhythms of Space (the Plastic Arts) and the Rhythms of Time (Music and Poetry)."[2] According to Canudo, film should not only turn into animated painting, but evolve into a "Sculpture developing in Time."[3] In a similar vein, Vachel Lindsay spoke a few years later of the alternation between long tableau shots and close-up shots in film as producing "dumb giants" and bodies "in sculptural relief."[4]

Hence, when in 1916 Hugo Münsterberg famously referred to both the visual arts and to stereoscopy as models for creating the perceptual illusion of plasticity and depth in order to distinguish between the film spectator's object of knowledge and his or her object of impression, he could already build on a well-established line of thinking about cinematic space as an interface for different media intertexts and modes of aesthetic experience. For Münsterberg,

> the stereoscope [...] illustrates clearly that the knowledge of the flat character of pictures by no means excludes the actual perception of depth, and the question arises whether the moving pictures of the photo play, in spite of our knowledge concerning the flatness of the screen, do not give us after all the impression of actual depth.[5]

Throughout the 1910s, both the visual and plastic arts and technological experiments with stereoscopic cinema played a key role in theoretical debates on the stylistic possibilities of carving out a three-dimensional perceptual space from what was essentially conceived as a two-dimensional image. Visual techniques

---

1 Ricciotto Canudo: The Birth of a Sixth Art [1911]. In: Richard Abel (ed.): *French Film Theory and Criticism. A History / Anthology, 1907–1939*, vol. 1. Princeton 1988, 58–66, here 59.
2 Canudo: The Birth of a Sixth Art, 59.
3 Canudo: The Birth of a Sixth Art, 59.
4 Vachel Lindsay: *The Art of the Moving Picture* [1915]. New York 2000, 68.
5 Hugo Münsterberg: The Photoplay. A Psychological Study. In: Allan Langdale (ed.): *Hugo Münsterberg on Film. 'The Photoplay. A Psychological Study' and Other Writings*. New York and London 2002, 43–162, here 66.

https://doi.org/10.1515/9783110613551-007

such as high-contrast cinematography and lighting, editing and masking shots, staging with several planes of action and pictorial framing, in addition to music and sound effects, effective narrative structure and 'deep' psychological characterization formed a set of stylistic options that were discussed and put into practice in order to overcome the material flatness of the filmic image. The aim was to create a 'virtual' experiential space that would enhance emotional involvement and offer the spectator a sense of embodied vision.

Consequently, it seems worthwhile to reconstruct the connection between early film style and the creation of a virtual and immersive narrative space during the 1910s. Against the horizon of what was essentially an international phenomenon, in German cinema the process of stylistic innovation of cinematic space took shape at the intersection of two interrelated discursive fields: the adaptation and appropriation of developments in the visual and performative arts on the one hand, and, on the other, technological experiments in stereoscopic photography and projection. The idea of a film style that would promote the plasticity of the filmic image, cast into the mold of the 'cinema as sculpture' analogy, was substantially informed by stereoscopic photography and stereoscopic vision. Stereoscopic vision was, in Jonathan Crary's words, an "inherently obscene" visual regime, which "shattered the *scenic* relationship between viewer and object that was intrinsic to the fundamentally theatrical [i.e. perspectival] setup of the camera obscura."[6]

6.2 'Total visual recall': Stereoscopic practice and binocular vision

The principle of stereoscopy was implemented in a popular optical device:

> when seen through a binocular stereoscope, paired images with a twin-lens camera produce a startling illusion of three-dimensionality, whereby the mind converts the flatness of the images set side by side on a piece of cardboard into a perception of depth.[7]

Therefore, stereoscopy – or "stereography," as it was sometimes called – primarily "refers to the optical process whereby two-dimensional images are designed to be

6 Jonathan Crary: *Techniques of the Observer. On Vision and Modernity in the Nineteenth Century*. Cambridge and London 1990, 127.

7 David Trotter: Stereoscopy. Modernism and the "Haptic." In: *Critical Quarterly* 4 (December 2004), 38–58, here 38.

perceived as having three-dimensional depth."[8] Physiologically, stereoscopic vision is based on the principle of binocular parallax, or the differential angle between the optical axes of each eye. In his treatise on optics from 1878, Hermann Helmholtz located stereoscopic vision at the intersection of physiological and mental processes: "Seeing the world with two eyes, we contemplate it at the same time from two slightly different viewpoints, thus obtaining two images from slightly different perspectives."[9]

Historically speaking, stereoscopy emerged as a viewing technology and perceptual model around the same time as photography and was based on Charles Wheatstone's theory of stereoscopic vision from 1838 and Sir David Brewster's development of the lenticular stereoscope in 1849. Stereoscopic practice can be divided into two different forms of viewing: one by means of a hand-held device (a 19th-century form of portable and home entertainment) and the other by means of projection upon a screen via the stereopticon (essentially equivalent to a double-projector Magic Lantern).[10] In both viewing contexts, according to historian Richard Kriebel, "the stereoscopic photograph, properly taken and presented, appears not as a picture, but as the recreation of the actual scene. It produces total visual recall – you are there."[11]

The stereoscope had its first major public debut at the Great Exhibition in London's Crystal Palace in 1851[12] and subsequently became a hugely successful medium of mass entertainment. The stereoscope had a number of scientific applications, the most prominent being medical surgery and military reconnaissance, but its primary use was in the field of popular culture. By the end of the 19th century, millions of stereoscopic images were in circulation. For the most part, these images were views of landscapes and architecture, but they also included representations of events, both real and staged for the camera. With regard to the latter, often called 'French tissues,' Brewster, in his essay "The Stereoscope: Its History, Theory and Construction" (1856), wrote that "the most interesting scenes in our best comedies and tragedies might be

---

8 William Uricchio: Stereography. In: Richard Abel (ed.): *Encyclopedia of Early Cinema*. London and New York 2005, 610–611.

9 Quoted from Renzo Dubbini: *Geography of the Gaze. Urban and Rural Vision in Early Modern Europe*. Chicago and London 2002, 204.

10 Uricchio: Stereography, 610.

11 Quoted from Nic Leonhardt: "…in die Tiefe des Bildes hineingezogen." Die Stereofotografie als visuelles Massenmedium des 19. Jahrhunderts. In: Christopher Balme and Markus Moninger (eds): *Crossing Media. Theater, Film, Fotografie, Neue Medien*. Munich 2004, 99–108, here 102.

12 The Crystal Palace was itself a visual spectacle as panoramic as it was immersive. Cf. Wolfgang Schivelbusch: *The Railway Journey. Trains and Travel in the 19th Century*. New York 1979.

represented with the same distinctness and relief as if the actors were on stage."[13] The most important features of stereoscopic vision were "the eerie paradox of tangibility, the illusion of an accessibility to touch, the sense of proximity of object to viewer."[14]

As a visual technology whose "pictures were not only informational, but [...] became keys to experience associated with the things that were pictured,"[15] stereoscopy's immense popularity undoubtedly helped "shape the horizon of expectations for early cinema."[16] As William Uricchio and others have pointed out, many pre-1906 actuality films adopted compositional conventions of the stereograph: "Rather than rely on stereographic projection, filmmakers seem quickly to have exploited the illusion of depth created by moving the camera towards the vanishing point (phantom train rides) or by allowing traffic to move towards the camera (the Lumière effect)."[17]

Examples of early cinema's striving for stereoscopic effects include a stereoscopic version of the Lumière Brothers' L'ARRIVÉE D'UN TRAIN À LA CIOTAT (ARRIVAL OF A TRAIN AT LA CIOTAT, 1895), made in a two-color format in 1903; the 'anaglyphic scenes' in films directed by Enrico Guazzoni between 1910 and 1918[18]; and Giovanni Pastrone's assertion that he chose to move his camera along curved rather than straight tracks in order to create the 'impression of relief' in approximation to stereoscopic effects in CABIRIA (1914). A number of early cinema scholars have referred to the cut-in enlargements of objects in GRANDMA'S READING GLASS (1900), THE GAY SHOE CLERK (1906) – which was probably even based on specific stereo-photographs – and in films by D.W. Griffith as further instances of early cinema's simulation of stereoscopic effects.[19]

As a form of visual representation, stereoscopy can, in art historian Ernst Gombrich's sense, justifiably claim to have established a powerful norm for technologically mediated forms of vision that had strong stylistic reverberations within early cinema and other arts.[20] As a particular way of perceiving the

13 Quoted from Leonhard: "... in die Tiefe des Bildes hineingezogen," 103.

14 Linda Williams: Corporealized Observers. Visual Pornographies and the "Carnal Density of Vision." In: Patrice Petro (ed.): *Fugitive Images. From Photography to Video*. Bloomington 1995, 3–41, here 12–13.

15 Edward W. Earle: *The Stereograph in America. A Cultural History*. New York 1979, 11.

16 Uricchio: Stereography, 610.

17 Uricchio: Stereography, 611.

18 Cf. *The Tactile Screen / Lo schermo tattile*, *Cinema & Cie* 2 (Spring 2003), supplement.

19 Cf. Trotter: Stereoscopy, 51.

20 Ernst H. Gombrich: Norm und Form. In: Dieter Henrich and Wolfgang Iser (eds): *Theorien der Kunst*. Frankfurt a. M. 1992, 148–178.

world, it has left its traces on the literary imagination of writers ranging from Marcel Proust and Walter Benjamin to Franz Kafka and James Joyce, to name just a few of the most prominent figureheads of modernism. And, as late as 1937, Sergei Eisenstein modeled his idea of the "multi-viewpoint, sequential montage" along the lines of the binocularity of stereoscopic vision, when he wrote: "Binocularity is the existence of two viewpoints that enable an object to be seen in relief. The same principle underlies the multi-viewpoint, sequential nature of montage, which also permits the object or event to be perceived, as it were, 'in relief.'"[21]

The history of stereoscopy's influence on popular fantasy, on cultural modes of visual representation and on artistic imagination thus reaches well beyond its 'physical life' as a media technology and mass medium, which dramatically declined during the first two decades of the 20th century. Whether this sudden demise as a distinct cultural practice was due to "the film medium's escalation of the terms of visual sensation" or "the rapid spread of home photography"[22] is open to debate and further research.

In any case, it seems reasonable to assume that stereoscopy had a substantial influence on the development of early film style in its attempts to overcome the material flatness of the cinematographic image. As I will show, this legacy was especially strong in German cinema. The stereoscope not only provided filmmakers with a stylistic model of visual composition prominent in such popular genres as melodramas, crime and fantasy films; it also contributed to an artistic paradigm of the early 1920s that would become widely known as cinematic expressionism.

---

21 Sergei M. Eisenstein: Unity of the Image. In: Sergei Eisenstein: *Selected Works*, vol. 2: *Towards a Theory of Montage*. London 1994, 268–280, here 269. On Eisenstein's later essay "O Stereokino" (1947), cf. Oliver Grau: *Virtual Art. From Illusion to Immersion*. Cambridge, Mass. and London 2003, 154–155: "The ultimate synthesis of all art genres would culminate the imminent realization Stereokino, stereoscopic cinema, which Eisenstein believed humankind had been moving toward for centuries and represented a further expression of a deeply human urge to create images. Then, the image, experienced as a 'real three-dimensionality' [...] would 'pour' from the screen into the auditorium. [...] [H]is reflections revolve around rendering images so powerful, with plasticity and movement, that they can tear the audience psychologically out of their actual surroundings and deliver them into the environment of the stereoscopic film."
22 Uricchio: Stereography, 611.

6.3 'Contact at a distance': The illusion of depth vs. the relief effect in early film style

In many studies on what is being referred to as the "transitional period" of the 1910s,[23] early film style is conceptualized in relation to the illusion of depth. Early cinema scholars have evaluated and acknowledged the international stylistic innovations and transformations of this period on the basis of devices for the creation of filmic space, such as staging in several planes of action, character movement along a diagonal axis, perspectival set design and lighting, the blocking of characters and overlap of objects, scene dissection and reverse-field editing. The concept of perspectival illusion to which these devices contribute, however, stays within the limits of the paradigm Crary would call "monocular vision."

Taking the binocular model of stereoscopic vision as the point of departure for an analysis of early film style constitutes a radical paradigm shift from 'perspectival illusion' to 'perceptual immersion.' Regarding this shift, a more suitable term to describe stereoscopic effects in films than 'illusion of depth' would be 'relief effect,' because it accurately describes the impression of the image protruding out of the screen towards the spectator, rather than the illusionary production of a deep space 'inside the image.' The relief effect thus refers to the visual gesture of reaching out into the auditorium and towards the spectator, rather than pulling the spectator out of his or her seat into the virtual world on the screen.

Such an understanding of stereoscopic effects as directly addressing spectators as physically present in the space of exhibition and appealing to their immediate sensorial perception, rather than imaginary investment into the filmic image, reveals their affinity to the "cinema of attractions" and its practices of immediate shock effects, direct address, acting towards the camera and persistent acknowledgment of the audience.[24] Like the shock effects of early cinema, relief effects aimed at sensorial immediacy in order to establish "contact at a distance" with the audience. The impact on the spectator is aptly evoked (in the slightly different context of a discussion of modernist literary

---

23 Cf. e.g. Barry Salt: Film Form, 1900–1906, 31–44, and Ben Brewster: Deep Staging in French Films 1900–1914, 45–55, both in: Thomas Elsaesser with Adam Barker (eds): *Early Cinema. Space, Frame, Narrative.* London, 1990; David Bordwell: *On the History of Film Style.* Cambridge, Mass. and London 1997; Yuri Tsivian: Cutting and Framing in Bauer's and Kuleshov's Films. In: *KINtop* 1 (1993), 103–113.
24 Tom Gunning: The Cinema of Attraction. Early Film, Its Spectator and the Avant-Garde. In: *Wide Angle* 3–4 (1986), 63–70.

tropes of visual perception) by Maurice Blanchot: "But what happens when what you see, although at a distance, seems to touch you with a gripping contact, when the manner of seeing is a kind of touch, when seeing is contact at a distance?"[25]

In order to understand how this "contact at a distance" can be established in film, early cinema scholars such as Antonia Lant, Laura Marks, Giuliana Bruno, Angela Dalle Vacche and David Trotter have recently drawn on art historian Alois Riegl's well-known concept of "haptic visuality," an idea he first developed in *Problems of Style. Foundations for a History of Ornament* (1893). Riegl describes two kinds of visual experience: on the one hand, the optical, "which delivers a survey, an account of [...] distinguishable objects in deep space"; and on the other, the haptic, "which feels its way along or around a world conceived as an infinitively variable surface," based on texture and surface effects rather than outline and perspectival illusion.[26] Riegl uses the term "haptic" (from the Greek word *hastein*: to fasten) rather than "tactile" to avoid being misunderstood as referring to actual touch in its literal sense. "[S]o fast in its fastening," as Trotter succinctly put it, the haptic was for Riegl a "form of attachment."[27] A form of *affective* attachment, one should add, which implies a strong connection between haptic visuality and a 'sentimental gaze' on the side of the spectator, engendered by the somatic exposure to the richness of the visual field.

In relation to early film style, the particular form of attachment between the film image and spectator can be seen to rest on the contrast and interplay between two regimes of stereoscopic vision: the *theatricality of the tableau*, i.e. the staging, gestures etc. and the *tangibility of embodied perception*, i.e. the visual impression of the objects seemingly protruding from the screen as if they were closing in on the spectator.[28] A film style based on stereoscopic vision emphasizes surface effects rather than the perspectival illusion of depth, texture rather than outline. It works with a layering of several spaces of action, organizing the image into "a sequence of receding planes."[29] It plays on a compositional and figurative contrast between background and foreground, as when a luminous figure or object 'stands out' from a dark backdrop in the tradition of the phantasmagoria.

---

25 Maurice Blanchot: *The Space of Literature*. Lincoln and London 1990, 32.

26 Trotter: Stereoscopy, 39.

27 Trotter: Stereoscopy, 39.

28 Trotter: Stereoscopy, 39–40.

29 Trotter: Stereoscopy, 41; cf. also Crary: *Techniques of the Observer*, 116–132, especially 123–124.

Trotter describes stereoscopic effects as both extremely variable and perfectly adjustable to a particular way of staging the action: "objects in the middle or far distance appear to be arranged along planes separated from each other by a void; while objects in the foreground, solid enough to touch, assume an astonishing palpability."[30] According to Trotter, stereoscopic effects are a "product of the assertiveness with which objects in the foreground occupy space," creating "the feeling that one could reach out and touch them, or be touched by them."[31] He sees this particular impression as being produced by the coexistence of the two visual systems of the haptic and the optical, rather than by the replacement of one with the other, as Crary suggests. In Trotter's opinion, of the two effects stereoscopy generated, "of tableau and of tangibility, the less memorable, the less disturbing, in 1850, or in 1900, or in 1910, must surely have been the former."[32] Trotter points to "the violence inherent in the stereoscopic foreground," as it forcefully penetrates into the perceptual space of the beholder. And he has convincingly demonstrated with specific stereoscopic photographs that low-angle framing is much more effective in this respect than eye-level view: "The lower the angle of the shot, the livelier the potential discomfort."[33]

6.4 Archaeology of cinematic expressionism: Haptic attachment and the sentimental mode

Tableaux and extreme close-ups, low-angle views instead of a balanced vanishing-point perspective – it is no coincidence that one is immediately reminded of Noël Burch's analysis of DAS CABINET DES DR. CALIGARI, with its extreme camera angles, distortions of vision and jumps from tableau-shots to extreme close-ups without intermediate stages.[34] In his essay "Primitivism and the Avant-Gardes. A Dialectical Approach," Burch addressed "the issue of haptic space" but without fully elaborating on the concept. Yet, what he wrote about

---

30 Trotter: Stereoscopy, 41.
31 Trotter: Stereoscopy, 41.
32 Trotter: Stereoscopy, 41.
33 Trotter: Stereoscopy, 48.
34 Noël Burch: Primitivism and the Avant-Gardes. A Dialectical Approach. In: Philip Rosen (ed.): *Narrative, Apparatus, Ideology. A Film Theory Reader*. New York 1986, 483–506, here 496: "Until around 1912 [...] the cinema was characterized by a sharp division between two types of pictorial space: 1.) emphasis on linear perspective and the rendering of haptic space in accordance with the model provided by the painting of the Renaissance. 2.) a pictorial approach which on the contrary emphasizes the picture plane."

the "ambiguous imagery in CALIGARI" as originating from uncertainness concerning the relationship between surface and depth can be understood in the context of stereoscopic vision as a powerful influence on the stylistic paradigm of expressionism. As Burch puts it:

> The film's famous graphic style presents each shot as a stylized, flat rendition of deep space, with dramatic obliqueness so avowedly plastic, so artificially "depth-producing" that they immediately conjure up the tactile surface of the engraver's page somewhat in the manner of Méliès. Yet at the same time, the movement of the actors within these frames is systematically perpendicular to the picture plane.[35]

If there is indeed a close connection between stereoscopic vision and the development of expressionist film style within an archaeology of cinematic expressionism, the theory, technology and cultural practice of stereoscopy could be seen as the 'missing link' between German expressionism's claims to establish film as a visual art in the early 1920s and the metaphor of film as a "plastic art in motion" in the mid-1910s. By triangulating stereoscopy, the plastic arts and early German film style into a culturally specific configuration, a number of contemporary ideas and experiments can be brought into constellation.[36]
In his 1893 book *The Problem of Form in Painting and Sculpture*, a work that strongly influenced Riegl, the sculptor Adolf Hildebrand argues that the eye perceives space in two modes: the optical and the kinesthetic, with the first mode appropriate to distance from the object, the latter to a close-up view. The specific term Hildebrand uses for the kinesthetic mode was "stereoscopic vision." A painting, he wrote, might belie its own flatness by an appeal to kinesthetic perception and thus produce a "stereoscopic impression."[37]

A concrete technological example is the *Photoskulptur* (photo sculpture), a procedure developed and patented in 1900 by the photographer and sculptor W. Selke in order to "remodel a plastic representation of the human body with the help of photography."[38] Selke's device consisted of a 'shadowing apparatus' into which the model to be portrayed was placed and a film camera that successively recorded the shadows cast by the apparatus (Fig. 6.1).

---

35 Burch: Primitivism and the Avant-Gardes, 497.
36 For other examples, mainly taken from the US context, cf. Gwendolyn Waltz: 2-D? 3-D? The Technology and Aesthetics of Dimension in Early Cinema and Turn-of-the-Century Stage Performance. In: *Cinema & Cie* 3 (Fall 2003), 26–38.
37 Quoted from Trotter: Stereoscopy, 40.
38 Cf. K. Rohwaldt: Photoskulptur. In: *Die Umschau* 6 (1900), 5–7; reprinted in: Albert Kümmel and Petra Löffler (eds): *Medientheorie 1888–1933. Texte und Kommentare*. Frankfurt a. M. 2002, 57–61.

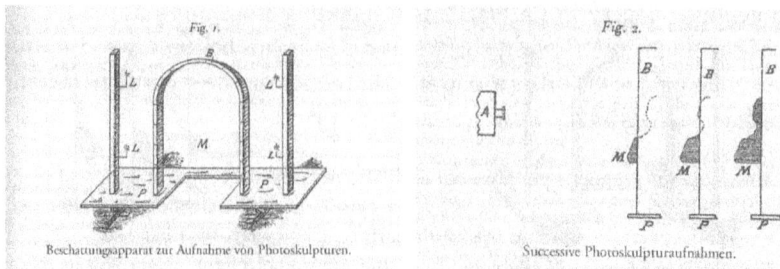

Fig. 6.1: W. Selke's "*Photoskulptur.*"

The resulting series of two-dimensional photographs would then be cut out, spliced together and finally molded in plaster, bronze, or ivory. In retrospect, this method seems to prefigure holographic imaging and 3D-printing technologies in the digital age as much as 'bullet time' motion capture à la THE MATRIX (1999), and it may have been influenced by Etienne-Jules Marey and Eadweard Muybridge. In fact, Selke's apparatus was modeled on an even earlier French device to turn photographic images into sculptured objects, which François Willème patented und commercialized under the name of "photosculpture" in the early 1860s, thus predating both Marey's and Muybridge's photographical experiments by roughly a decade (Fig. 6.2).

Another pre-cinematic technological marvel with some relevance in this context is "Pepper's Ghost," one of the most famous of the 19th-century phantasmagoria techniques (Fig. 6.3). In the early 1910s, a cinematic imitation of 'Pepper's Ghost' was developed and patented in Germany: the 'Kinoplastikon,' promoted as "Pepper's Ghost on the Motion Picture Screen."[39] The device used "a partially reflecting screen of glass to conceal the actual location of the movie screen and give the impression of projected actors moving about the real space of the screen."[40] Around the same time, film producer Oskar Messter developed what he came to call 'Alabastra-Theater,' which premiered publicly in Berlin in 1910 (Fig. 6.4). Messter used a similar set-up of partly semi-transparent mirrors to inscribe the filmic space into the space of the auditorium and achieve a synthetic

---

39 Quoted from William Paul: Uncanny Theater. The Twin Inheritances of the Movies. In: *Paradoxa* 3–4 (1997), 321–347, here 324.

40 Paul: Uncanny Theater, 324. Paul identifies the "twin inheritance for cinema" (327) as, on the one hand, the tradition of magic lantern shows (phantasmagoria, the uncanny) and, on the other, the theatrical tradition of Belasco.

Fig. 6.2: The "photosculpture" by François Willème.

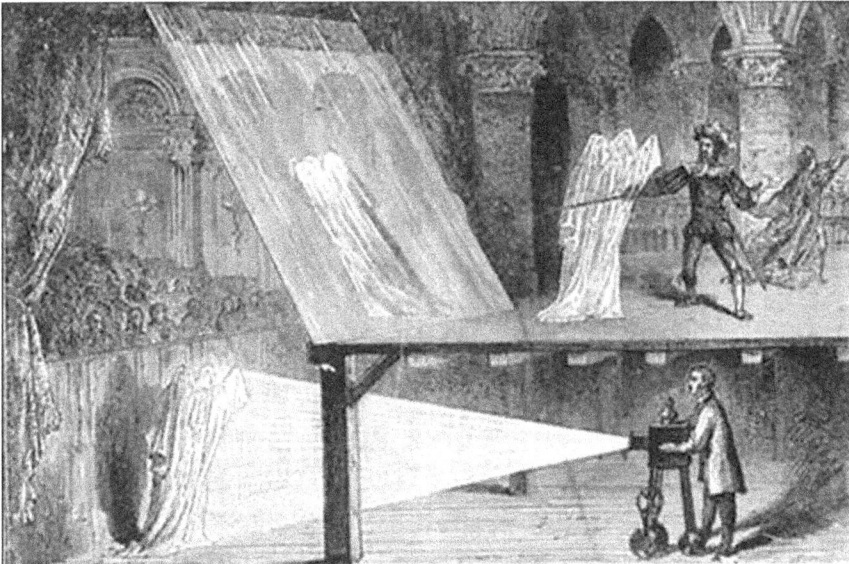

Fig. 6.3: 'Pepper's Ghost.'

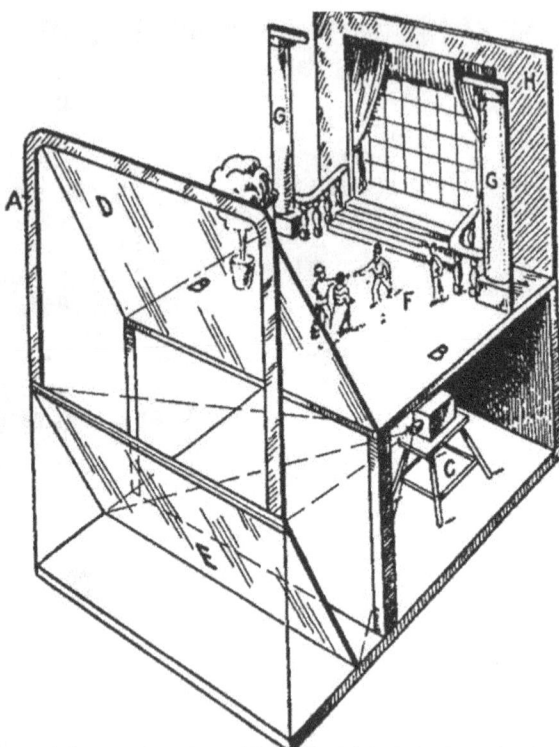

Fig. 6.4: Oskar Messter's 'Alabastra-Theater.'

effect of three-dimensionality.[41] Theater director Max Reinhardt also repeatedly employed such effects during the early 1910s, for example in his productions of *Hamlet* (1912) and *Richard III* (1913). In turn, these theatrical experiments held significant interest for film directors and therefore constitute a useful starting point for reconsidering Reinhardt's influence on German film style.[42]

When one sets out to trace the impact such experiments had on contemporary innovations in film style, one discovers many theoretical texts and

41 On Messter's Alabastra theater and the tradition of 3-D-projection arts, cf. Ludwig Vogl-Bienek: Die historische Projektionskunst. Eine offene geschichtliche Perspektive auf den Film als Aufführungsereignis. In: *KINtop* 3 (1994), 11–32.

42 The classic account of Reinhardt's importance for filmmakers in Germany is Lotte H. Eisner: *The Haunted Screen. Expressionism in the German Cinema and the Influence of Max Reinhardt.* Berkeley and Los Angeles 2008. Originally published in French in 1952, in English in 1969.

practitioners' statements as evidence. Max Mack, for example, reflected on Messter's and Reinhardt's experiments in his essay "The Conquest of the Third Dimension" (1914). Mack acknowledged that filmmakers were already striving for relief effects, but only "when it will be feasible to produce truly stereoscopic recordings on film, the plasticity of the image will be far more real, far more tangible."[43] Two years earlier, a comprehensive overview of the artistic possibilities of film direction culminated in a consideration of the "question of the plastic, corporeal organization of the filmic image."[44] While the experiments with the 'Kinoplastikon' may not have had a great technological influence on the cinema, the essay argued that directors should nevertheless draw on all the options at their disposal, whether *mise en scène*, lighting, or expressive shot compositions, in order to achieve comparable effects of relief and plasticity.[45] In the German debates on directorial styles and cinema aesthetics from around 1910 until the mid- to late 1920s, the problem of how to create the impression of three-dimensionality emerged time and again. Answers to this question were sought and found with explicit reference to stereoscopy and the plastic arts, which had crucial implications for shaping horizons of experimentation and expectation in the development of a recognizable German film style, in evidence as much in popular genre filmmaking as in art cinema.

Among the stylistic devices that contributed to the creation of plasticity for dramatic and aesthetic effects, the interplay between acting, *mise en scène* and lighting was perhaps most common. With regard to lighting, one can generally distinguish two different layouts for the period in question: diffuse lighting and three-point-lighting. As Kristin Thompson has pointed out, diffuse lighting was arranged "so as simply to make everything in the shot *visible*. Walls, actors, furniture, props, all receive an overall, diffuse light, usually coming from the front and top." In diffuse lighting, "the notion of creating atmosphere, depth modelling, and other effects [...] was distinctly secondary."[46] By contrast, in the layout of three-point-lighting a primary light or key light would be concentrated on the main actors, whereas the

---

43 Max Mack: Die Eroberung der dritten Dimension. In: *B.Z. am Mittag* 131 (8 June 1914), supplement 1. A translation of this text can now be found in Anton Kaes, Nicholas Baer and Michael Cowan (eds.): *The Promise of Cinema. German Film Theory, 1907–1933*. Oakland 2016, 578–579.
44 Otto Th. Stein: Ueber Regiekunst im Lichtbildtheater. In: *Erste Internationale Film-Zeitung* 48 (30 November 1912), 51.
45 Stein: Ueber Regiekunst im Lichtbildtheater, 51.
46 Kristin Thompson: *Herr Lubitsch Goes to Hollywood. German and American Film After World War I*. Amsterdam 2005, 38.

setting, which might be rather busy in its design and hence might draw the eye away from the actors, would be lit with a somehow dimmer [...] *fill light*. A slightly darker set would create a sense of greater relief when the brightly-lit actors stood in front of it. Fill light could also be cast on the actors from the side opposite the key light, softening shadows and creating an attractive, modeled look.[47]

The third method was back-lighting, where "lamps could be placed on the top of the set at the rear or directed though windows or other openings in the set; these would project highlights onto the actors' hair and trace a little outline of light around their bodies, often termed 'edge light.'"[48] Back-lighting, or more specifically, edge lighting, was one way "in which light could set the figures apart [...] by emphasizing their three-dimensionality," using highlights on the hair and shoulders to "pick their outlines out against the darkness."[49]

Before it can be made productive for analytical purposes, Kristin Thompson's detailed account of historical lighting practices in German film around 1920 should be accompanied by the methodological distinctions between three different dimensions of light in the cinema: light in a physical-technological sense as taken from a natural source during shooting or produced artificially in the studio; light in a semiotic sense as part of a given film's representation of a fictional world, attributable to the objects and phenomena which shape this world and thus contributing to the construction of the diegetic universe; and, finally, light as an aesthetic means of expressiveness, integrating the first two dimensions but producing a perceptual surplus beyond its representational function, geared towards the audience's sensory experience and potentially meaningful in itself.[50] In the context of the present chapter, it is this aesthetic dimension of light and lighting that is of primary interest.

Fritz Lang, a trained painter and former sculptor, often lit his superimposition shots in the phantasmagoria tradition. So too did director Joe May, as in the shot with the highlight on the approaching ghost in HILDE WARREN UND DER TOD (HILDE WARREN AND DEATH, 1917), a film on which Lang collaborated as script writer (Fig. 6.5).[51] Such compositions were deliberately evocative of

---

47 Thompson: *Herr Lubitsch Goes to Hollywood*, 39.
48 Thompson: *Herr Lubitsch Goes to Hollywood*, 39.
49 Thompson: *Herr Lubitsch Goes to Hollywood*, 41.
50 For a similar, but slightly different set of distinctions, cf. Frances Guerin: *A Culture of Light. Cinema and Technology in 1920s Germany*. Minneapolis and London 2005, xviii–xix. On the semiotics of lighting in German cinema of the 1920s, cf. Piotr Sadowski: *The Semiotics of Light and Shadows. Modern Visual Arts and Weimar Cinema*. London et al. 2018.
51 On the phantasmagoria and its impact on fantasy and mental imaging, its strong influence on early cinema's representation of dreams and subjective visions co-inhabiting the space of the action, not isolated and detached in the form of flashbacks or dream sequences as in

Fig. 6.5: Phantasmagoric shot from HILDE WARREN UND DER TOD.

effects created by showmen such as Étienne-Gaspard Robert (aka Robertson) that involved using a mobile projector to produce the illusion of a ghost coming straight toward the audience (Fig. 6.6).

The compositional logic behind this kind of superimposition, common in German films of the 1910s, and the symmetrical arrangements found in Franz Hofer's WEIHNACHTSGLOCKEN 1914 (CHRISTMAS BELLS 1914, 1914) seem less concerned with the creation of deep space than with the juxtaposition and layering of two or more autonomous planes of action with a visible rupture or void in between. In a signature shot from WEIHNACHTSGLOCKEN, the characters in the extreme foreground (and especially their hands) are clearly lit and arranged in order to achieve a high degree of plasticity (Fig. 6.7). Moreover, the motif of the arc formed by the hands of the two main characters is echoed by the gestures of the couples in the background – a doubling effect reminiscent of contemporary stereo-photographs.[52]

---

classical cinema, cf. Terry Castle: Phantasmagoria. Spectral Technology and the Metaphorics of Modern Reverie. In: *Critical Inquiry* 1 (Autumn 1988), 26–61.

52 On the effects of symmetrical shot compositions in Hofer, cf. Yuri Tsivian: Two "Stylists" of the Teens. Franz Hofer and Yevgenii Bauer, 264–275, and Elena Dagrada: The Voyeur at Wilhelm's Court, 277–284, both in Thomas Elsaesser with Michael Wedel (eds.): *A Second Life. German Cinema's First Decades*. Amsterdam 1996.

Fig. 6.6: Étienne-Gaspard Robert's phantasmagoria show.

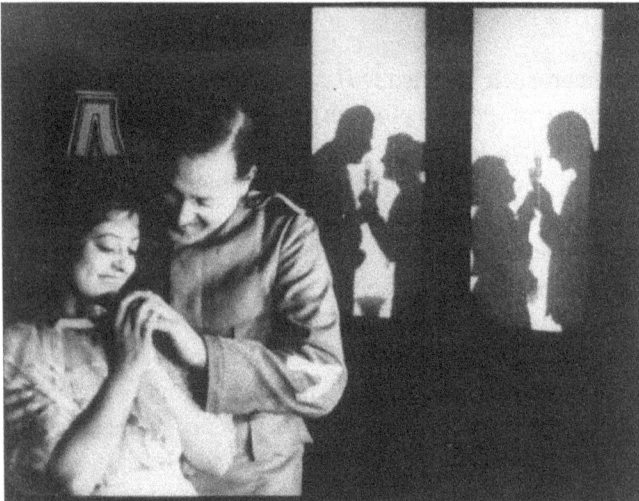

Fig. 6.7: WEIHNACHTSGLOCKEN.

In a shot from Richard Oswald's UNHEIMLICHE GESCHICHTEN (UNCANNY TALES, 1919), there is a similar arrangement and lighting pattern set against a dark background, only this time in closer framing and limited to the foreground action (Fig. 6.8). Conrad Veidt's stare, and especially his hand, appears to reach beyond

Fig. 6.8: UNHEIMLICHE GESCHICHTEN.

the picture plane into a virtual space and towards the spectator. This excess of plasticity is emphasized and enhanced by the contrast to the gaze and posture of the woman, who is safely contained 'within the image.'[53]

A director of special interest in this context is William Wauer, who was not only a filmmaker, but also a theater director, expressionist painter and sculptor who wrote extensively on film as an art form born out of visual technologies[54] and on lighting practices, corporeality and the perception of plasticity in the theater.[55] In a key scene from RICHARD WAGNER, a film Wauer wrote and co-directed with Carl Froelich in 1913, we once more find an arrangement utilizing separate planes of action, high-contrast set-design, compositional symmetry

---

53 On the plastic effects of Conrad Veidt's acting, cf. Klaus Kreimeier: Notorisch anders – Conrad Veidt. Zur schauspielerischen Repräsentation der Devianz. In: Christiane Rüffert et al. (eds): *Unheimlich anders. Doppelgänger, Monster, Schattenwesen im Kino.* Berlin 2005, 69–76.

54 Cf. e.g. William Wauer: Die künstlerischen Grundlagen des Films. In: *Erste Internationale Filmzeitung* 21 (1915), 15–21; William Wauer: Die Wirklichkeit des Films. In: *Illustrierte Filmwoche* 27 (6 Juli 1918), 184–185; William Wauer: Filmkunst: Kunst oder Nicht-Kunst? In: *Illustrierte Filmwoche* 38 (21 September 1918), 271.

55 Cf. William Wauer: *Der Kunst eine Gasse! Kritische Beiträge zur Theaterreform.* Berlin 1906, 36–38; William Wauer: *Die Kunst im Theater: Bemerkungen und Gedanken.* Berlin 1909; William Wauer: Die Theaterkunst. In: *Der Sturm* 76 (September 1911), 605; William Wauer: *Theater als Kunstwerk.* Berlin 1919.

Fig. 6.9: A sense of spatial expansion in a key scene from RICHARD WAGNER.

and expressive lighting (Fig. 6.9). The two knights in the right foreground are in high relief, marking a compositional trajectory that a dove, just released from the cup and as shiny as the two knights, is about to reiterate by flying right past the camera and off-screen. The prominence of the columns underscores a sense of spatial expansion, drawing on what Ernst Gombrich in his essay "Ambiguities of the Third Dimension" called the "column paradox," which "is caused by the beholder's difficulty in interpreting the projection of a shape extending in depth but giving no clues as to its orientation," since "Columns or spheres look the same from any angle" and therefore produce "a special case of ambiguity."[56] Similar compositions mark other points in RICHARD WAGNER, as in a shot where the lighting picks out the leaves of the bushes on both sides of the foreground in order to simulate a binocular relief effect (Fig. 6.10).

With respect to another of Wauer's films from the mid-1910s, SO RÄCHT SICH DIE SONNE (HOW THE SUN TAKES REVENGE, 1915), it is worth noting that Wauer collaborated at this time not only with Axel Gratkjaer, but also with cameraman and photographer Helmar Lerski, who is today best known today for his portrait

---

56 Ernst H. Gombrich: Ambiguities of the Third Dimension. In: Ernst H. Gombrich: *Art and Illusion. A Study in the Psychology of Pictorial Representation*. London 1994, 204–244, here 216.

Fig. 6.10: Simulation of a binocular relief effect in RICHARD WAGNER.

photographs of common people from the 1920s and early 1930s.[57] Toward the narrative climax of this murderous melodrama, lighting patterns increasingly divide the space into different planes of action to emphasize an 'impossible' foreground that seems to protrude into the space of the auditorium. This spatial logic is especially evident in a shot where a table and the main character in the foreground, emphasized by the lighting, are separated from the deep space by a compositional void across which there is no diagonal character movement (Fig. 6.11). This pattern is taken up again in another shot, with edge lighting placed not only on the figure on the left, but also on the curved armrest of the chair on the right-hand side of the foreground, creating a complex and plastic space (Fig. 6.12). In another shot from the same film, the poignant edge lighting is again directed on an object, this time a lamp. As in the previous shot, the edge light intensifies what is already foregrounded by the composition (the character holding the lamp); as a result, the lamp appears to protrude from the screen (Fig. 6.13). When the film finally reaches its violent climax, the axe, as the soon-to-be murder weapon, is represented only in the graphic silhouette of

---

57 On Lerski, cf. Jan-Christopher Horak: *Making Images Move. Photographers and Avant-Garde Cinema*. Washington and London 1997, 55–78.

Fig. 6.11: Compositional void in SO RÄCHT DIE SONNE.

Fig. 6.12: Plastic space as an effect of edge lighting.

a shadow. Thus, as a physical object, the axe remains as abstract and invisible as the off-screen act of murder itself. According to this spatial logic, which increasingly collapses the perspectival deep space for the sake of a virtual space reaching beyond the screen towards the spectator, the haptic surface of the cloth on the wall carries all the 'material' weight of the scene's emotional turmoil and physical violence (Fig. 6.14).

Fig. 6.13: The lamp protrudes from the screen.

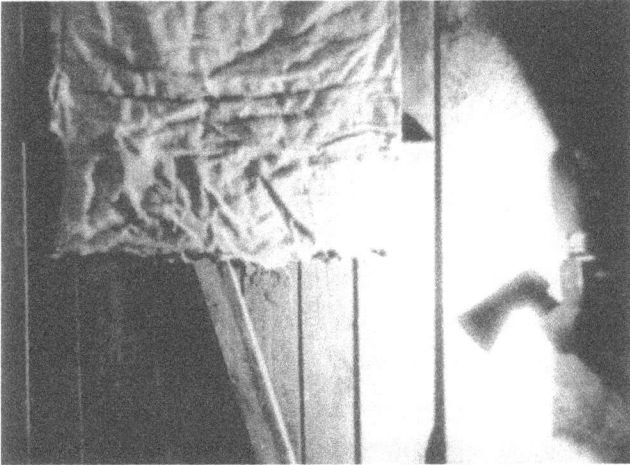

Fig. 6.14: Haptic surfaces and physical violence.

Other films by Wauer, above all PETER LUMP and IM BEWUSSTSEIN DER SCHULD (CONSCIOUS OF GUILT), both from 1916, were praised by critics as "creations of a new art of light," bringing forth "the magic of a Rembrandt-like chiaroscuro" and evoking an "atmosphere of indescribable allure."[58] Among

---

[58] Julius Urgiß: William Wauer. In: *Illustrierte Kino-Woche* 32–33 (25 August 1916), 210.

Wauer's later surviving films, the correlation between simulated plasticity modeled on sculpture, stylistic expressivity and the enhancement of the spectator's perceptual and affective experience becomes most palpable in the Albert Bassermann film DR. SCHOTTE (1918). DR. SCHOTTE tells the story of an assistant doctor of the same name (played by Bassermann) who attends to the young Charlotte Heyl (Käte Wittenberg). Charlotte is pregnant from Schotte's superior, head physician Dr. Torsleff (Joseph Klein), and was paid by him to silence her and avoid a scandal. After Dr. Schotte successfully performs a number of effective treatments on members of the local aristocracy, he is promoted to head of the university hospital, where he employs Charlotte as a children's nurse. A little later he asks her to marry him if she promises that the lapse with Dr. Torsleff was the only one.

Motivated in equal parts by professional envy and personal jealousy, Dr. Torsleff and the former head nurse Johanna (played by Bassermann's wife Else Bassermann, who also wrote the script to this film) procure the ruin of Dr. Schotte's marriage. When Torsleff invites Schotte to a party to celebrate the delivery of an oil painting (possibly painted by Wauer himself) commissioned by a painter he knew had been involved with Charlotte years ago, he reveals another affair from her past. Schotte casts Charlotte and her child out on the street. Agonized by his own decision, he commits several instances of medical malpractice, one of which leads to the death of a patient. Over the course of sleepless nights, Schotte wanders through the halls of his empty house, seeking relief in the bible and pondering over a human skull that lies on the desk next to the book (Fig. 6.15) – adopting a pose reminiscent of Hamlet during his famous monologue "To be or not to be...," a role Bassermann played countless times on Max Reinhardt's stage. Gloomy moments also occur during the day in his office, when Schotte stares at the preserved heart of a young woman and asks himself how much depravation and virtuosity it might have once hidden.

Wauer's film reaches its climax when the board of the local medical association, growing suspicious of Schotte's increasingly hazardous methods of surgery, asks Schotte to perform a public demonstration to prove his unimpaired competence at the operation table. The corpse that is put in front of the visibly tormented Schotte is in fact Charlotte, who, he learns, committed suicide out of despair. With the words (communicated in the film's final intertitle), "It is only on a living body that I can execute such a complicated surgery in front of such a critical audience. And if there is no other body at hand...," Schotte turns the scalpel against himself and follows Charlotte into death. "At several points in the film," one critic noted after witnessing the premiere of Wauer's DR. SCHOTTE, "the devout audience displayed a breathless, nerve-wrecking, almost eerie silence,

Fig. 6.15: Sleepless nights.

due to the gradual intensification of the dramatic tension."[59] But the dramatic effect was also heightened by an increasing amount of high-contrast backlighting on Bassermann's face and body. This backlighting seems to have cinematically simulated the emotionally-charged multi-dimensionality of Wauer's celebrated expressionist bust of Bassermann, which was commissioned during shooting and possibly modeled on the actor's highly expressive acting in a number of the film's close-ups (Fig. 6.16).[60]

---

59 *Die Lichtbild-Bühne* 34 (23 August 1918), 102.
60 On Wauer's bust of Bassermann, cf. Klaus Hammer: William Wauer – ein Propagandist europäischer Avantgarde. In: *Bildende Kunst* 3 (1990), 56–59. On Wauer's work as a sculptor, cf. Marc Wellmann (ed.): *William Wauer und der Berliner Kubismus. Die Plastischen Künste um 1920.* Cologne 2011.

Fig. 6.16: Wauer's bust of Bassermann.

6.5 Film style, embodied vision and 'mental magic'

Wauer's work can be taken as a particular example of a more general insight: that in a particular historical constellation – characterized by competing technologies, arts and forms of entertainment, as well as specific creative environments and cultural pressures – stylistic paradigms take shape in variable degrees, depending on current aesthetic debates and generic horizons, but also on personal dispositions and cross-medial concerns.[61]

At the historical juncture between the dominant visual regime of stereoscopy, the rhetoric of film as a "plastic art in motion" and the transition from the "cinema of attractions" to a cinema of dramatic effect and sensory affect, film style, understood as a distinct set of artistic choices at a particular moment in time, was neither fixed nor was it an end in itself. Instead, film style itself ought to be understood as a making – a *poiesis* – and thus as a process meant to encompass an audience whose modalities of feeling and understanding film

---

61 Similar assumptions generally guide David Bordwell's concept of a "historical poetics" of cinema. Cf. David Bordwell: Historical Poetics of Cinema. In: Richard B. Palmer (ed.): *The Cinematic Text. Methods and Approaches.* New York 1989, 369–398. Cf. also David Bordwell: *Poetics of Cinema.* New York and London 2008, 23–29.

included sensations from other cultural experiences. In the end, any type of visual effect – perspectival, stereoscopic, or otherwise – involves the spectator's sensory perception and mental processing of stimuli. This fact holds especially true for stereoscopic effects, as both Münsterberg and Eisenstein remind us. Münsterberg's psychological theory of cinema's mode of spectatorial address rests on what William Paul once called cinema's "mental magic"[62]: "Depth and movement alike come to us in the moving picture world, not as hard facts but as a mixture of fact and symbol. They are present and yet they are not in the things. We invest the impressions with them."[63]

For Eisenstein, in turn, cinema's temporality adds a metaphorical dimension to stereoscopy's relief effect:

> If there is a greater divergence between [binocularity's] two viewpoints – both of angle and of the time of vision – there is a shift in the perception of the resultant image, which thereby forfeits its immediate *physical* relief in favor of a relief effect that is *metaphorical*.[64]

The aesthetics of German film of the transitional and early Weimar period have often been called "magical" or "metaphorical."[65] The double impact of stereoscopy's embodied vision and the plastic arts on cinema might be taken together as one key to unlock the historical dimension of those attributes.

---

62 Paul: Uncanny Theater, 326.
63 Münsterberg: The Photoplay, 78.
64 Eisenstein: Unity of the Image, 270 (emphasis in the original).
65 As discussed in chapter 5.

7 Permanent Transition: Techniques and technologies of the early German music film

7.1 Mediation, representation, synchronization

In recasting the problem of cinematic sound in terms of different audio-visual delivery systems, recent film historiography has called into question the traditional opposition and chronological split between 'silent' and 'sound' film into a variety of more gradually shifting industrial practices and often-competing devices for the representation of sound in the cinema. Visual sound cues matched by live musical or sound accompaniment, recorded phonographic sound with post-synchronized images, the parallel experimentation and development of sound-on-disc and sound-on-film systems – these are only a few of the many technical and cultural practices which have constantly defined and redefined cinematic experience – or, in Rick Altman's words: the identity of cinema – throughout the so-called 'silent' era.[1]

The growing awareness of silent cinema's multiple sound identities has led to a radical revision of a number of methodological assumptions that have had crucial implications for historical research into early sound practices. Among these implications two general theoretical premises serve as useful conceptual entry points into the history of German cinema's early experiments with synchronized music during the 1910s and 1920s.[2]

In order to be rediscovered as a meaningful cultural practice, the early sync-sound systems of the German music film call for the development of a 'historical poetics' or 'historical pragmatics' of cinematic sound: an explanatory

---

1 I am alluding here to what Altman as described as a "crisis model of film historiography." Cf. Rick Altman: The Silence of the Silents. In: *The Musical Quarterly* 80:4 (Winter 1996), 648–718, here 689. For an overview of sound practices in silent cinema, cf. Richard Abel and Rick Altman (eds.): *The Sounds of Early Cinema*. Bloomington and Indianapolis 2001.

2 My use of the term 'synchronization' is narrower than the definition suggested by James Lastra, who contends that "any fixed or purposeful relationship between sound and image legitimately may be thought of as synchronized. From this perspective 'lip-synch' is only one, rather banal possibility." In the following, I distinguish between illustrative film musical accompaniment and the synchronized music film; however, the particular sound systems discussed below only underscore Lastra's point that "it is better to focus on representational effects, putting the emphasis back on the film experience and moving it away from potentially irrelevant issues concerning, among other things, the arena of the profilmic." James Lastra: *Sound Technology and the American Cinema. Perception, Representation, Modernity*. New York 2000, 94.

https://doi.org/10.1515/9783110613551-008

model that sets out to reconstruct the options available to a filmmaker at a given historical moment, a model that would attempt to relocate empirical evidence in the context of historically-specific industrial imperatives, aesthetic standards and cultural conventions. Rather than producing teleological or retrospective readings and explanations, historical agency and change would be accounted for by a model that highlights individual acts of choice or of avoidance and that regards cinema's institutional dynamics. Such an approach would provide specific and historically definable constraints and preferred options via given industrial standards and representational norms.[3]

This approach alone runs the risk of focusing too closely on (textual) production, or, indeed, relying too much on textual analysis to account for the complex utilizations and applications of sound effects in early cinema. It therefore seems necessary to open up the methodology of a historical poetics towards the exhibition context and the audiovisual experience in the movie theater. This shift would first imply, following Rick Altman, a redefinition of the object of study not in terms of 'film as text' but in terms of 'cinema as event.' As Altman writes:

> In this three-dimensional Moebius-strip world [of the cinematic event], the textual center is no longer the focal point of concentric rings. Instead, like the pinhole in the hourglass, it serves as a point of interchange between two 'V' shapes, one representing the work of production, the other figuring the process of reception. Beginning as a subset of culture at large, one 'V' progressively narrows as the work of film production runs its course [...] until eventually the work of production has been resolved into a single narrow product: the text. The process of reception then broadens out again, eventually reaching the point where it is indistinguishable from the culture in general.[4]

One conclusion to be drawn from Altman's hourglass model of interchange between the sound spaces of production and reception across the pinhole of the text is the non-identity between the recorded pro-filmic sound and the represented/exhibited sound in the cinema experienced by the audience. As a number of scholars, including Altman, Tom Levin, Allan Williams and James Lastra have pointed out, it is far more accurate to speak of cinematic sound not in terms of the reproduction of an original sound or of sound experience, but rather in terms of representation. This also means that we must conceive of the relationship between the sound produced during the production of a film and

---

3 Cf. David Bordwell: Historical Poetics of Cinema. In: R. Barton Palmer (ed.): *The Cinematic Text. Methods and Approaches.* New York 1989, 369–398.
4 Rick Altman: General Introduction. Cinema as Event. In: Rick Altman (ed.): *Sound Theory / Sound Practice.* New York and London 1992, 1–14, here 3–4.

the sound produced in the cinema on their own terms. A representational or non-identical approach to cinematic sound is thus less concerned with issues of 'fidelity' and 'authenticity' of a represented sound in relation to any original than it is with the technologies and institutions mediating the process of sound representation and shaping its experiential dimensions.[5]

7.2 The early German music film: A genre in transition

The synchronized German music film of the years between 1914 and 1929 constitutes something of a permanent crisis formation within the development of the genre. The extent of the film historical lacunae surrounding the music film is of almost exactly inverse proportion to the attention paid by film historians to the earlier experiments and applications of the German film pioneer Oskar Messter, after whom, one would have to infer, no major developments occurred until the early 1930s. What this scenario tends to overlook is the strong presence and durable persistence of the musical intertext, particularly the influence of the well-developed Wilhelmine and Weimar opera and operetta culture, on German narrative filmmaking throughout the 'silent' period. More specifically, this configuration casts a shadow over the manifold technological practices that accompanied experimentation with and production of synchronized musical, opera and operetta films throughout the 'silent' era.

In fact, the development of synchronized music films in Germany hardly ever came to a standstill in the years after the production of Messter's *Tonbilder* (sound pictures), nor was the genre first constituted only after the industrial standardization of the Triergon System in Germany in the early 1930s.[6] Instead, German production companies released on average two or three music films – film operas, film operettas, *Filmsingspiele, Singfilme* and *Gesangsfilme* – every year between 1914 and 1929. Three systems are particularly significant for the development of the music film genre and its sub-genres in Germany: the Beck patent, with which more than 30 film operas, film operettas, *Gesangsfilme, Singfilme* and *Filmsingspiele* were produced between 1914 and 1929; the Lloyd-Lachmann device, which was used only once in 1918/19 for the film operetta DAS

---

5 For an excellent discussion of 'representational' or 'non-identity' sound theory, cf. Lastra: *Sound Technology and the American Cinema*, 123–153.
6 For an extended account and critical reassessment of the development of the music film genre in Germany, cf. Michael Wedel: *Der deutsche Musikfilm. Archäologie eines Genres 1914– 1945.* Munich 2007.

CAVIARMÄUSCHEN (THE CAVIAR MOUSE); and the Notofilm system, used to produce one dance film, four film operettas and one film opera between 1919 and 1924.[7]

This chapter discusses the different practices of the German music film of the 'silent' era and the aesthetic horizons these films opened up for contemporary audiences. In order to account for why they could become an acceptable *technological* solution for the film industry in the mid-1910s and early 1920s, they need to be understood within a particular historical and cultural constellation. This constellation informs my reading of the music film genre mainly in respect to three general characteristics of what is commonly labeled 'transitional cinema.'[8] *Aesthetically*, the development of the synchronized German music film traces the conflict between the demands of developing narrative integration, on the one hand, and the lasting attraction value of the experience in the cinema, on the other. *Economically*, we must see the music film in the context of the crucial battles waged over aesthetic control and its consumption by audiences between the production and exhibition sectors. More specifically, this conflict can be regarded as a variation on contemporary debates surrounding film's musical accompaniment, which critics and practitioners in Germany and elsewhere fought over intensely, whether for (compilatory) illustration or (original) composition.[9] Finally, the *critical discourse* about this particular genre reflects strongly the cultural tension between the established parameters of musical theater and an increasingly confident, artistically independent film culture.

7.3 Mirroring sound: The Beck system and the negative legacy of the *Tonbild*

When former stage manager Jacob Beck applied for a German *Reichspatent* for his "Device for the Achievement of Simultaneity between a Cinematographic

---

7 In 1921, another patented device, the 'Hans Reichmann system,' was employed for the exhibition of the *Filmsingspiel* QUELLEN DER LIEBE (FOUNTAINS OF LOVE). This system was not, however, a synch-sound technology comparable to the other three. It used instead a seemingly mobile room divider-like screen installed a few steps in front of the film screen to hide the live singers during the musical numbers. In order to maintain the fictional illusion, its design matched the diegetic sets. Cf. Johann E. Reiff: Quellen der Liebe. *Film-Kurier* 249 (25 October 1921).

8 For a useful summary of the extensive historical debate over the determining features of "transitional Cinema," cf. Roberta Pearson: Transitional Cinema. In: Geoffrey Nowell-Smith (ed.): *The Oxford History of World Cinema*. Oxford 1996, 23–42.

9 For a theoretical discussion of this debate on an international scale, cf. Martin Miller Marks: *Music and the Silent Film. Contexts and Case Studies, 1895–1924*. New York 1997.

Representation and hereto referring Natural Sound Performances" in 1911,[10] the *Tonbild* era in Germany was drawing to a close. In the years between 1903 and 1909, the *Tonbild* enjoyed immense popularity with German audiences and featured as a main attraction in the short film program structure. From 1907 onwards, the combination of filmed operetta and cabaret stars with synchronized speech, singing and music, had briefly set the economic and aesthetic standard for filmmaking and film exhibition in Germany.[11] The industrial conversion to longer narrative formats in 1910/11 – and the changes in program structure it entailed – gradually rendered the short, but expensive and technologically sophisticated format of the *Tonbild* unprofitable.

Most closely associated with the name of producer-inventor Oskar Messter and his Biophon system,[12] the *Tonbilder* consisted primarily of either short musical numbers adopted from Berlin variety and cabaret theaters or well-known pieces from popular operas and operettas. These were usually taken from existing recordings but were also occasionally recorded in the film studio, either simultaneously with or after the shooting of the visual 'accompaniment.'[13] The rise and

---

10 Moritz Adam: Das Musik-Chronometer von Carl Robert Blum im Dienste der Filmkunst. In: *Die Kinotechnik* 4 (1927), 94.

11 As Corinna Müller has shown, this is indicated by the price per film meter. At 2.50 Marks (plus the rent for the sound record), the price was more than twice as high as the 'silent' film rate of 1.00 Mark. The fierce competition brought about in 1907/08 by newly developed sound picture systems such as Duske's Cinephon, Karl Geyer's Ton Biograph (for Deutsche Mutoskop & Biograph), and Guido Seeber's Seeberophon (for Deutsche Bioscop) led to a rapid decrease in quality and rental rates, sinking to the same level of the silent film price by 1911. Cf. Corinna Müller: *Frühe deutsche Kinematographie. Formale, wirtschaftliche und kulturelle Entwicklungen 1907–1912*. Stuttgart and Weimar 1994, 80.

12 For useful accounts of Messter's manifold activities, including his development of the Biophon system, in English, cf. Albert Narath: Oskar Messter and his Work. In: Raymond Fielding (ed.): *A Technological History of Motion Pictures and Television. An Anthology from the Pages of the Journal of the Society of Motion Picture and Television Engineers*. Berkeley, Los Angeles and London 1967, 109–117; Martin Koerber: Oskar Messter, Film Pioneer. Early Cinema between Science, Spectacle, and Commerce. In: Thomas Elsaesser with Michael Wedel (eds.): *A Second Life. German Cinema's First Decades*. Amsterdam 1996, 51–61.

13 Cf. Harald Jossé: *Die Entstehung des Tonfilms. Beitrag zu einer faktenorientierten Mediengeschichtsschreibung*. Freiburg i. Br. and Munich 1984, 69. The fact that both the record industry and the film industry settled in Friedrichstraße in Berlin around the turn of the century surely contributed to the emergence of the sound picture. Friedrichstraße was also where the major variety and operetta theaters were situated, creating a common milieu of popular entertainment in which collaborations and joint ventures flourished. The close topographical connection between the film and record industries and the popular musical and variety stages functioned as a forceful media machine that fostered the popularity of international stars like Enrico Caruso or Emmy Destinn, whose Berlin guest performances were often used for sound

decline of the sound picture format is well documented in Messter's business records: in 1907, sound pictures made up 83 percent of his company's sales, a figure that rose to 90 percent the following year, before dramatically decreasing in 1909, the first year they resulted in substantial losses. While Messter produced 40 sound pictures in 1908, he cut the production of sound pictures to only 3 in 1909; by 1911, they made up only 8 percent of his company's overall sales.[14] After 1911, only a few production companies still provided the market with sound pictures, among them Jules Greenbaum's Vitascope.[15] During the 1913/14 season, the production of sound pictures in Germany came to a virtual standstill.[16]

The recording and exhibition of the *Tonbild* was based on connecting a gramophone to the camera and projector respectively over a mutual driving-belt (Fig. 7.1) and was thus bound to the time limits of the existing sound recording technologies of 4 to 5 minutes.[17] Longer formats could only be achieved in the form of a series, as with the Messter 1908 productions of the abridged second act of DIE FLEDERMAUS (THE BAT) and his five-part adaptation of EIN WAL-ZERTRAUM (A WALTZ DREAM), which had a running time of 15 to 20 minutes. Exhibiting such *Tonbild* series required the use of two alternating turntables, but the necessary readjustment in the fine-tuning between gramophone and projector inevitably led to frictions and interruptions during the screening.[18] Although the synchronicity between sound and image generally seemed to work satisfactorily, the large distance between screen and gramophone, due to the fact that the latter had to be placed close to the projector, had a negative effect on the intended audiovisual illusion. Contemporary audiences were also

---

recordings at the Deutsche Grammophon (founded in 1898) and for film recordings at Messter, only a few blocks away. Cf. e.g. the documents collected in Ruth Glatzer (ed.): *Das Wilhelminische Berlin. Panorama einer Metropole 1890–1918.* Berlin 1997, 219–234.

14 Cf. Müller: *Frühe deutsche Kinematographie*, 83.

15 Greenbaum had marketed his own sound picture system from 1908 under the name of the Synchronoscope, which he was even able to export to Carl Laemmle in the United States. Cf. Jossé: *Die Entstehung des Tonfilms*, 92; Scott Eyman: *The Speed of Sound. Hollywood and the Talkie Revolution, 1926–1930.* New York 1997, 29.

16 Just as his early counterpart Gaumont did in France, Messter continued to experiment with synch sound devices until the early 1920s, but without being able to put his refinements of the sound picture system into production on a broader scale On Messter's later experiments, cf. his memoirs *Mein Weg mit dem Film.* Berlin 1936, 61–73; on Gaumont, cf. Martin Barnier: Le Cinéphone et l'ideal-sonore. Deux appareils sonores Gaumont des années 1920–1930. In: *1895* 24 (June 1998), 37–53.

17 Jossé: *Die Entstehung des Tonfilms*, 68.

18 Messter: *Mein Weg mit dem Film*, 66; Friedrich von Zglinicki: *Der Weg des Films.* Hildesheim and New York 197, 282–283; Konrad Ottenheym: *Film und Musik bis zur Einführung des Tonfilms. Beiträge zu einer Geschichte der Filmmusik.* PhD Berlin 1925, 25.

Fig. 7.1: Recording a late Messter-*Tonbild* in 1913.

bothered by the mechanical, slightly croaking quality of the sound, especially in the case of arias adopted from famous operas and operettas.[19]

The sound picture came to a determinate end with the arrival of longer narrative films in the German national market during the early 1910s, but it did not vanish without a trace. Jacob Beck had recourse to the sound picture as a historical precedent for his own system. Before devising his system, which was geared towards musical and vocal quality representations in the cinema, he carefully analyzed the sound picture's shortcomings.[20] Beck's idea was to use a concave mirror to reflect the conductor directing the musical performance during filming into the field of the camera so that the conductor would be visible at the bottom of the image during the projection of the film.[21] In this way, the

19 Cf. Friedrich Weber-Robine: Das Tonbild und die Sprechmaschine. Eine knappe Darstellung der Kontrollmittel des Tonbild-Theaters. In: *Der Kinematograph* 196, 198, 200, 204 (28 September 1910 – 23 November 1910).

20 Cf. Jacob Beck: Wie die Lichtspiel-Oper entstand. In: *Delog-Post* (June 1917), 1–3; Beck: Wie die Lichtspiel-Oper entstand: Schluss. In: *Delog-Post* (July 1917), 4–8. Also cf. Deutsche Lichtspiel-Oper. Denkschrift Anläßlich der Erstaufführung der ersten deutschen Lichspieloper Lohengrin am 21. Januar 1916 in Berlin. In: *Die Film-Börse* 3 (1916), 9–10.

21 Cf. Marc Roland: Gleichlaufsysteme. In: *Die Filmtechnik* 17 (1926), 348–349. The Beck System must not be confused with the system of the *Dirigentenfilm* (conductor film), developed in 1914 by Oskar Messter and Giuseppe Becce. In the conductor films, a publicly famous conductor was filmed simultaneously by two cameras from the front and the back, with both images projected with the back view (visible to the audience) on top of the frontal view (visible only to

conductor's instructions could be transmitted to either the conductor of the theater orchestra or directly to musicians and soloists performing live on site and who ideally remained hidden from the audience in an orchestra pit.[22] Additionally, a metronome was used at the time of shooting and appeared beneath the filmed conductor to insure the exact correspondence of rhythm and tempo between the filmed conductor and his counterpart in the theater.[23]

Beck's initial idea to shoot the soloists and the conductor with two cameras simultaneously and then insert the film strip with the conductor at the lower edge of the frame proved far less feasible than the mirroring method, because it was nearly impossible to achieve adequate synchronicity between the two recording apparatuses.[24] Replacing all technological sound recording and reproduction devices by an optical-rhythmical mediation made it possible to meet the new demands in film length and continuously adapt and project entire operas and operettas.[25] By replacing the sound picture's gramophone (phonographic sound) with real musicians and singers (live sound) in the reproduction – or rather representation[26] – of the acoustic dimension in the theater, the quality of the musical performance was no longer inferior to stage productions of the same opera or operetta.[27]

It was only at the beginning of 1914 that Beck had secured the financial means to set up his own production company, which would be especially

---

the cinema orchestra) to mimic the 'real' view of famous musical personalities conducting a performance in front of the audience. On this technology, cf. Harald Pulch: Messters Experiment der Dirigentenfilme. In: *KINtop* 3 (1994), 53–64.

22 In order to circumvent the problem of a contradictory orchestra arrangement in the theater, smaller orchestras were instructed to follow the filmed conductor directly, whereas full orchestras were meant to follow a live conductor who would 'translate' the movements of his celluloid colleague according to the individual circumstances. Cf. Karl Otto Krause: Der Lichtspielopern-Kapellmeister. In: *Delog-Post* (October-December 1917), 4–5; Ottenheym: *Film und Musik bis zur Einführung des Tonfilms*, 25.

23 Ottenheym: *Film und Musik bis zur Einführung des Tonfilms*, 25.

24 See Dr. E. Neumann: Die Technik des Opernfilms. In: *Illustrierte Filmwoche* 43 (17 November 1916), 280.

25 On the change in program structure and the importance of longer film formats in German cinema at that time, see Corinna Müller: Variationen des Kinoprogramms. Filmform und Filmgeschichte. In: Corinna Müller and Harro Segeberg (eds.): *Die Modellierung des Kinofilms. Zur Geschichte des Kinoprogramms zwischen Kurzfilm und Langfilm, 1905/6–1918*. Munich 1998, 43–76.

26 To speak of 'sound representation' seems especially accurate in this context, as it is, strictly speaking, with cinematic sound in general. Cf. James Lastra: Reading, Writing, and Representing Sound. In: Altman (ed.): *Sound Theory, Sound Practice*, 65–86.

27 Musicus: Die Lichtspiel-Oper. In: *Illustrierte Filmwoche* 43 (17 November 1916), 278.

equipped to produce film operas. On April 24, 1914, the Deutsche Lichtspiel-opern-Gesellschaft (Delog) presented its first production in Munich.[28] It was a version of Friedrich von Flotow's 1847 romantic-comical opera MARTHA ODER DER MARKT VON RICHMOND (MARTHA, OR, THE MARKET AT RICHMOND). The trade press greeted this first German film opera as pointing the way toward the development of a new musical film genre at the same time it criticized it as "unfilmic."[29] The outbreak of war prevented the distribution of MARTHA, which required a large cast and crew, and at first postponed further production. In July 1916, apparently unimpeded by such aesthetic objections and encouraged by audience interest in his second film opera in the spring of 1916 – an adaptation of Siegfried Wagner's *Lohengrin* – Beck expanded and restructured his business and moved it to the Reich's capital city, Berlin.[30] In late summer 1916, a second version of MARTHA was produced, which at last met with wide public acclaim. Beck's repeated choice of Flotow's opera can be explained by the fact that it was often performed in Berlin in recent theater runs and it was therefore possible to use the best-known soloists from various opera houses as 'silent' actors. At the film premiere, Delog could therefore offer a 'top cast' that would not have been possible at any of the opera houses because of contractual reasons.[31] At the regular screenings, in which an ensemble hidden from the spectators sung the parts, the recognition effect of the stage stars was meant to create the illusion of hearing them really sing. These performances drew on the appeal of famous soloists. That local soloists could concentrate wholly on their singing when performing at the film projection and not irritate the spectators with a possible lack of acting ability was also considered to have an advantage over stage productions of the same opera in small towns.

Because the pro-filmic sound dimension – including the quality of song and music during the shooting – was of no significance for the audiovisual experience of the film in the cinema, the outdoor scenes could be shot in the open air, a novelty compared to stage productions of the same opera.[32] In this earliest surviving film opera, it is also clear that current film aesthetic standards were

28 Karl Zimmerschied: *Die deutsche Filmindustrie. Ihre Organisation und Stellung im deutschen Staats- und Wirtschaftsleben.* Stuttgart 1922, 26.

29 Die neuen Opernfilms. In: *Der Artist* 1525 (3 May 1914).

30 For a more detailed account of the organizational development of Delog, cf. Wedel: *Der deutsche Musikfilm*, 79–85.

31 Cf. Die Filmkünstler der Lichtspieloper MARTHA. In: *Delog-Post* (November 1916), 10–12.

32 Julius Urgiss: Die Aufnahmen für die Film-Oper MARTHA in Wernigerode a. Harz. In: *Der Kinematograph* 510 (4 October 1916); E.A. Dupont: Kinofahrt nach Wernigerode. In: *Illustrierte Filmwoche* 43 (17 November 1916), 281.

hardly considered. The complicated mirroring method used during filming allowed for no camera movement or montage within a scene, resulting in a static filmic space. Even the film's photographic quality was not altogether impressive, unlike the color effect of a "powerful tinting" which, largely unmotivated by any narrative causality, was meant to emphasize the spectacle of the live musical presentation.[33]

Although Delog initially focused on competing with stage operas rather than the rest of the film industry, it soon reacted to the criticism of their "unfilmic" productions by assigning two experienced feature film directors, Rudolf Meinert and William Wauer, to direct DER FREISCHÜTZ (THE MARKSMAN, dir. Meinert, 1917/18), DER WAFFENSCHMIED (THE ARMOURER, dir. Meinert, 1918) and DIE LUSTIGEN WEIBER VON WINDSOR (THE MERRY WIVES OF WINDSOR, dir. Wauer, 1918).[34] In the eyes of the critics, these directors had an extremely advantageous effect on the stylistic quality of Delog's comic film operas.[35] In addition, the latter two films diverged from the principal of 'pure' opera. They contained narrative scenes without a filmed conductor, a fact that makes evident the beginnings of a transition to the lighter generic formula of the film operetta.[36]

Although Delog planned to add film operettas to its output when it was restructured and renamed Deutsche Lichstpielopern und -operetten GmbH in summer 1916, a change in production strategy was not carried out until two years later – and spearheaded by another company.[37] In June 1918, shooting had wrapped on the first German film operetta with synchronized singing and music, WER IN DER JUGEND NICHT KÜSST (WHO HASN'T KISSED WHEN YOUNG). The newly founded production company of Karl Otto Krause, chief composer at Delog since 1916, acted as producer for Delog's distribution arm. Operetta stars Molly Wessely and Paul Westermeier debuted as screen actors when the film opened in Berlin in August 1918. Critical reception focused less on the technical method behind the film– which was by this time a well-established synch system – and more on its success at meeting requirements of the number principle of popular hit operettas.[38] In September 1918, Delog announced a business deal

---

33 Die Lichtspieloper MARTHA. In: *Die Lichtbild-Bühne* 45 (11 November 1916), 20.

34 Meinert's views on the special requirements of directing film operas are expressed in: Lichtspiel-Opern-Regie. Eine Unterredung mit Rudolf Meinert. In: *Delog-Post* (June 1917), 4–6.

35 Cf. the reviews in *Der Film* 16 (20 April 1918), 59; *Der Kinematograph* 621 (27 November 1918).

36 Cf. Die erste Lichtspiel-Operette. In: *Der Kinematograph* 605 (7 August 1918).

37 For a more detailed account of the concrete occasion for this shift in production strategy, cf. Wedel: *Der deutsche Musikfilm*, 98–116.

38 Cf. Die erste Lichtspiel-Operette. In: *Der Film* 32 (10 August 1918), 70. "Number principle" here refers to the internal structure of the hit operetta (*Schlager-Operette* or "revue operetta,"

with more than 51 "large cinemas" throughout Germany, including 9 Ufa theaters and 6 venues belonging to the Heuser chain.[39] That same month, eight prints of WER IN DER JUGEND NICHT KÜSST 'toured' Germany with eight complete vocalist ensembles, sets of sheet music and program notes with instructions for the local cinema owners, musicians and bandleaders.[40] With this enormous success, the film operetta had definitively replaced the film opera. In the following years, there was not a single film opera produced using the Beck method; in the years between 1918 and 1922, a combination of narrative and single singing scenes, film comedy and operetta hits became the primary mode of the synchronized music film.

In 1919, thanks to director Edmund Edel (active in feature film production since 1913[41]), Delog's WENN MÄNNER STREIKEN (WHEN MEN GO ON STRIKE) and LACHENDE HERZEN (LAUGHING HEARTS) fully converged with contemporary standards of narrative filmmaking.[42] Even today, the attempt to balance cinematic and musical demands is strikingly visible in the surviving print of WENN MÄNNER STREIKEN (Fig. 7.2). Through montage, the intermittent attractions of the tableau-like singing scenes are coherently integrated into the diegetic space of the narrative, and classical shot/counter shot patterns and parallel editing sequences clearly reveal the characteristics of an approach to the popular genres of comedy and operetta films à la Ernst Lubitsch, Max Mack, or Friedrich Zelnik.[43] In their duets, the stars of the Berlin operetta stage, Lotte Werckmeister and Paul Westermeier, use the absence of

---

as is was called at the time), where the individual songs/musical numbers alternate with spoken dialogue. This new stage practice was opposed to the classic operetta format, which only included music and singing, and thus reflects the influence of the contemporary variety and cabaret programs, which also mixed comedy numbers with music and singing.

39 *Die Lichtbild-Bühne* 37 (14 September 1918), 16.

40 *Der Kinematograph* 618 (6 November 1918). About the contents of the 'packages' (the non-filmic constituents) which Delog distributed with the film material and which belonged to the 'final product,' cf. J. M. Jacobi: Propaganda und Reklame. In: *Delog-Post* (Januar 1917), 4–9.

41 First as a scriptwriter, and from 1916 on also as a director. On Edel's previous career, cf. the entry in Hans-Michael Bock (ed.): *CineGraph. Lexikon des deutschsprachigen Films*. Munich 1984-. In May 1917, Edel had contributed a comic feature article on the phenomenon of the Beck film opera in the pages of the *Delog-Post* by the title "Lieschen Schultz auf dem Fünfund-sechzig-Pfennig-Platz" (14–17).

42 This was also noted in the trade press. Cf. Sbt.: Eine neue Filmoperette – Das berliner Ereignis der Woche. In: *Der Film* 32 (1919), 24; and the reviews in *Film-Kurier* 51 (5 August 1919), 1; *Der Kinematograph* 658 (13 August 1919); *Die Lichtbild-Bühne* 47 (22 November 1919), 22.

43 For a more explicit distinction between the genre of the synchronized film operetta and the contemporaneous 'silent' (i.e. musically illustrated) German operetta film, cf. Wedel: *Der deutsche Musikfilm*, 329–332.

Fig. 7.2: The conductor visible at lower edge of the image in WENN MÄNNER STREIKEN.

the pro-filmic sound level to insert many dance sequences, which add a comical effect through their grotesquely excessive choreography, particularly compared to the stage. With WENN MÄNNER STREIKEN, the Beck film operetta reached the height of public acceptance. For the first time, even the specialist press recognized the film operetta as an independent film genre and autonomous form of cinematic expression rather than as a mere substitute for real operetta (*Operettenersatz*). Compared to the genre of the silent operetta film, the film operetta had the additional advantage of offering a high degree of interactivity. In keeping with the conventions of stage operetta, it offered this surplus entertainment value on demand: the film's hit songs, edited together on a separate reel, could be repeated at the end of the program.[44]

Whereas Delog remained committed to a strategy of compromise between the varying expectations of the operetta and the cinema audience with HANNE-MANN, ACH HANNEMANN (HANNEMANN, OH, HANNEMANN, 1919) and WENN DIE LIEBE NICHT WÄR (IF LOVE DIDN'T EXIST, 1921), other production companies working with the Beck system aimed to meet the aesthetic expectations of highbrow music theater audiences, something that was also reflected in their exhibition sites of converted stage venues. To distance themselves from the strategy of Delog, Karl Otto Krause-Film and Sing-Film (which operated the Beck system from 1921 onwards) no longer called their productions film operettas but rather

---

44 Cf. Dr. J.B.: WENN MÄNNER STREIKEN: Die Filmoperette. In: *Film-Kurier* 51 (5 August 1919), 1.

Filmsingspiele or *Gesangsfilme*.[45] In scantily dramatized plots of such films as
DAS ALTE LIED (THE OLD SONG, 1919), ZIGEUNERBLUT (GYPSY BLOOD, 1920) and IN
EINEM KÜHLEN GRUNDE (DOWN IN THE COOL VALLEY, 1921) entire opera scenes were
often restaged without narrative intermissions. The medium of film was only
required to function as a hinge between the fictional world and the real theater
reality, both on and in front of the screen. Accordingly, professional film critics
who showed little understanding for such specialist productions questioned the
quality of these films:

> Unfortunately, we see what we do not want to hear, and hear what we absolutely do not
> want to see. If we were deaf, we would see, if we were blind we would hear. There is no
> escape, unless we are both blind and deaf, but then in any case we would be lucky
> enough not to find the venue.[46]

The reaction of the Berlin critics should not be understood, however, as representative of the actual popularity of such productions, especially in small
towns and rural areas, as is evident in the persistence of this sub-genre until
the end of the 1920s.

In retrospect, the Beck system reminds us that the mirror has always been
a powerful visual medium. For centuries of art and popular culture, mirrors related distinct spaces to each other and created strong imaginary, sometimes
even magic (or phantasmagoric) effects.[47] More specifically, early narrative
films used mirrors as a device for internal montage, an alternative (or functional equivalent) to editing. Frontally positioned mirrors came into standard
use in European films in the early 1910s as a way of distinguishing themselves
from contemporary stage conventions:

> Because of their restricted use on stage, filmmakers of the teens seized the opportunity to
> appropriate real mirrors. [As opposed to 'blind mirrors,' M.W.] Typically, a reflected

---

45 A notable exception was Carlo Emmerich's Musica-Film: with the abundant use of trick-
photography and a dash of self-irony, the film operetta TRICK-TRACK (1921, dir. Emil Albes, cinematography by Guido Seeber) integrated the individual singing scenes into a fantastic narrative surrounding a youth elixir which "makes people as old or as young as the respective song
text demands." Cf. Willy Haas: TRICK-TRACK – Pressevorführung in der Schauburg. In: *Film-Kurier* 216 (16 September 1921), 1.
46 *Film-Kurier* 212 (10 September 1921), 1 (about Karl Otto Krause's DER SPIELMANN, 1921).
47 On the cultural uses of mirrors generally, cf. Benjamin Goldberg: *The Mirror and Man.*
Charlottesville 1985. On the tradition of "magic mirrors" from Athanasius Kircher's *Ars magna
lucis et umbrae* (1646) to 19th-century phantasmagorias, cf. Laurent Mannoni: *The Great Art of
Light and Shadow. Archaeology of the Cinema.* Exeter 2000, 3–27 and 136–175; Ulrike Hick: *Geschichte der optischen Medien.* Munich 1999, 115–156.

fragment of the space 'behind the viewer' would appear in these cinematic mirrors, in order to inscribe the viewer into the space of the action, imbue him with the same sense of 'being there' as painters were used to doing. To make the reflective space more functional or even dramatic, an off-screen door would often appear reflected in this cinematic mirror, motivating exits and entrances past the camera.[48]

In German narrative films of the 1910s, mirrors were also used to relate the diegetic space of the film to the space of the spectator in novel ways. In Max Mack's ZUM PARADIES DER DAMEN (THE LADIES' PARADISE, 1913/14), for instance, the placement of a mirror creates a sense of suspense as to whether the female character will discover her fiancé hidden in the wardrobe. In the culminating sequence of the film, the older fatherly character, who has brought the audience in the execution of his master-plan, blocks her view with his body, just as he previously related the narrative meanings of his actions to the audience by looking, smiling and nodding into the camera, thereby establishing a record of sharing his privileged knowledge with the audience.

Another example from the early 1910s, more closely related to the logic of the Beck system, was Oskar Messter's so-called *Alabastra-Theater*, which premiered in Berlin in 1910. The system used a mirror to radically inscribe the filmic space into the theatrical space of the audience to achieve an effect of three-dimensionality.[49] What Messter's *Alabastra Theater* attempted for visual 3D-effects, the Beck system set out to accomplish for sound: in contrast to the diegetic effect of integrating the (space of the) spectator into the imaginary 'textual' space of the film, the Beck system sought to inscribe the absent sound space of production into the exhibition space of an audience imagined as physically and collectively present in the theater.

Significantly, this process reverses the traditional relationship between sound recording and sound reproduction. The goal is not to reproduce in the film theater an original, pro-filmic sound space with the highest possible 'fidelity'; instead, the sound produced during exhibition in the theater sets the standard of musical quality and creates the 'original' sound experience to which the production is referring through the 'text.' Put differently, the Beck system, in imagining the reflective space of the mirror as the space of the auditorium, marks pro-filmic sound as the copy to which the original needs to be restored.

---

48 Yuri Tsivian: Two Stylists of the Teens. Yevgeni Bauer and Franz Hofer. In: Thomas Elsaesser with Michael Wedel (eds.): *A Second Life. German Cinema's First Decades*. Amsterdam 1996, 264–276, here 269–270. Cf. also Yuri Tsivian: Portraits, Mirrors, Death. On Some Decadent Clichés in Early Russian Films. In: *Iris* 14–15 (Autumn 1992), 67–83; Barry Salt: *Film Style & Technology. History & Analysis*. 2nd ed. London 1992, 70.
49 Cf. above chapter 6.

7.4 From the sound clue to the diegetic relay: The Lloyd-Lachmann device

In spring 1921, Beck's successor as managing director of Delog, Joseph Max Jacobi, stopped production on music films and set about making "all kinds of films."[50] This decision was partly due to a new competitive situation brought about by the success of a format that fused feature-length visual story-telling and synchronized live musical entertainment into a new cinematic experience for which there was a large paying audience in Germany. One of the producers, composers and inventors who entered the arena with alternative synch systems was Julius Lachmann, who took over the Lloyd Kinofilm company in November 1918 with the intention of changing the current production output of generically diverse entertainment films to primarily film operettas.[51]

Within four weeks, Lachmann had registered a patent for his own method of synchronizing film image and live cinema music and singing, and began production on the film operetta DAS CAVIARMÄUSCHEN (THE CAVIAR MOUSE, 1918/19).[52] Lachmann considered one of the main failings of the Beck method that the song scenes remained too isolated from the narrative flow, because it did not allow a transition from song scene to narrative scene within a single shot. He also disliked the conductor's appearance in the filmed music scenes because it signaled a break in the narrative before the live musical performance could compensate for the break. Lachmann therefore transposed the movement of the filmed conductor into an abstract rhomboid-formed lighting system integrated into the diegetic sets that would supply the musicians and soloists in the cinema with the time signature and bar and that could be switched on and off during the transition between narrative and singing scenes without necessitating a cut (Fig. 7.3). The method was also designed to be suitable for smaller cinemas with one pianist and one vocal soloist only. For this reason, it was important that the film operettas using this system also offered entertainment value separate from faithful musical reproduction. Consequently, a Lloyd Kinofilm advertisement on occasion of the first day of shooting for DAS CAVIARMÄUSCHEN, emphasized the quality of the film's screenplay, set design and photography.[53] According to the same advertisement, Lachmann wrote the "highly original comic manuscript" in collaboration with Erich Schönfelder, co-author of

---

50 Delog-Film-Vertriebs-G.m.b.H. (Die Filmindustrie im Handelsregister). In: *Film-Kurier* 209 (7 September 1921).
51 *Die Filmwelt* 44 (2 November 1918), 25; *Der Kinematograph* 618 (6 November 1918).
52 *Die Filmwelt* 47/48 (30 November 1918), 52.
53 *Die Lichtbild-Bühne* 48 (30 November 1918), 50–52.

Fig. 7.3: The rhomboid lighting system hidden in the set of DAS CAVIARMÄUSCHEN.

Lubitsch's SCHUHPALAST PINKUS (SHOE PALACE PINKUS, 1916), DER BLUSENKÖNIG (THE BLOUSE KING, 1917) and WENN VIER DASSELBE TUN (WHEN FOUR DO THE SAME, 1917). Another member of the Lubitsch team, Hanns Kräly, wrote the song texts, and the film's cameraman was Mutz Greenbaum, a recognized professional. Its director was Gerhard Dammann, known as a versatile director of comedies, whose popular screen character "Bumke" had already entertained cinema audiences in "Operettas without Words" before the war.[54] Much attention was given to the dance scenes, choreographed by the Berlin dance instructor Georges Blanvalet, who appears briefly in the film in that role.

Compared with the Beck system, the restrained displays of time signature and bar were much better suited to aid the synchronized musical accompaniment of dance scenes. Karl Alfredy wrote the compilations of well-known popular songs. To prepare the audience for these songs, the film begins with an emblematic shot of Alfredy in front of a picture of Jacques Offenbach and followed by an intertitle reading: "In the spirit of Offenbach...." Quickly picking up the popular tunes during the first screening of DAS CAVIARMÄUSCHEN on April 1, 1919, "the audience sang along enthusiastically in places and applauded heartily."[55]

Although reviewers were satisfied with the synchronicity of sound and image, one disadvantage of the Lachmann system in comparison to the Beck

---

54 On Damman's earlier career, cf. Hans-Michael Bock (ed.): *Der komische Kintopp*. Hamburg and Berlin 1997.

55 Hans Richter: *Kinobriefe* 9 (16 April 1919). Another reviewer commented: "Well, poetry is not exactly Kräly's strong point. [...] Still, some of the songs were successful, and the audience sang them in the intermissions. The highlight is, 'Nicki, Du bist nicht ohne. Nicki, du bist 'ne Kanone!' [...] Other refrains were also heard and sung with enthusiasm.' Egon Jacobsohn: DAS CAVIARMÄUSCHEN. In: *Der Kinematograph* 639 (2 April 1919).

system was the impossibility of filming outdoor scenes.[56] It seems as though DAS CAVIARMÄUSCHEN was the only film produced according to this method and, with Edmund Edel's less tableau-oriented Beck operettas, the modest success of the new system was quickly forgotten. In 1921, however, the specialized film journal *Die Kinotechnik* ran a piece about an unnamed inventor who had recently registered a patent for a variation on the Lachmann device, in which the light system was shifted back outside the diegetic world into the lower right corner of the screen. The decisive difference between this method and both the Beck system and the original Lachmann system was that there was no need to take account of a conductor or a lighting system during the shooting or when constructing the set: the synchronization mechanism could be "copied in" during post-production, and it was even thought feasible that the small light system (ca. 10 x 20 cm) could be projected via a mirror onto the desk of the cinema conductor to keep it from the eyes of the spectators.[57]

The idea behind the Lloyd-Lachmann system constitutes something of a paradox: the integration of the mediating device into the diegesis was meant to make transitions from narrative to singing scenes more fluent and the synchronization signal less conspicuous, thus fostering narrative coherence *and* the spectator's involvement into the action. As in many narrative films with illustrative musical accompaniment, the musical clues are shifted back into the fictional universe from which the sound is assumed to emanate. Erasing the mediating space of the mirror, integrating the signal into the fictional space of the action and pushing it back from the foreground into the design of the diegetic background sets all seems to account for an individualized spectator whose attention is focused on smooth narrative development and directed towards the foreground action of characters as narrative agents. As a soundtrack within the image, Lachmann's synchronization device appears to have become part of the film 'text' to be decoded and reproduced by theater conductors, singers and live musicians instead of modulators, amplifiers and loudspeakers.

In another crucial respect, however, the mode of experience DAS CAVIARMÄUSCHEN creates is far from being 'classical.' As a film operetta geared towards the event of exhibition, it retains the Beck system's catering for audience participation and does not silence the audience, as classical cinema's dominantly instrumental symphonic soundtracks would do.[58] On the contrary, by repeating

---

56 Jacobsohn: DAS CAVIARMÄUSCHEN.
57 Dipl.-Ing. Hans Kellner: Kino und Musik. In: *Die Kinotechnik* 8 (1921), 294–295.
58 Rick Altman has described "the changing modes of exchange between screen and audience" in the transition to classical sound in the context of early American cinema: "With popular music it was hard to keep the audience from singing or humming along, but there was no

the hit songs more than once and drawing on popular musicals themes and melodies, it played on the audience's familiarity and encouraged them to sing along with the professional singers hidden in the orchestra pit.

The interactive mode of reception implied by these sync systems corresponds to what Daniel Dahan and Elihu Katz in their classification of different media events have described as the mode of "festive viewing." In contrast to mere spectacle, the "festival" mode is characterized by a high level of interaction on the part of the audience.[59] In light of this definition, the paradox of the Lloyd-Lachmann system seems to operate using a double strategy of address, creating multi-media events that oscillate between the spectacle of fictional illusionism and the festival of participation and interaction, between the pleasures of classical spectatorship and the pleasures of being part not of the 'text,' but of the event.

7.5 Inscribing the score: The Notofilm system

"For the living film, the living note!" was the slogan that accompanied the June 1920 announcement of the first film operetta to be produced under a new music film system.[60] The Notofilm system, developed in 1919 by film director and erstwhile operetta director Ludwig Czerny and composer Tilmar Springefeld, consisted of an apparatus constructed by Ernst Lucht that coupled a second smaller device to the front of the camera. The rotation of the device allowed the recording of the musical notes simultaneous to the action.[61] The advantages of the highly usable and portable Notofilm system over the Beck and Lachmann

---

danger of the audience joining in the chorus of a song without words. [...] By folding the audience into the diegesis, the film's story line, the new accompaniment standard simultaneously achieved several important goals. First, it carefully reduced real spectator individuality, substituting instead a temporary fictional homogeneity based on the audience's common immersion in the film and its emotions. Second, it transformed each spectator from recognized (audible) interlocutor in an overtly discursive situation to (invisible) voyeur and (silent) *écouteur* of a distanced history. Third, by effacing cinema sound's direct address to the audience, it removed overt interpellation's invitation to respond." Rick Altman: Sound – All of it. In: *Iris* 27 (Spring 1999), 31–48, here 42–43. For an extended argument, cf. Rick Altman: *Silent Film Sound*. New York 2004, 231–286.

59 Danial Dayan and Elihu Katz: *Media Events. The Live Broadcasting of History*. Cambridge, Mass. 1994, 119–146.

60 *Die Lichtbild-Bühne* 23 (5 June 1920), 79.

61 Cf. Notofilm. In: *Film-Kurier* 107 (9 October 1919); St. R.: Die erste Filmoper. In: *Allgemeine Kino-Börse* 36 (1922), 5.

Fig. 7.4: The Notofilm system.

systems was that operettas could be synchronized throughout – including inter-titles, outdoor shots, trick shots and close-ups – without limiting the formal range of the filmic medium. The Notofilm system therefore retained the combi-nation of acting and singing scenes, but aimed also for synchronized musical accompaniment during the acting scenes, something that was not possible with the Beck or Lachmann systems.[62] With the aid of a line of music moving from right to left beneath the film image throughout (Fig. 7.4) and containing the melodies of the musical score as well as the entry and recital signs indicated by a stable vertical marker in the center,[63] Czerny and his composers, Springefeld and Hans Ailbout, intended a synthesis of the competing demands for musical quality on the one hand and narrative filmmaking on the other.[64] In this re-spect, the Notofilm system reflected a more general trend in film musical ac-companiment during the 1920s: "Like the images it accompanied, silent film music moved from a mode of intermittent 'attractions,' or a mode of stressing

---

[62] Cf. promotion brochure of the Noto-Film-Gesellschaft [1920], Archive Deutsche Kinema-thek, Berlin.

[63] Marc Roland: Gleichlaufsysteme, 348–349, and Adam: Das Musik-Chronometer von Carl Robert Blum im Dienste der Filmkunst, 94, attribute the basic technical idea behind this device to a certain Paulo Benedetti, who in 1912 had claimed a patent in Brazil. In 1924, a similar de-vice with a running score printed on the film frame was apparently used for the Argentine film LA MUJER DE MEDIANOCHE (MIDNIGHT WOMAN), which points to another history of the genre in South America. The film's director, Carlo Campogalliani, later worked in Germany as the co-director of the comedy ICH HAB' MEIN HERZ IM AUTOBUS VERLOREN (I HAVE LOST MY HEART IN A BUS, 1929).

[64] Cf. Ludwig Czerny: Film und Musik. In: *Der Film* 35 (27 August 1923), 31; Hans Ailbout: Mu-sikfilme. In: *Filmland* 4 (February 1925), 64.

the autonomy of individual elements, to a form that stressed the absolute continuity of the music from one end of a picture to another."[65]

The Notofilm system was first tested in late 1919 in the main scene of the dance film DAS MENUETT, produced by Cela Film and directed by Czerny.[66] Its success must have been promising because in the following spring, Czerny and Springefeld founded the Notofilm company.[67] With Czerny at its head, the company was to produce music films using its patented system. For the production of a Notofilm, the director used the manuscript to work out the length of the single scenes. Then, with the help of a metronome, the composer would write the musical arrangement and the piano score to fit with the individual scene's images. The musical notation was then copied from the score and filmed beneath the scene. This method also ensured that the original music was played throughout the screening, whereas with the other systems which only gave the musical key, the choice of music during narrative scenes was often left to the orchestra in the cinema.[68]

Between 1920 and 1924, Notofilm produced one film per year from original compositions, written primarily by Ailbout with Springefeld's occasional collaboration. The main actress in Notofilms was Ada Svedin, an excellent dancer with a second-rate singing voice, who was dubbed in the cinema by professional operetta singers, whereas most of the other actors sang their own parts, at least at the film premieres.[69] The *Biedermeier* operetta DAS KUSSVERBOT (KISSING PROHIBITED, 1920) was both a critical and box office success, although the size of the clearly visible music strip met with criticism. The presence of the music strip was corrected in subsequent productions, and in the spectacular and hugely successful MISS VENUS (1921), set in America, the note strip system was reduced in size so that "it was only visible to the conductor and at the most to the first rows in the auditorium."[70]

---

65 Lastra: *Sound Technology and the American Cinema*, 115.

66 Cf. the advertisement in *Das große Bilderbuch des Films*. Berlin 1920.

67 *Film-Kurier* 54 (4 March 1920).

68 Cf. Noto-Film-Gesellschaft. In: *Film-Kurier* 143 (21 June 1921); Czerny: Film und Musik, 31. This was a problem Beck and his collaborators were aware of very early on. In order to assure that no other music was played than the one delivered with the film, they told theater owners very clearly – and repeatedly – that no programs or musical instructions except those issued by Delog must be given out to the audience and the musicians before or during the screening. Cf. *Delog-Post* (November 1916), 18.

69 Cf. hfr.: Die blonde Geisha. In: *Die Lichtbild-Bühne* 11 (17 March 1923), 29.

70 MISS VENUS: Die neue große Filmoperette. In: *Bühne & Film* 17 (1921), 10. Some critics commented effusively: "A new film operetta – an absolute victory all the way along the line. Its conscientious brisk composition makes it an operetta from the first bar until the last pause

Notofilm's first failure came in 1922 with the expensive "fantastic film opera" JENSEITS DES STROMES (BEYOND THE STREAM), composed by Ferdinand Hummel. It was a fruitless attempt to reanimate a genre that Delog had given up on six years earlier, among whose advocates Hummel was counted.[71] The greater filmic possibilities of the Notofilm system were neglected in favor of filming Hummel's original score, and the direction was done with hardly any regard for contemporary conventions of cinematic representation.[72] In respect to the famous composer, rapid scene changes were avoided.[73] Visually, the film was orientated towards the symbolic world of the painter Arnold Böcklin, resulting in a cascade of histrionic double exposures and lighting effects.[74] Because the quality of the musical performance was of utmost importance, JENSEITS DES STROMES was distributed to large cinemas along with a conductor, song soloists and complete musical notation. For smaller cinemas that did not have a complete orchestra, a second version of the film was produced: "in its dramatic creation it is a four-part play about fate, also with professor Hummel's music [but] with a series of fine suggestive titles instead of songs to link the images."[75]

The practice of substituting intertitles for sung lyrics is instructive because it adds further evidence for a rationale that works with a set of options and functional equivalents. More importantly, however, it suggests an affinity between the symbolic codes of written language and musical notation in the task of anchoring the imaginary realm of the visual representation.[76] In this context, the Notofilm system becomes legible as a diachronic extension of those occasional intertitles that in the 'silent' era served to indicate the desired musical accompaniment for individual scenes by giving the lyrics and a few bars of music of well-known tunes. This feature sets the Notofilm system apart from the Beck and the Lloyd-Lachmann devices, both of which worked with an imaginary space of

---

[…]. It is also a film wonderfully directed, acted and photographed; pure in every scene and amusing in its burlesque, eccentric ideas. […] This balanced and colorful film promises to become a hit with the public. I cannot think of any conditions it does not fulfill." *Film-Kurier* 223 (24 September 1921).

71 Cf. Ferdinand Hummel: Musik und Kino. In: *Delog-Post* (May 1917), 1–3. On Hummel's work for the cinema, cf. Herbert Birett: *Stummfilm-Musik. Materialsammlung.* Berlin 1970, 199.

72 Cf. *Jenseits des Stromes. Vollständiges Textbuch mit musikalischen Erläuterungen und Leitmotiven.* Berlin 1922). A copy is held at the Bundesarchiv-Filmarchiv, Berlin, Documentation Dept., Sign. 8244.

73 St. R.: Die erste Filmoper, 6.

74 Ferdinand Hummel: Die Filmmusik. In: *Der Film* 36 (3 September 1922), 28–31.

75 *Der Film* 25 (18 June 1922), 60.

76 Cf. Friedrich Kittler: *Grammophone, Film, Typewriter.* Stanford 1999.

visual mediation. In contrast, the Notofilm system seems to have found the appropriate textual model against which to develop its mode of sound representation in the symbolic code of language and the contemporary use of intertitles.[77]

With DIE BLONDE GEISHA (THE BLONDE GEISHA, 1923) and DAS MÄDEL VON PONTECUCULI (THE GIRL FROM PONTECUCULI, 1924), Notofilm produced only two more films using this system. Early in 1924, Springefeld joined the Dewesti Film company to compose DIE BRIGANTIN VON NEW YORK (THE BRIGANTINE FROM NEW YORK) and make use of the system he had developed with Czerny.[78] Czerny also left Notofilm shortly after the failed premiere of DAS MÄDEL VON PONTECUCULI.[79] Apparently forbidden by the two renegade inventors to use the system after which the company was named, the new management at Notofilm returned to the Beck system to produce its last Singfilm in 1926: GRETCHEN SCHUBERT.

7.6 The shifting terms of the 'audiovisual pact'

Thanks to Karl Otto Krause's obstinate belief in the Beck device, the 'silent' *Gesangsfilm* with its 'sound-on-screen' practice managed to last until the international standardization of sound-on-film systems in Germany in 1929/30.[80]

---

77 Intertitles still served as a forceful model for the aesthetics of the early sound film. Cf. Mary Ann Doane: The Voice in Cinema. The Articulation of Body and Space. In: *Yale French Studies* 60 (1980), 33–50; Lastra: *Sound Technology and the American Cinema*, 148.

78 Cf. *Filmland* 6 (April 1925), 65, 72; Ernesto Bernardy: Kalauer bei Tilmar Springefeld. In: *Filmland* 7 (May 1925), 64.

79 Cf. Robert Volz: Die Filmoperette. In: *Der Bildwart* 2 (1925); reprinted in: Katja Uhlenbrok (ed.): ... *aus dem Geiste der Operette. Musiktheater und Tanzkultur im deutschen Film 1922–1937*. Hamburg 1997, 4–7. In 1930, Czerny adapted his sync system to the new demands of the sound film industry and converted it into a device facilitating the dubbing of foreign film imports. Cf. Wedel: *Der deutsche Musikfilm*, 165–168. On the connection between the sync systems of the 'silent' music film and technical aids for dubbing foreign films cf. the role Carl Robert Blum's device played in the production of the German version of ALL QUIET ON THE WESTERN FRONT, discussed below in chapter 8.

80 In September 1929, Josef Max Jacobi's now renamed "Delog-Tonfilm" once more revived the production of synchronized musical films with ZAPFENSTREICH AM RHEIN (TATTOO AT THE RHINE). A 'silent' version as well as two sound versions of this film were produced, the latter using the Tobis electrical optical sound system and General Electric's needle device respectively. Despite its illustrious professional crew – including director Jaap Speyer, cinematographers Franz Planer and Friedl Behn-Grund, set designer Walter Reimann and composer Friedrich Hollaender – ZAPFENSTREICH AM RHEIN premiered on December 1, 1930, to little success. In the wake of this public failure, the planned production of a follow-up film seems to have been canceled. Cf. the advertisement for Delog-Tonfilm in: *Film-Kurier* 223 (19 September 1929); Was die Delog verspricht. In: *Kinotechnische Rundschau* 38 (21 September 1929).

Krause's films of the late 1920s, WIR ARMEN KLEINEN MÄDCHEN (WE POOR LITTLE GIRLS, 1926), ICH HAB DICH LIEB (I AM FOND OF YOU, 1926) and EINMAL UM MITTERNACHT (ONCE AT MIDNIGHT, 1929), gave well-known stage soloists ample space for self-presentation within loosely linked narratives, providing the *Sängerfilme* of the early 1930s with their recipe for success.[81] Critics saw EINMAL UM MITTERNACHT as a contribution to a film genre and technology paradoxically poised between a distant past, a transitional present and an eternally utopian future. Immediately after the film's premiere in October 1929, the film critic from the *Deutsche Filmzeitung* judged it "an average product of the growing genre of the *Singfilm* which still appeals to a large audience."[82] Yet, by the end of February 1930, Siegfried Kracauer regarded the two levels of sound and image as an "anachronistic product," going on to say:

> As the motorbike is the poor man's car, so the Singfilm is the poor man's talkie. It is not a real sound film. Two singers in the orchestra sing the hits and the songs that have been put into the mouths of the people on screen. They sing perfectly in time to produce the illusion of a sound film.[83]

Significantly, Kracauer did not criticize any failure in the construction of the audiovisual illusion but, acknowledging the existence of newly available sound-on-film systems, he announced that unlimited pleasure at the illusion produced by the Beck system might now be over. As early as 1921, Ernst Jäger described as a necessary condition for the perceptual integration of sound and image what one might call a successful 'pact' between the music film genre and its cinema audience:

> First, we have to overcome the irritation resulting from critical thinking about the artificiality of the experience. We must allow ourselves to be duped into thinking that sound and image come from the same source. If we stop watching to see whether in fact every lip movement and arm movement of an actor corresponds to the singing in front of the screen, we will willingly experience sound and image as one, and then this system of the Beck "film operetta" will meet with undivided applause.[84]

---

81 On the genre of the *Sängerfilm*, cf. Michael Wedel: *Der deutsche Musikfilm*, 61, 359–362. Krause himself switched over to the Tobis-Klangfilm system in 1933 with his last production, LIEBESFRÜHLING (SPRING OF LOVE).

82 [René Prévot]: EINMAL UM MITTERNACHT. In: *Deutsche Filmzeitung* 45 (8 November 1929); reprinted in Gero Gandert (ed.): *Der Film der Weimarer Republik. Ein Handbuch der zeitgenössischen Kritik*, vol. 1: 1929. Berlin and New York 1993, 144.

83 Raca. [Siegfried Kracauer]: EINMAL UM MITTERNACHT [1930]. In: *Werke*, vol. 6.2: *Kleine Schriften zum Film 1928–1931*, ed. Inka Mülder-Bach. Frankfurt a. M. 2004, 338–339.

84 J. [Ernst Jäger]: BANDITEN. In: *Film-Kurier* 60 (11 March 1921).

Only with the industrial standardization of the Triergon-Klangfilm system would this 'audiovisual pact,'[85] grounded in a particular cultural framework and a determinate set of historical pressures, tensions and desires pervading German cinema from the early 1910s well into the 1920s, meet opposition on the side of the audience. Constantly transforming and permanently co-existing, as it were, in the physical space of the auditorium and the imaginary space on screen, the inventors and practitioners of the transitional synch systems of German music films between the early *Tonbild* and the later *Tonfilm* may appear not as insignificant after all, since their products seem just as ambiguously poised between a craving for cultural legitimacy and an urge towards stylistic autonomy as the national cinema to which they belong. Indeed, they are no less obsessed by the medium's contesting poetic and popular potentials as a linear story-telling machine, on the one hand, and as a generator and catalyst of live performances, audience interactions and (multi-)media events, on the other.

---

[85] As a number of film scholars have pointed out, the willingness to enter into an 'audiovisual pact' in the cinema has always remained subject to conventionalization, and its significance has not vanished even in the present day. Cf. e.g. Michel Chion: *Audiovision. Sound on Screen.* New York 1994, esp. Part 1: "The Audiovisual Contract."

8 Ruptures in the nation's "experiential economy": Universal in Germany and ALL QUIET ON THE WESTERN FRONT

"Crisis" becomes a fundamental historico-philosophical concept on the basis of which the claim is made that the entire course of history can be interpreted out of its diagnosis of time. Since then, it is always one's own particular time that is experienced as crisis. [...] The assumption that every crisis is a final decision is easily revealed as a perspectival illusion.[1]

R. Koselleck

A strange phenomenon in contemporary historiography must be observed. The historian is no longer a person who shapes an empire. He or she no longer envisages the paradise of a global history. The historian comes to circulate around acquired rationalizations. He or she works in the margins. In this respect the historian becomes a prowler.[2]

Michel de Certeau

Between the years 1928 and 1932, the arrival of the sound film substantially changed the international film industry. As the film industry's new standard product, the sound film provoked fundamental changes not only in production and exhibition, but also in distribution practices. With regard to transnational film distribution, the film industry's new commodity threatened Hollywood's hegemony in a world market that was about to diversify into countless distinct language areas. As would soon became clear, the hope (voiced by Louis B. Mayer in 1928) that the sound film would help to re-enforce English as cinema's "universal language"[3] thanks to the worldwide popularity of Hollywood productions (and thus seamlessly continuing the internationalism of the silent picture) was based on a false assessment of the impeding market situation and its economic determinants and cultural dynamics. It would instead be innovation and instability, creativity and crisis management that would govern the international film business for years to come.

The conceptual framework within which I want to account for this complex situation is that of a "crisis historiography." In doing so, I draw from a revisionist notion of the logic driving historical change in the cinema, which Rick

---

1 Reinhart Koselleck: Some Questions Regarding the Conceptual History of "Crisis." In: Koselleck: *The Practice of Conceptual History. Timing History, Spacing Concepts*. Stanford 2002, 239, 244.

2 Michel de Certeau: *The Writing of History* [1975]. New York 1988, 79.

3 Quoted in Kristin Thompson: *Exporting Entertainment. America in the World Film Market, 1907–1914*. London 1985, 158.

https://doi.org/10.1515/9783110613551-009

Altman forcefully casts in terms of the medium's shifting identities as a "crisis model of film historiography"[4]:

> This model recognizes that cultural changes (and especially the introduction of new tech-nologies, such as new sound recording and reproduction devices) sometimes plunge rep-resentational systems into an *identity crisis* during which they are sequentially and even simultaneously imaged as belonging to several different categories, each with its own separate (and sometimes contradictory) set of practices.[5]

Defined in multiple terms, the system in crisis becomes the site for what Altman calls a *jurisdictional conflict* among various actors and practices vying for con-trol. Stability is achieved (if ever) only after a series of redefinitions, model shifts and *negotiated settlements*:

> Because the system in crisis always engages several different reality codes or representa-tional models, involves multiple diverse identity frameworks, and happens over an extended time frame in many different locations, the identity crisis – jurisdictional con-flict – negotiated settlement process never appears as a linear progression but instead as fragmented, contradictory, even chaotic.[6]

Charting transitional developments in a more linear fashion, most film histori-cal accounts of the American film industry's efforts to protect its interests in for-eign markets have centered on Hollywood's leading studio conglomerates. The scholarly debate around the film industry's transition to sound and its impact on the film export business has revolved around Paramount and MGM's at-tempts to safeguard their hegemonic positions in the international market or on Fox, Warner and RKO's efforts to expand their market shares and standings within studio hierarchies and as major new players in the international film trade.[7]

In contrast to the companies that would emerge from the commotion of the early sound years as Hollywood's "big five," we know relatively little about the role of Carl Laemmle's Universal Pictures, the largest of the "small three" stu-dios – Universal, Columbia and United Artists – in 1928. How specifically did Universal react to the introduction of sound? In what ways was Universal's ex-port policy affected by the tussle over patent rights and import quotas between Hollywood and Europe? What strategies of adaptation did Universal develop

---

4 Rick Altman: Crisis Historiography. In: *Silent Film Sound*. New York 2004, 15–23.

5 Rick Altman: The Silence of the Silents. In: *The Musical Quarterly* 80:4 (Winter 1996), 648–718, here 689.

6 Altman: The Silence of the Silents, 689.

7 Douglas Gomery: *The Coming of Sound. A History*. New York and London 2005.

and employ to overcome language barriers and to counter points of cultural resistance? Finally, what was the 'product' – in terms of style, subject and genre – with which Universal thought it would meet the fresh expectations European audiences would bring to the sound film?

To answer some of these questions, I will look at Universal's activities in the German market between 1928 and 1932. In light of the exceptional interest and attention that the studio of the Swabian emigrant Carl Laemmle had always shown towards Germany as a film economic and cultural point of reference, this case study might not qualify as representative for Universal's European policy as a whole. With the figurehead character as Universal's most important European market (a point that the company's leading representatives emphasized), Germany should, however, be instructive as a starting point for further comparative research.

At the heart of Universal's activities in Germany after 1928 was its local subsidiary firm "Deutsche Universal." This subsidiary's repeatedly reorganized and redefined internal structure formed part of a specific and identifiable strategy aimed at the protection of the company's interest in the German market. As I will argue, this strategy constituted a distinct alternative to the adaptation policies of the two leading Hollywood studios for the same market and in the same historical situation.

In order to reconstruct how this alternative approach came about, it is necessary to address the technical, aesthetic and cultural implications of Universal's market strategy in Germany. My first step will be to consider the historical rationale behind relocating the production of German-language export versions from Hollywood to Berlin. Next, I will investigate the technical system used by Universal to produce German versions of their early sound films and discuss how exactly they carried out studio work in Berlin. Originally developed in the context of the musical film production during the silent era, the device used by Universal points back to a longer, rather convoluted, history of audiovisual synchronization practices in the German film industry. While the previous chapter traced the emergence of the most prominent sync-sound systems of the "silent" music film, the present chapter draws out the latter's historical legacies for the early sound film era and its multiple practices of language adaptation.

Universal's German import strategy set its films apart from those of other Hollywood studios, not only in terms of their formal and aesthetic features and the technological practice of production. As I will demonstrate with the example of the reception of the German version of ALL QUIET ON THE WESTERN FRONT (IM WESTEN NICHTS NEUES, 1929/30), this import strategy also had a considerable impact on the cultural and political debates of the late Weimar Republic. Toward the end of the chapter, I will discuss the lessons Universal learned and the conclusions they drew from the turmoil surrounding the German version of ALL QUIET ON THE WESTERN FRONT with regard to the problem of language adaptation. I will also describe how Universal tried to reposition itself in Germany in the years 1931 and 1932 within an ideologically over-determined social force field.

8.1 The transition to sound and the 'Universal model'

The foundation of a German distribution branch named "Universal-Matador" in May 1927 was still in tune with general American studio practices at this point in time. As such, there was nothing particularly exceptional or unique about Universal's export policy at this time.[8] Likewise, the expansion of this branch into a full-blown distribution company that also worked with German films (implemented a year later with the establishment of the "Deutsche Universal-Film-Verleih GmbH") can be seen in the context of a more general shift in the American film industry in the wake of the recent amendment of the German quota laws and the crisis of the domestic market leader Ufa.[9] As was characteristic for Universal, however, Carl Laemmle wanted German theater owners to understand the exceptional engagement of the company as a token of his personal attachment to German culture.[10]

In the years 1930 and 1931, Deutsche Universal expanded into a production and distribution company for self-made or commissioned domestic films as well as for dubbed German language versions of American Universal features. Along with their expansion and reorganization, which we should understand as a consequence of the transition to sound, Universal's German subsidiary implemented

---

8 On the development of German subsidiary firms of American studios in the 1920s, cf. Thomas Saunders: *Hollywood in Berlin. American Cinema and Weimar Germany.* Berkeley, Los Angeles and London 1994, 51–53.

9 In October 1925, Universal contracted Filmhaus Bruckmann to handle the German distribution of their productions (after April 1926 the company was also in charge of the German distribution of Warner Bros. films). In return for a 15 million Reichsmark credit, Ufa distributed 10 Universal pictures in Germany between 1926 and 1927. Universal cancelled their agreement with Ufa in November 1927, likely in order to begin preparations for the establishment of a German subsidiary. Establishing a German subsidiary was in large part a response to the introduction of a new quota law in November 1927 that required the number of imported films between April 1, 1928, and June 30, 1929, to be 50 percent of the total number of domestic productions.

10 Carl Laemmle: Die Internationalisierung des Films und Deutschland. In: *Film-Kurier* 1 (1 January 1928), 1.

a strategy that deviated considerably from the export practices of the leading Hollywood studios. Universal's strategy distinguished itself from the "Paramount model" of a centralized production of European language versions in the studios in Paris-Joinville (acquired by Paramount and rented out to other companies for this very reason) and from the "MGM model" of importing European personnel to Hollywood for the production of multiple-language versions at the studio's home base just outside of Los Angeles.[11]

The alternative strategy of what we might call the "Universal model" consisted of two main aspects. First, instead of falling back on the production of multiple-language versions, Universal used dubbing from the very beginning of the sound film era. Second, from fall 1930 onwards, Universal produced synchronized German versions of talkies not in Hollywood or at one central European studio but at the German subsidiary Deutsche Universal in Germany – that is, decentralized on location in the country of destination.

The exceptional design of Universal's strategy becomes clear if one considers the options available to Hollywood studios to adapt their films to the European market broadly and the German market specifically. Relating the original dialogue via live commentary, intertitles, or subtitles, as was done in countries with smaller film industries and smaller language areas, was not a feasible option for a market as big as Germany.[12] The two remaining options consisted of producing multiple-language versions, in which both American and German or German-speaking actors performed the roles, or dubbing, where only the dialogue (that is, the actors' voices) was replaced.[13]

---

11 Douglas Gomery: Economic Struggle and Hollywood Imperialism. Europe Converts to Sound. In: Elizabeth Weis and John Belton (eds.): *Film Sound. Theory and Practice*. New York 1985, 25–36, here 27; Ginette Vincendeau: Hollywood Babel. The Coming of Sound and the Multiple-Language Version. In: Andrew Higson and Richard Maltby (eds.): *"Film Europe" and "Film America." Cinema, Commerce and Cultural Exchange, 1920–1939*. Exeter 1999, 207–224, here 207; Nataša Ďurovičová: Translating America. The Hollywood Multilinguals 1929–1933. In: Rick Altman (ed.): *Sound Theory / Sound Practice*. New York and London 1992, 139–153, here 147.

12 Thompson: *Exporting Entertainment*, 163; Ruth Vasey: *The World According to Hollywood, 1918–1939*. Exeter 1997, 97.

13 In contrast to European studios that shot their foreign language versions parallel to the original versions, American studios usually shot them as remakes of the originals. Cf. Michaela Krützen: "Esperanto für den Tonfilm." Die Produktion von Sprachversionen für den frühen Tonfilmmarkt. In: Michael Schaudig (ed.): *Positionen deutscher Filmgeschichte. 100 Jahre Kinematographie: Strukturen, Diskurse, Kontexte*. Munich 1996, 110–154, here 134–135. On the production of multiple language versions at the Ufa studios in Babelsberg, cf. Chris Wahl: *Multiple Language Versions Made in Babelsberg. Ufa's International Strategy, 1929–1939*. Amsterdam 2015.

If one traces the quantitative proportions of multiple-language versions and dubbed versions over the first two sound film seasons in Germany, it becomes clear that multiple-language versions were the dominant solution for the German market. Only 10 percent of all foreign films entering the German market in German language versions in 1930–31 were dubbed. Of the 24 foreign feature films that had their premiere in German cinemas in 1930 as "100%-talkies" (including dialogue, sound effects and music), only four were shown in their original English version with German titles or uniquely devised German-language framing sequences. Of the 19 films shown in a German-language version, only two had been post-synchronized into a dubbed German version in Germany itself (the Universal features CAPTAIN OF THE GUARD directed by John S. Robertson [German release title: DER KAPITÄN DER GARDE] and ALL QUIET ON THE WESTERN FRONT directed by Lewis Milestone). Finally, of all the 64 foreign sound film imports which premiered in Germany in 1931, 52 were shown in a German language version while only six of those 52 were dubbed.[14] Three of these six dubbed versions were the Universal imports HELL'S HEROES directed by William Wyler (German release title: GALGENVÖGEL), STORMS (also directed by Wyler, German release title: STÜRME) and RESURRECTION directed by Edwin Carewe (German release title: WO DIE WOLGA FLIESST). These figures reflect a conscious import strategy in the years 1930 and 1931 in which Universal became the only Hollywood studio to dub its feature films for the German market in the country of destination.

8.2 'American capital to Germany': Dubbing in Berlin

In 1929, Universal's production of dubbed German language versions happened in Hollywood, which caused two basic problems. First, this practice conflicted with the international patent law situation in technical sound equipment and became entangled in the Tobis-Klangfilm group and the Western Electric/RCA Photophone group's fight over the European (and German) exhibition market. The second problem was German audiences' low tolerance for foreign films dubbed into German.

Among the first of Universal's talkies dubbed into German were the musicals SHOWBOAT and BROADWAY (both 1929). For BROADWAY, Carl Laemmle Jr. contracted the Hungarian director Paul Fejos, who had been working in Hollywood

---

14 Karl Wolffsohn (ed.): *Jahrbuch der Filmindustrie*, vol. 5. Berlin 1933, 259.

since 1926 but returned to Europe in 1931.[15] The German dialogue for the dubbed version of BROADWAY was directed by Friedrich Zelnik and Kurt Neumann.[16] In early October 1929, the German trade press reported from the dubbing stage in Universal City:

> Quite naturally, the actors and actresses have been speaking in English during the shoot. [...] Miraculously, they now all of a sudden speak German, as if it was their mother tongue. And they do so throughout the whole film, which is quite packed with dialogue. Furthermore, what is surprising is that close-up shots have not been avoided at all.[17]

In German cinemas, however, BROADWAY could be commercially exploited only in a silent version, which premiered in November 1929. In the German press, the version shown to German audiences was therefore ironically referred to as "silenced Broadway."[18] In 1930, the film daily *Film-Kurier* wrote:

> As is well known, Universal has produced a sound version of BROADWAY in German. Here in Germany this version cannot be seen in the cinema – it is shown, however, in America, for numerous American cities have a high percentage of German-speaking inhabitants. In Milwaukee, for example, the German BROADWAY version is a record breaking box-office hit. For how long will the patent war go on?[19]

SHOWBOAT, a "part-talkie" (a silent film with intertitles and only a few post-dubbed sound sequences), had become victim to the unresolved patent situation. Internal test screenings of the dubbed German version took place on a Klangfilm-sound projector in the Berlin Zoopalast in June 1929 and revealed serious acoustic shortcomings. Since the German-language print was tested only a day later on a Western Electric machine, the cause for the deplorable sound reproduction quality clearly laid in the incompatibility of the American (Western Electric) sound recording system and the European (Tobis-Klangfilm) reproduction apparatus. As a consequence, Universal withdrew the film from distribution, having already relinquished to Ufa the responsibility for promoting

---

15 Fejos made only one more film for Universal in 1929, THE LAST PERFORMANCE, before he returned to Europe. He was briefly considered as director of ALL QUIET ON THE WESTERN FRONT.
16 Krützen: "Esperanto für den Tonfilm," 148.
17 Ch.: Optimismus der Jugend. Universal synchronisiert Sprechfilme deutsch. In: *Film-Kurier* 234 (2 October 1929).
18 Cf. e.g. in *Der Kinematograph* 279 (29 November 1929).
19 Deutschsprachige Tonfilme laufen in Amerika, aber nicht bei uns. In: *Film-Kurier* 7 (7 January 1930).

the film in Germany.[20] SHOWBOAT (German release title: DAS KOMÖDIANTENSCHIFF) had to wait a whole year before it was finally released to German cinemas in July 1930 – and then only, and by then somewhat anachronistically, in a silent version.

In the 1929–1930 season, Universal's place in the German market was a highly contradictory one. Although they produced dubbed German language versions of films, the international patent situation and the technical incompatibility between Western Electric recordings and Klangfilm sound projectors (the issue of "interchangeability") made it impossible for these prints to be commercially exploited in German cinemas.[21] For the upcoming season 1930–1931, Universal sought to resolve this extremely unfortunate export situation through a twofold strategy. Universal relocated its production of dubbed language versions from Hollywood to Germany and, by doing so, moved from Western Electric to Tobis-Klangfilm recording technology. Next, Universal expanded its own distribution activities in the German market by affording Deutsche Universal a broader financial basis.[22]

In August 1930, the new head of production at Deutsche Universal Paul Kohner summarized Universal's response to the current situation on the European and German markets:

> In Hollywood, I was one of the first to make use of dubbing [...]. But we were on the wrong track, and we knew it. We forced language into an unwanted marriage. BROADWAY and SHOWBOAT were the results. [...] I am convinced only of a production [of dubbed foreign language versions] in Europe. The import of German actors to Hollywood is not commercially viable. [...] The solution: American capital to Europe. To carry out production, where one can choose from a rich arsenal of actors, where the current taste of the audience is immediately felt. Everything else is an experiment.[23]

Earlier that year, in a general meeting on their export policies, American producers noted that after only a short period of time in the United States, an alienating resonance would enter the native language of the actors brought to Hollywood. They estimated that in the long run this would lead to considerable

---

20 Wolfgang Mühl-Benninghaus: *Das Ringen um den Tonfilm. Strategien der Elektro- und der Filmindustrie in den 20er und 30er Jahren.* Düsseldorf 1999, 119–121.

21 The problem of the so-called "interchangeability" between American and European systems (a major issue in the context of the "patent war") was settled in the Paris agreement in July 1930. Cf. Mühl-Benninghaus: *Das Ringen um den Tonfilm*, 171.

22 Deutsche Universal AG now had a budget of two million Reichsmark at its disposal. Cf. Karl Wolffsohn: *Jahrbuch der Filmindustrie*, vol. 4. Berlin 1930, 109.

23 Paul Kohner: Hollywood sagt: Nur in Europa produzieren! In: *Film-Kurier* 184 (6 August 1930).

financial loss in the European market in comparison to local language versions produced in Europe.[24] Of course, this conclusion concerned multiple-language versions as much as dubbed export versions.[25]

Legal measures taken by Tobis against German language versions dubbed on American sound recording systems caused additional problems. For example, in May 1930, Tobis sued the Artiphon-Record Company for releasing William Wellman's film WINGS, which was dubbed in America, onto the German market. As a result, the film had to be withdrawn from German distribution.[26]

Against the horizon of these events and deliberations, Universal's change of strategy reflected a more general trend within the American film industry's export policy. In contrast to the vast majority of American studios, Universal did not swing over to multiple language versions but continued instead to produce dubbed versions. Kohner's analysis of Universal's erroneous policy in 1929–1930 was not so concerned with the practice of dubbing itself as it was with the fact that the production of dubbed versions had been carried out at Universal City on American recording systems with actors assimilating too rapidly rather than in Germany on recording devices that were compatible with local sound reproduction technology and complied with German patent law. These considerations led Universal to move the production of post-synchronized German language versions to Germany within weeks of the publication of Kohner's article. In making this move, Universal was the exception among the Hollywood studios, which only started dubbing their German language versions in Germany after being forced to do so by a new quota law in the summer of 1932.[27]

In the earlier quoted text, Kohner also writes about Universal's experimentation with a technical system that would perfect the practice of post-synchronization. The technical system to which he was referring, without giving any concrete information in order to keep it secret from competitors,[28] was Carl Robert Blum's "rhythmographic apparatus." Blum's device was to be used for

---

24 Cf. W. Engelhard: Hohe Politik des Tonfilms. In: *Berliner Börsen-Courier* 209 (7 May 1930); Peter Murr: Film als Mißton. Diktatur der Patente. In: *Vossische Zeitung* 232 (18 May 1930).

25 Press reports from Hollywood had already drawn attention to this problem in April 1930. Cf. Dr. F.K.: So geht es nicht. Die Voraussetzungen für eine deutsche Sprechfilmproduktion sind gegeben; allein die bisherigen Versuche sind untauglich. In: *Der Kinematograph* 86 (11 April 1930).

26 Cf. Mühl-Benninghaus: *Das Ringen um den Tonfilm*, 163.

27 Thompson: *Exporting Entertainment*, 163; Markus Spieker: *Hollywood unterm Hakenkreuz. Der amerikanische Spielfilm im Dritten Reich*. Trier 1999, 26.

28 Kohner: Hollywood sagt: Nur in Europa produzieren!

all of Universal's dubbed German language versions of the 1930–1931 season, including ALL QUIET ON THE WESTERN FRONT.

Blum's system represented a technical transformation and new industrial application of his 1926 "musical chronometer," which was tested a year later by composer Edmund Meisel in preparation for the premiere of Walter Ruttmann's BERLIN – DIE SINFONIE DER GROSSSTADT (BERLIN, SYMPHONY OF A BIG CITY), among a number of other practical implementations including the production of synchronized musical films.[29] On the occasion of the premiere, Blum had already conceived of what he called the "universal applicability" of his device and predicted its later development in the early sound era.[30] With this apparatus, Blum wrote in 1927, "any rhythmically structured sequence in motion – filmic, acoustic or linguistic – can be analyzed and synchronized."[31]

The first Universal feature to be dubbed in Germany with the help of Blum's rhythmographic system was CAPTAIN OF THE GUARD, released in October 1930. Reports in the trade press paid attention to exactly how the dubbing work was carried out on the sound stage.[32] A rhythmographic track with a coded transcription of the original dialogue, reminiscent of Morse code and visible through a thirty-centimeter small outlet, was synced with the projected film. On the basis of the rhythmographic track, coded according to the length of each syllable in the original dialogue, the script for the German dialogue (which was not a literal translation but rather a German equivalent in terms of phonetic length and emphasis) could then be developed. Finally, the German dialogue was recorded with the help of a marker at the center of the opening that indicated to the actors which syllable was to be spoken and what length it should have in order to line up perfectly with the lip movements and the action on the screen.[33]

---

29 For a more extensive account cf. Michael Wedel: *Der deutsche Musikfilm. Archäologie eines Genres 1914–1945*. Munich 2007, 192–217.

30 Kohner's attention could have been drawn to Blum's device by a series of articles in the trade press. Cf. for example E. Palme: Das Rhythmographie-Verfahren. In: *Kinotechnische Rundschau* 28–29 (12 and 19 July 1930).

31 Blum: Zeit wird Raum. In: *Der Film* 11 (15 June 1927), 26.

32 In 1930–1931, dubbing was done in the studio of Blum's Rhythmographie GmbH in Berlin. Only when dubbing became the standard solution were all major German film studios equipped with the necessary technology. The Jofa-studios, later used by Deutsche Universal, were among the leading facilities in this respect. Cf. Wolffsohn: *Jahrbuch der Filmindustrie*, vol. 5, 309–311.

33 Cf. C.R. Blum: *Die Herstellung von Tonfilmen mittels Rhythmographie, System C.R. Blum*. Berlin 1930.

Blum's system was only one among a number of similar synchronization devices. For all of these systems, including Blum's device, it was much more important for the German dialogue to correspond exactly to the word length and phonetic articulation of the English original than it was to provide a close literal translation.[34]

8.3 The problem of cultural acceptability

The rhythmographic device seems to have produced more than satisfactory results, if one takes contemporary reviews of the German versions at their word.[35] Regardless of the technical quality of Universal's dubbed versions, their releases were met with resistance from German critics and audiences in the earliest years of the sound period.[36] The German public's initial reluctance and even hostility toward dubbing is an important reason why multiple-language versions remained the dominant solution for foreign import versions until 1932.

What the early reception of dubbed versions suggests is that the so-called delay of dubbing as the standard technique of language adaptation for Germany was not due primarily to unsurpassable technical difficulties of post-synchronization. The main reason for any "delay" was German audiences' discomfort with the split between body and voice on which post-synchronization as a technological practice fundamentally relies. In this respect, multiple-language versions seemed more acceptable to German audiences because they kept intact the imaginary unity of the actor's body and voice. Dubbing and post-synchronization, by contrast, fused the body of the American actor and the voice of the German actor into a hybrid cultural identity.

It was only in the course of the industrial standardization of dubbed language versions and the concomitant conventionalization of an audience

---

34 Cf. Das Rhythmoband im Dienste des Tonfilms. In: *Kinotechnische Rundschau* 42 (15 November 1930). For an overview of these synchronization devices cf. Michael Wedel: Okkupation der Zeit. In: *Schnitt* 29 (Winter 2003), 10–15.

35 Cf. the review of INSURRECTION in *Der Kinematograph* 250 (28 October 1931). Cf. also the various production reports, e.g. Die neue Universal-Staffel. In: *Der Kinematograph* 279 (29 November 1930); Rhythmographie-Arbeiten. In: *Der Kinematograph* 139 (18 June 1931). Universal also distributed silent versions of their films to satisfy the considerable demand of theaters that had not yet converted to sound equipment. Cf. Der stumme Film in U.S.A. In: *Der Kinematograph* 233 (24 September 1930).

36 Some of the films, including HELL'S ANGELS, were offered to German theater owners in synchronized versions "without dialogue" – that is, in versions that only contained music and sound effects. Cf. *Der Kinematograph* 36 (12 February 1931).

disposition towards readily believing in the illusion of imaginary unity of body and voice that audience resistance to dubbing could be counter-acted and gradually decreased during the course of 1932. As film historian Joseph Garncarz succinctly puts it:

> The refusal of dubbed versions of foreign films goes back to the cultural problem, that for a contemporary audience, it was not easily possible to ascribe the "borrowed voice" of the post-synchronization to the actor on screen. [...] If one relates this refusal of dubbing back to the non-identity of body and voice, then one has to understand the gradual acceptance of dubbing as a cultural learning process, in which the knowledge about the non-identity between the one who is visibly speaking, and the invisible source of the spoken word, is filtered out in the consciousness of the spectator.[37]

One way to enhance and accelerate this cultural learning process was to naturalize the split between body and voice (and image and sound) by making it a topic of the films themselves. This practice contributed to the development of a self-reflexive tendency in many early sound films.[38] It is no surprise that Universal was particularly active in this area of cinematic self-promotion. Consider, for example, an all-star production like the film DIE GROSSE SEHNSUCHT (THE GREAT LONGING) from 1930, a film-within-a-film whose action is set almost entirely in a sound film studio. Also significant were the marketing strategies and PR events Universal orchestrated in 1930 and 1931.

With regard to marketing and promotion, a number of press reports provide striking examples of the ways Universal sought to naturalize both the practice and the effects of post-synchronization as a new aesthetic possibility and technological marvel. In October 1929, Deutsche Universal invited more than 40 journalists to witness a post-production sound recording for THE LAST PERFORMANCE (German release title: ILLUSION). The recording was allegedly necessary because an important sentence of Conrad Veidt's dialogue during the central courtroom sequence was not audible to viewers at a test screening in Hollywood. Veidt, the only German-speaking actor on set,[39] had in the meantime relocated in Berlin and so said the line over a radio-telephone that transmitted

---

37 Joseph Garncarz: Die bedrohte Internationalität des Films. Fremdsprachige Versionen deutscher Tonfilme. In: Sibylle M. Sturm and Arthur Wohlgemuth (eds.): *Hallo? Berlin? Ici Paris! Deutsch-französische Filmbeziehungen 1918–1939*. Munich 1996, 127–140, here 132–133.
38 Cf. Jörg Schweinitz: "Wie im Kino!" Die autothematische Welle im frühen Tonfilm. Figurationen des Selbstreflexiven. In: Thomas Koebner (ed.): *Diesseits der dämonischen Leinwand. Neue Perspektiven auf das späte Weimarer Kino*. Munich 2003, 373–392.
39 This may have been one reason why THE LAST PERFORMANCE became the first Universal picture to be dubbed into German. Whereas Veidt's voice was replaced in the English version, the dialogue of the other actors was dubbed into German. Cf. Conrad Veidt telephoniert mit

his voice via London and New York to Universal City where the actual recording took place, according at least to the ensuing press reports.[40]

A year later, during the opening of the 1930–1931 season, Universal fell back on a similar marketing stunt. The company placed an article written by its contract director John M. Anderson in German trade journals that reported on how the company solved an issue that occurred during the shooting of the Paul Whiteman-Musical THE KING OF JAZZ, which was soon to premiere in Germany under the release title DER JAZZKÖNIG. This time there was a gap in the musical score of one particular scene. A replacement was quickly composed, arranged and recorded in New York and transmitted, again via telephone, in real time onto the Hollywood set, allegedly enabling the actors to sing and dance in perfect synchronicity.[41]

8.4 Language adaptation and the controversy around ALL QUIET ON THE WESTERN FRONT

Promotion stunts like the two discussed here did not significantly change the general reservations and skeptical attitudes German critics and moviegoers held against American movies dubbed into German. Indeed, Universal would soon learn just how socially and politically explosive the problem of language adaptation could be with its release of the dubbed German version of ALL QUIET ON THE WESTERN FRONT – Universal's only A-picture of the season. The controversial reception of the first German version of ALL QUIET ON THE WESTERN FRONT has been extensively documented and discussed in light of the rise of National Socialism and the general radicalization of the political arena in the final years of the Weimar Republic.[42] Less attention has been paid, however, to the technical and

---

Hollywood. In: *Der Kinematograph* 240 (14 October 1929); Universal Takes Lead in Foreign Version Films. In: *Universal Weekly* 5 (8 March 1930).

40 The press reports reveal the strong tendency to transform an attitude of cultural resistance into a modern and universal fascination with technology. Cf. al.: Tonfilm-Aufnahme über 10.000 Kilometer. In: *Die Lichtbild-Bühne* 245 (14 October 1929).

41 Cf. J.M. Anderson: Komposition durchs Telephon. In: *Der Kinematograph* 242 (16 October 1930).

42 Cf. e.g. J. Simmons: Film and International Politics. The Banning of ALL QUIET ON THE WESTERN FRONT. In: *Historian* 52 (1989), 40–60; Andrew Kelly: ALL QUIET ON THE WESTERN FRONT. Brutal Cutting, Stupid Censors and Bigoted Politicos (1930–1984). In: *Historical Journal of Film, Radio and Television* 2 (1989), 135–150; Andrew Kelly: *Filming ALL QUIET ON THE WESTERN FRONT*. London and New York 1998, 103–132; Peter Dörp: Goebbels' Kampf gegen Remarque (2). Eine Untersuchung über die Hintergründe des Hasses und der Agitation Goebbels' gegen den

aesthetic aspects that informed the debate about the film. As I would like to suggest, the critical and at times almost hysterical reactions to the German version of ALL QUIET ON THE WESTERN FRONT – while doubtlessly initiated by Nazi provocations and demonstrations against the film's first public screening – should also to a certain degree be seen as a reflection of the problem of language adaptation and the lack of a cultural acceptance of dubbing in Germany.

As a matter of fact, the German premiere of ALL QUIET ON THE WESTERN FRONT, on December 4, 1930, took place precisely at a moment in time when the rejection of dubbed import versions of foreign films reached its peak. Critics widely complained that audiences would be annoyed by the "non-sense" of dubbing that would never truly achieve a neat synchronization.[43] One critic even went so far as to argue that German audiences would never accept the "biologically impossible" division of body and voice. He claimed that the practice of dubbing would constitute a serious violation of the social fabric and national body of the Germans by literally tearing apart the German people's "experiential economy."[44]

Therefore, what was at stake for many German critics in the debates over the practice of dubbing was nothing less than the coherence of the nation's collective experience – that is, Germany's national identity and cultural distinctiveness. With its division of voice and body, image and sound and visual and acoustic perception, the trans-cultural practice of dubbing was understood as a traumatic threat to the idea of a coherent national identity, a threat that could easily be instrumentalized to ideological and political ends. In order to fully capture the historical dynamics and cultural reverberations of the public controversy surrounding the release of the German version of ALL QUIET ON THE WESTERN FRONT, it is necessary to locate it within a multi-causal framework and to consider it as a complex phenomenon of cultural interference at the intersection of socio-political, cultural, technological and aesthetic discourses.

In triggering such a debate, ALL QUIET ON THE WESTERN FRONT was like no other film of the time. Based on a German novel depicting the First World War from the perspective of a German soldier and adapted by an American film

---

amerikanischen Spielflm IM WESTEN NICHTS NEUES nach dem gleichnamigen Bestsellerroman von Erich Maria Remarque. In: *Erich Maria Remarque-Jahrbuch* 3 (1993), 45–72; John Whiteclay Chambers II: ALL QUIET ON THE WESTERN FRONT (1930). The Antiwar Film and the Image of the First World War. In: *Historical Journal of Film, Radio and Television* 4 (1994), 377–411. The most comprehensive collection of documents about the German reception of both novel and film is Bärbel Schrader (ed.): *Im Westen nichts Neues – Eine Dokumentation.* Leipzig 1992.

43 Hans Pander: Die Illusion beim Tonfilm. In: *Die Kinotechnik* 17 (5 September 1930), 471.
44 Harald Landry: Der Synchronisierungs-Unfug. In: *Vossische Zeitung* (30 November 1933).

company with American actors (who, in the dubbed version, speak fluent German), the question of who is speaking for whom and who is representing whom is at the heart of the whole enterprise, in an aesthetic as much as in a political sense. The fact that the film was the very first A-picture from Hollywood to enter the German market in a dubbed version only added to the critical potential of this question.

It is interesting to note that Universal representatives seemed to have anticipated the problems a dubbed version of ALL QUIET ON THE WESTERN FRONT might encounter. The studio initially considered shooting a German language version with German actors in Germany, which would keep both the unity of body and voice and the national imaginary of the whole film intact and coherent.[45] In the public debate following the scandal surrounding the German premiere of ALL QUIET ON THE WESTERN FRONT, Universal was criticized for a number of cuts in the German version as compared to the international version. Universal was, above all, accused of many subtle and not so subtle changes in the dialogue. These changes were due in part to considerations of political correctness from a German perspective but also, as was noted in connection to Blum's rhythmographic post-synchronization device, a common practice in the process of dubbing. The result was that the film was banned in Germany for almost a year before it was re-released in a substantially altered version and became a major box office hit.

Particularly instructive about the blind spots and inherent contradictions in the debate over the German soundtrack of ALL QUIET ON THE WESTERN FRONT is the fact that critics railed against the film's German dialogue but praised and celebrated as authentic and realistic other acoustic elements – such as the noise and sound effects of the battle scenes. This praise came even from extremely conservative and right-wing critics, who ignored the fact that the film's sound effects had already been synthetically produced and post-synchronized to the action in the original American version of the film.[46]

8.5 Reactions and consequences

For Universal, the events surrounding the German release of ALL QUIET ON THE WESTERN FRONT made it painstakingly clear that the problem of language

---

45 Cf. Deutsche Universal verfilmt *Im Westen nichts Neues*. In: *Film-Kurier* 158 (5 July 1929).
46 Cf. G.J. Mitchell: Making ALL QUIET ON THE WESTERN FRONT. In: *American Cinematographer* 66:9 (September 1985), 34–36.

adaptation could produce serious cultural, ideological and political reverberations. Parallel to the attempt to get clearance for the film from the German censorship boards, Universal implemented two measures it hoped would provide a
better protection of its future investments in Germany.

One of the actions Deutsche Universal took was to move away from dubbing toward the production of multiple-language versions for the European and
German markets, a decision discussed in a meeting of Universal's European
heads of production and communicated to the public in April 1931.[47] In order to
put this new directive into practice, Universal signed a contract with the Societé
Internationale Cinématographique in Paris. Following the Paramount model,
this contract intended for the central production of French and German language versions to be carried out in Paris.[48] The search for an appropriate studio
space, however, yielded no results, and the production of Universal's European
language versions remained decentralized in the two respective countries of
destination – France and Germany – under the umbrella of the Societé Internationale Cinématographique. In a statement given to the press in June 1931, S.D.
Wilson, the head of the Societé Internationale Cinématographique, described
the rationale behind Universal's future production policy, particularly with respect to different European language versions:

> We want to produce films with themes appropriate to the countries in question, Germany,
> France, England, and America. [...] A well-organized production should make it possible
> that an interesting subject matter, elaborated in a proper way for each country, becomes
> a success.[49]

As early as February 1931, the Universal comedy THE BOUDOIR DIPLOMAT,
adapted from a German stage play and shot in Hollywood the previous year,
had its premiere in a German version.[50] As an exception to Universal's general
practice at that time, the German version was produced – following MGM – by
flying in the German actors (Olga Tschechowa, Johannes Riemann, Arnold
Korff and Hans Junkermann) to shoot at Universal Studios in Hollywood. The
German press welcomed Universal's transition from dubbing to the production

---

47 Cf. Revirement bei Universal. In: *Der Kinematograph* 41 (18 February 1931); F. Keller: Universal – Paris – Berlin. In: *Film-Kurier* 86 (14 April 1931); Donald Crafton: *The Talkies. America's Transition to Sound, 1926–1931*. Berkeley, Los Angeles and New York 1999, 438.
48 Cf. Carver produziert für die Universal in Frankreich. In: *Film-Kurier* 100 (30 April 1931).
49 Universal-Kombination plant 10 Filme – für den 1. Teil der Saison. In: *Film-Kurier* 144 (22
June 1931).
50 Apart from a German version, Universal produced French and Spanish versions of this film
in Universal City in October and November 1930.

of multiple-language versions early in 1931: "The good quality of German language versions that Hollywood has always promised in theory has this time been delivered by Universal."[51] Concurrent to the disaster with ALL QUIET ON THE WESTERN FRONT in the German market was the considerable success of the German version of THE BOUDOIR DIPLOMAT. This film's success doubtlessly reinforced Universal's decision to switch from dubbing to producing multiple-language versions.[52]

With the transition from dubbing to multiple-language versions, Universal was again going against the grain of general Hollywood practice at this time. Universal and its European subsidiaries intensified their production of multiple-language versions precisely at a historical juncture (Spring/Summer 1931) when all the other Hollywood studios abandoned the production of multiple-language versions for the European market and made their transition – in the opposite direction, as it were – to dubbing as the standard format for foreign language versions of their product.[53]

Examples of German and French language versions produced or co-produced by Deutsche Universal and/or Societé Internationale Cinématographique for Universal between 1931 and 1933 include a French version of ICH GEH AUS UND DU BLEIBST DA under the title INCONSTANTE; French versions of G.W. Pabst's DIE HERRIN VON ATLANTIS (L'ATLANTIDE, 1932) and Carl Boese's PAPRIKA (1932); German and English versions of Kurt Bernhardt's and Luis Trenker's DER REBELL (THE REBEL, 1932–1933); and, in Spring 1933, the German and English versions of S.O.S. EISBERG (SOS ICEBERG). The last multiple-language version distributed by Deutsche Universal was the German version of SKANDAL IN BUDAPEST (SCANDAL IN BUDAPEST), which was produced by Universal's Hungarian subsidiary Universal-Hunnia RT in summer 1933.

Apart from halting the dubbing practice and making the belated and utterly anachronistic transition to multiple-language versions, Universal's crisis management included two other strategies, both of which can be seen as consequences of the ban of ALL QUIET ON THE WESTERN FRONT. Universal cut a deal with Tobis to exclusively use Tobis-Klangfilm technology for production in their studios across Europe without having to pay license fees in cash. This deal allowed Universal to create a homogenous technological framework that avoided problems of adaptability and interchangeability.[54] After their experience with

---

51 Ein deutscher Tonfilm aus Hollywood. In: *Der Kinematograph* 43 (20 February 1931).
52 Cf. LIEBE AUF BEFEHL im Deutschen Reich. In: *Der Kinematograph* 46 (24 February 1931).
53 Cf. Hollywood dreht keine "Versionen" mehr. In: *Der Kinematograph* 215 (17 September 1931); Crafton: *The Talkies*, 436–437.
54 Cf. Wolffsohn: *Jahrbuch der Filmindustrie*, vol. 5, 41, 225, 262.

ALL QUIET ON THE WESTERN FRONT, Universal also sought to adapt to what it considered a particular sensibility and mental disposition of the German public toward the representation of military conflict and issues of national identity. We can see this reflected to some extent in the style and subject matter of films either produced or distributed by Deutsche Universal in 1932–1933, with such titles as UNTER FALSCHER FLAGGE (UNDER THE WRONG BANNER, 1932), DIE UNSICHTBARE FRONT (THE INVISIBLE FRONT, 1932), or the nationalist epic DER REBELL – which had the rather dubious honor of becoming Hitler's favorite movie.[55] All of Universal's efforts to cater to the tastes of the new political and administrative elites in Germany did not save them, however, from being placed under the control of the National Socialist State and renamed "Rota-Film AG" in July 1934.

8.6 Crisis historiography

There are as many ways to research and interpret the role ALL QUIET ON THE WESTERN FRONT has played for the German film market as there are approaches to writing film history. The film is as much part of a history of media and technology as it is part of the histories of economics, society and culture. ALL QUIET ON THE WESTERN FRONT can be interpreted as an allegory of political developments or as indexical of changing ideas and shifts in collective mentalities. Finally, Lewis Milestone's early sound film can be studied as both aesthetic object and in the context of the history of film as a specific art form. Doing so helps us trace transitions in film form and define individual stylistic developments along patterns of influence and rejection, as well as moments of cultural change and technological innovation. As a concept that cuts across traditional areas of film historical reasoning, the notion of "crisis historiography" is a conceptual and methodological tool to observe the in-between points where various levels of historicism and their corresponding interpretive systems intersect and interact.

As historian Reinhart Koselleck has pointed out, the term "crisis" stems from the Greek *krino* and refers to a whole spectrum of activities: to cut, to select, to decide, to judge and by extension to measure, to quarrel, to fight.[56] In its original meaning, then, the concept of "crisis" implies radical alternatives and final decisions that permit no revisions. A second dimension of the concept, however, tends to divest this notion of target-oriented vectorization on the diachronic time axis by infusing it with a strong sense of synchronic

---

55 Cf. Spieker: *Hollywood unterm Hakenkreuz*, 47.
56 Koselleck: Some Questions Regarding the Conceptual History of "Crisis," 237.

dispersion. In this sense, crisis always refers to more than one area of life at the same time, whether politics, psychology, economics, culture, the arts, or historical consciousness itself. As a key concept in the writing of film history, crisis can thus serve to bring different heuristic paradigms and areas of investigation usually kept apart – the history of film aesthetics, the history of film technology, the history of film economics and the social history of film – into a critical constellation.[57]

Rick Altman's plea for a "crisis model of film historiography" that would consider the medium as beset with an unresolved identity crisis from its historical beginnings right up to its digital present, where stability on one level (e.g. in the areas of film technology or the film industry) runs parallel to contradictions between others (e.g. in film style or politics), closely relates to the threefold semantics of crisis as it is discussed by Koselleck. This semantics includes crisis as a multi-dimensional process that interprets history as a permanent crisis; as an "iterative periodization concept" that characterizes "a singular, accelerating process in which many conflicts, bursting the system apart, accumulate so as to bring about a new situation"[58]; and as "the final crisis of all history that precedes it." This final point opens up a future-oriented, utopian horizon of meaning, suggestive of the idea that technical media (and film in particular) have taken the place of historical consciousness, traditionally understood as being built on the assumption that historical progress is based on the linear-causal succession of 'real' events.[59]

In order to constitute more than a conceptual metaphor and to become an operational heuristic instrument for the examination of clearly circumscribed case studies like the one presented in this chapter, crisis as a historiographic concept has to meet a number of criteria. Historical processes that are characterized as crisis-laden must be limited in time. They must substantially affect and significantly change the society or the social environment in which they occur, without necessarily assuming 'revolutionary' status. Casting a historical instance or process in terms of crisis ought to help define its singularity and to delineate its causes, structure and effects. The concept of crisis subsumes change and rupture but it must also be able to account for stability and continuity, in order to allow for the observation and

---

57 Cf. Robert C. Allen and Douglas Gomery: *Film History. Theory and Practice*. New York et al. 1986.
58 Koselleck: Some Questions Regarding the Conceptual History of "Crisis," 240.
59 CF. Robert Rosenstone: *Visions of the Past. The Challenge of Film to Our Idea of History*. Cambridge and London 1995.

theoretical reflection of different temporal logics and various levels of meaning existing parallel to each other.[60]

Once these criteria are met, the idea of a "crisis historiography" can contribute to our understanding of particular film-historical processes and constellations by giving us a renewed sensibility for their constitutive openness, irreducible complexity and inherent multi-dimensionality. This sensibility should be paired with a deep-rooted skepticism toward any attempts to dissolve the intricate singularity of a historical phenomenon by dividing it up either synchronously (into the allegedly distinct areas of the social, the economic, the political and the aesthetic) or diachronically (into distinct 'periods' and their specific interpretational systems).

We find this mixture of sensibility and skepticism in the writings of the eminent 19th-century historian Jacob Burckhardt, who saw historical crises as "nodal points" of multiple developments, particularly in regard to the insights offered by a non-restrictive "crisis phenomenology." Following Burckhardt, the task of the historian lies not in disentangling – let alone cutting – the Gordian knot at hand but rather in bringing its singular, complex intertwinement to the fore.[61]

60 Cf. Rudolf Vierhaus: Zum Problem historischer Krisen. In: Karl-Georg Faber and Christian Meier (eds.): *Historische Prozesse. Beiträge zur Historik*, vol. 2. Munich 1978, 313–329, here 320–321.
61 Jacob Burckhardt: *Gesammelte Werke*, vol. 4: *Weltgeschichtliche Betrachtungen*. Darmstadt 1956, 138.

9 Epilogue: Fritz Lang, double vision and the place of rupture

We feel authorized to reconstruct the image of long-forgotten epochs from documents handed down to us in architecture, works of art, and writings. Their value, however, is determined only by the subjective attitude of the viewer. In the future, when our chaotic era has long been reduced to a static formula, scholars will find it much easier to bring it [to] life once again. They will open a box full of condensed life wherever they play a film. There will be a piece of history from former times.   Fritz Lang, 1924[1]

9.1 Inside film history

With his notion of the "historical imaginary," Thomas Elsaesser has provided a forceful figure of thought to reconceive cinema's place in and contribution to the formation of history and of cultural memory. More specifically, it has helped us overcome a number of conceptual deadlocks in rethinking the history of German cinema, beset as this national cinema is by questions of continuity and discontinuity, ideological over-determination and political representation, historical trauma and new beginnings. Elsaesser takes Weimar cinema – the most celebrated period of German film history in view of its peak artistic achievements and its most controversial with regard to its social and political meanings – as the looking-glass through which German cinema's complex correlations to national (and international) society and culture at large are reconsidered: "Unique among film movements, Weimar cinema came to epitomize a country: 20th-century Germany, uneasy with itself and troubled by a modernity that was to bring yet more appalling disasters to Europe."[2] In looking at films from the Weimar period through the prism of the historical imaginary, a "Möbius strip is forming before one's eyes, which catches a nation's history in a special kind of embrace"[3] whose powerful grip seems to have the alluring

---

1 Fritz Lang: Kitsch – Sensation – Kultur und Film. In: Edgar Beyfuss and Alex Kossowsky (eds.): *Das Kulturfilmbuch*. Berlin 1924, 28–31. English translation quoted from Fritz Lang: Kitsch – Sensation – Culture and Film. In: Anton Kaes, Nicholas Baer and Michael Cowan (eds.): *The Promise of Cinema. German Film Theory, 1907–1933*. Oakland 2016, 210–212, here 210–211.
2 Thomas Elsaesser: *Weimar Cinema and After. Germany's Historical Imaginary*. London and New York 2000, 3.
3 Elsaesser: *Weimar Cinema and After*, 4.

https://doi.org/10.1515/9783110613551-010

power of renewing its strength for each generation of cinéphiles and film historians alike. As such, Elsaesser contends,

> Weimar cinema is not just (like) any other period of German cinema, it is this cinema's *historical imaginary*, which suggests that it is "the German cinema and its double": in fact, it became a *Doppelgänger* of its own pre-history: foreshadowed in the "kino-debate" of the 1910s, it shadowed the Nazi cinema that selectively tried to (dis)inherit it in the 1930s. On the other side of the Atlantic, in the 1940s, it legitimated – almost equally selectively, as film noir – the work of German émigré film makers, before it was dug up again in the 1970s, to lend a historical pedigree to the New German Cinema of Syberberg, Herzog and Wenders.[4]

In its particular logic of self-definition and otherness, Elsaesser's elaboration of a cinematic "historical imaginary" as a cultural temporality evading traditional notions of chronological progress or retrospective teleology cuts across the art cinema vs. popular cinema divide that has defined much of the writing the history of German cinema. Rather than discarding the basic assumptions from Siegfried Kracauer's *From Caligari to Hitler* and Lotte Eisner's *The Haunted Screen*, it consciously builds on, works through and pushes further these two seminal accounts of Weimar cinema.[5]

One of the greatest conceptual achievements of Elsaesser's notion of the "historical imaginary" – an idea that builds on some of Kracauer and Eisner's central insights – lies in its capacity to locate Weimar cinema's cultural influence, its historical meaning and socio-political dimension in the specific aesthetic form of the films themselves. It is not only on the level of their narratives and modes of production, but also in their concrete cinematic articulation and their self-reflexivity that

> the films usually indexed as Weimar cinema have one thing in common: they are invariably constructed as picture puzzles. Consistently if not systematically, they refuse to be tied down to a single meaning. [...] Kracauer's Möbius-strip effect is [...] due to a set of formal and stylistic devices, whose equivalences, inversions and reversals facilitate but also necessitate the spectator constructing "allegories of meaning." [...] Apart from the ambiguity after which all art strives, Weimar cinema's rebus images – readable, like

---

4 Elsaesser: *Weimar Cinema and After*, 4. Cf. also Thomas Elsaesser: The New German Cinema's Historical Imaginary. In: Bruce A. Murray and Christopher Wickham (eds.): *Framing the Past. The Historiography of German Cinema and Television.* Carbondale and Edvardsville 1992, 280–307.
5 Siegfried Kracauer: *From Caligari to Hitler. A Psychological History of the German Film.* Princeton 1947; Lotte H. Eisner: *The Haunted Screen. Expressionism in the German Cinema and the Influence of Max Reinhardt.* Berkeley and Los Angeles 2008 (originally published in French 1952).

Wittgenstein's duck-rabbit picture as either the one or the other, but not both at the same time – have to do with mundane matters of film economics and marketing, with the film industry and its objectives and constraints. These function as the "historical symbolic," the limits and horizons that outline and yet vanish in the historical imaginary.[6]

Far beyond qualifying merely as some descriptive term for the aesthetic complexities and manifold cultural inscriptions and re-inscriptions of Weimar cinema, the "historical imaginary" as it is conceived by Elsaesser forms a meta-theoretical horizon, a fantasy formation and dialectical contraption that keeps in check more common empirical modes of film historiography. The duplicity restored to Weimar films folds itself onto the heuristic efforts of the film histori-cal discourse to which it has given rise. The latter in turn appears less authori-tative or objective and closer to its object, affected – as much it might seek to deny it – by cinema's phantasmagorial powers and part of a mutual historical logic and cultural formation.[7] In its meta-theoretical implications, the idea of a "historical imaginary" offers an effective tool for deconstructing the implicit myths and underlying fantasies behind film historical reasoning and causation, the building of traditions and the formation of a cultural heritage, while at the same time acknowledging their power as the founding impulse and ultimate justification for why we should care not only about writing but "doing" and even "living" and "experiencing" the history of cinema: "The cinema is part of us, it seems, even when we are not at the movies, which suggests that in this respect, there is no longer an outside to the inside: we are already 'in' the cin-ema with whatever we can say 'about' it."[8]

Adding another conceptual layer to the idea of a "crisis historiography" dis-cussed at the end of the previous chapter, I would like to trace the reverbera-tions of the shift in film historiographical thinking marked by Elsaesser's notion of the "historical imaginary" and consider some of the consequences that can be drawn from it. With the example of Fritz Lang – one of Weimar cin-ema's iconic auteur filmmakers, but also one of its most prolific popular genre

---

6 Elsaesser: *Weimar Cinema and After*, 4–5.

7 Elsaesser's prime example for this phenomenon is film noir, a genre invented after the fact in a particular historical situation. Cf. Elsaesser: *Weimar Cinema and After*, 420–444

8 Thomas Elsaesser: The New Film History as Media Archaeology. In: *CiNéMAS* 14:2–3 (2004), 75–117, here 76. The concept of the "historical imaginary" can be brought into a fruitful con-stellation with Elsaesser's more recent writings on early cinema, new media, and archival poli-tics; his ongoing critical engagement with the "New Film History"; and his programmatic model of "Media Archaeology," first formulated in his general introduction to Elsaesser (ed.): *Early Cinema. Space, Frame, Narrative*. London 1990, 1–7, and later fully explored in Elsaesser: *Film History as Media Archaeology. Tracking Digital Cinema*. Amsterdam 2016.

directors – I use the theoretical framework of the "historical imaginary" to show how it not only transcends traditional ideas of cinematic authorship as a revelation of the artist's personality (e.g. in Patrick McGilligan's biographical study of Lang), but also adds an important dimension to accounts of the auteur as textual effect and discursive agency, most vigorously put forward in relation to Lang by Tom Gunning.

9.2 The enigma of Fritz Lang

The spell of fascination cast by Fritz Lang and his films has remained one of cinema's most forceful and enigmatic.[9] Elsaesser characterizes Lang as "the most flagrantly intelligent as well as self-reflexive representatives of the enlightened false consciousness" that philosopher Peter Sloterdijk has identified as the ultimate index of Weimar culture's quintessential modernity: "Lang could have been on Sloterdijk's mind when he says that we need a 'logical and historical cubism, a simultaneous thinking and seeing in several dimensions' if we are to understand 'the Weimar symptom.'"[10]

Like Alfred Hitchcock and Jean Renoir (with whom Lang is often compared and whom he both influenced and was influenced by), Lang's artistic signature has proven difficult to pin down down in traditional terms of stylistic continuity or biographical self-reference.[11] There are simply too many shifts and outright breaks that mark Lang's career: from his silent epics DER MÜDE TOD (DESTINY, 1921) and DIE NIBELUNGEN (NIBELUNGEN, 1924), science-fiction fantasies METROPOLIS (1926/27) and DIE FRAU IM MOND (WOMAN IN THE MOON, 1929), crossbreeding popular kitsch-sensibility with stark symbolism (and therefore often misplaced in the vicinity of German expressionism[12]) through his experiments with early sound technology and the thriller genre in M (1931) and DAS TESTAMENT DES DR. MABUSE (THE TESTAMENT OF DR. MABUSE, 1932) to the almost classical, but increasingly bleak American genre pieces of the 1940s and 1950s, the West-

---

9 Elsaesser speaks of "the enigma of Lang" (*Weimar Cinema and After*, 148).

10 Elsaesser: *Weimar Cinema and After*, 10. Elsaesser refers to Peter Sloterdijk: *Critique of Cynical Reason*. Minneapolis 1988, originally published in German in two volumes under the title *Kritik der zynischen Vernunft* (Frankfurt a. M. 1983).

11 Cf. Thomas Elsaesser: Too Big and Too Close. Alfred Hitchcock and Fritz Lang. In: *Hitchcock Annual* 12 (2003), 1–41.

12 Lang's relationship to German expressionist film has always been somewhat vexing; for a revisionist account of Lang's work that situates him closer to the aesthetics of *Jugendstil* than to expressionism cf. Elsaesser: *Weimar Cinema and After*, 185–188.

German remakes DER TIGER VON ESCHNAPUR and DAS INDISCHE GRABMAL (THE TIGER OF ESCHNAPUR and THE INDIAN TOMB, 1958/59) and sequels (DIE 1000 AUGEN DES DR. MABUSE / THE THOUSAND EYES OF DR. MABUSE 1960). For the majority of critics, especially in Germany and Britain, Lang's career appeared to describe the parabola of a decade-long decline after he left Germany (and divorced his second wife and co-author of most of his German films, Thea von Harbou) at the peak of his creative power. What followed is commonly characterized as a dramatic loss of artistic vision and control within the constraints of the Hollywood studio system, culminating in nostalgic pastiche and self-parody at the end of his career.

Film scholars have not ceased to hunt for a common denominator unifying this body of work, looking for the hidden key with which to unlock the mysterious core of the Langian universe.[13] Along the lines of traditional auteur theory, Patrick McGilligan believes to have found Lang's "Rosebud" in a personal trauma caused by the violent and mysterious death of his first wife Elisabeth Rosenthal, which occurred after she had caught Lang and von Harbou making love in Lang's Berlin residence. For McGilligan, this early incident pre-shadowed Lang's obsession with love triangles, covered-up murders and personal guilt, which pervades almost all of his films.[14]

Only a few years after the publication of McGilligan's biography, the curators of the Fritz Lang exhibition held in Berlin in 2001 were able to present new pieces of evidence regarding the circumstances of the death of Elisabeth Rosenthal on September 25, 1920. Unknown to McGilligan at the time he was writing his biography, this evidence included a document confirming police registration of Rosenthal's funeral that was issued by the criminal investigation department on September 29 and an application form for her burial at the Jewish cemetery in Berlin-Weißensee dated October 1 that records the cause of death as "shot in the chest, accident." To the curators of the exhibition and the authors of the accompanying book, this evidence, taken alongside the conspicuous absence of other official documents, suggests neither murder nor suicide, but a third scenario:

> The word "accident" in connection with such an unusual death caused by a shot in the chest might also mean: there was a struggle in the apartment during which one party tried to prevent the other – who in the heat of the moment was about to commit a crime – from pulling the trigger, but the gun went off, firing the fatal shot.[15]

---

13 Cf. e.g. the contributions to Joe McElhaney (ed.): *A Companion to Fritz Lang*. Malden 2015.
14 Patrick McGilligan: *Fritz Lang – The Nature of the Beast. A Biography*. New York 1997. Cf. also Thomas Elsaesser's review essay on McGilligan's book: Traps for the Mind and the Eye. Fritz Lang. In: *Sight & Sound* 7–8 (August 1997), 28–30.
15 Rolf Aurich, Wolfgang Jacobsen and Cornelius Schnauber: *Fritz Lang – His Life and Work. Photographs and Documents*. Berlin 2001, 60–61.

Whatever impact this early traumatic experience might have had on Lang's artistic development, McGilligan's spectacular re-grounding of Lang's major themes and cinematic obsessions in his wife's death – an incident that occurred early on in Lang's "real" life – is driven by exactly the opposite logic of a cinematic effect desperately seeking a (real life) cause. The temporally-inverted logic of "life imitating art" is shaped, all too clearly, by an imaginary that wants to identify the biographical "origin," "historical reality," and psychological *Ur-Szene* of the key dramatic triangulation of pleasure, violence and guilt that Lang's cinema incessantly worked through and made to be felt so "real" over and over again. The irony behind this particular historical imaginary lies in the fact that it ultimately corresponds to Lang's oft-stated desire to survive in his films alone. Lang always refused to reveal much of his personal life to professional interviewers and to film historians. This practice has bred infinite speculation, often based on a handful of biographical legends carefully planted by Lang himself.[16] "Tell her some nice lies about me," he once suggested to an old lady friend whose daughter was interested in what kind of a man he was.[17] This stance might well come to represent Lang's motto in all things personal.

9.3 Double vision

In another attempt to unravel the conundrum posed by trying to think together Lang and his films, constructing, as Foucault would call it, the "fundamental" but always imaginary "unit of the author and his work,"[18] Tom Gunning has rooted his speculations less in biographical research than in theoretical reflection. Following a structuralist approach to the idea of the cinematic auteur, he is less interested in Lang as a biographical person than in the artistic persona 'Fritz Lang' inscribed in and to be read from his films. Thus reconstructed and placed within the cultural context of 20th-century media modernity, Gunning's "emblematic" Lang re-emerges as a historical agency of much wider implications than reflected by any study of his artistic background or personal surroundings. For Gunning, the imprint Lang has left behind in his work consists above all in an invitation to closely read and reflect on his films, whose

---

16 Most exemplary in this respect is perhaps Lang's autobiographical note published in Lotte Eisner: *Fritz Lang*. London 1976, 9–15

17 Quoted in Bernard Eisenschitz: Flüchtlingsgespräche. Die Briefe von Fritz Lang an Eleanor Rosé. In: *Filmblatt* 6:15 (Winter/Spring 2001), 54–59, here 55.

18 Michael Foucault: What is an Author? In: Foucault: *Aesthetics, Method, and Epistemology*. London 1998, 205–222, here 205.

representational economy and mode of address are consequently defined as allegorical, in the sense given to the term by Walter Benjamin and Siegfried Kracauer: as hieroglyphic images to be contemplated and deciphered by the spectator beyond their literal (narrative) meaning.[19]

Gunning's analysis of Lang's cinematic meditations on modernity's basic effects – the commodification of culture and the alienation of subjective experience – looks beyond the traditional level of thematic or stylistic continuities. What Gunning identifies as the driving force behind Lang's cinema is the concept of the 'destiny-machine' which over the years has taken on various narrative forms and audiovisual figurations: Gunning's catalogue of instantiations includes the hourglass and the watchman's cry in DER MÜDE TOD; the *Gesänge*-fatefully sub-dividing the two-part NIBELUNGEN; Moloch and the recurring steam whistle in METROPOLIS; the false bottoms, spinning wheels and locked doors in DR. MABUSE, DER SPIELER (1921/22); the urban cobwebs of criminal control systems, counter-information highways and intersecting phone calls in M, DAS TESTAMENT DES DR. MABUSE and THE BIG HEAT (1953); the media dissemination of individual identity in FURY (1936), YOU ONLY LIVE ONCE (1937), or WHILE THE CITY SLEEPS (1955); Chris Cross's gold watch timing his manipulation of the electricity circuit in SCARLET STREET (1945); the eternally returning, floating corpse in HOUSE BY THE RIVER (1950); the 'unholy' architecture of the ancestral house in SECRET BEYOND THE DOOR (1948) and the Hotel Luxor in DIE 1000 AUGEN DES DR. MABUSE.

According to Gunning, the ultimate image of the Destiny machine in Lang's films is the clock, a machine whose rationale is, by definition, beyond the control of individual characters.[20] As much as his famous master criminals and media moguls, obsessed painters, novelists and architects believe in their intellectual and technological mastery of the Destiny machine and the course of the narrative, all of Lang's characters are caught in the workings of a cinematic system controlled by Lang alone. This hidden hierarchy is built into every single

---

19 Tom Gunning: *The Films of Fritz Lang. Allegories of Vision and Modernity*. London 2000. David Levin, Catherine Russell, Tom Conley, Garrett Stewart, and Jacques Rancière, among others, have connected Lang's films to the idea of 'allegorical cinema' from various, interpretative vantage points. Elsaesser first suggested such a reading in a series of essays on Weimar cinema written in the 1980s, perhaps most thoroughly in: Cinema – The Irresponsible Signifier or "The Gamble with History." Film Theory or Cinema Theory. In: *New German Critique* 40 (1987), 65–89.

20 Gunning delivers an almost encyclopedic account of the many instances in which clocks of all shapes and sizes assume central roles in Lang's oeuvre. One important figuration of the clock as Destiny machine in the opening sequence of *M* is not, however, identified by Gunning but finds its precise description in Anton Kaes: *M*. London 2000, 10–11.

Lang film, introducing a struggle between different narrational agencies that trap not only its characters but also its audience in a complex game of deception and recognition. Here, Gunning seems to align with Elsaesser, for whom "To see, to know, to believe [...] is the triad whose contending claims on perception and reason the radical sceptic in Lang never ceases to play off against each other."[21]

According to Gunning, Lang's films occasionally grant glimpses into the structure of the Destiny machine. In such rare "visionary moments," both characters and viewers of a Lang film find themselves in an unreliable world scattered with false traces and wrong tracks, plunged into an unstable universe full of black holes that suck the individual into ever deeper layers of contingency.[22] Along similar lines, Elsaesser relates the "mesmerizing or hallucinatory effects on spectators so often attributed to Lang's films" to be the result of two kinds of violence: "the film viewer's interpretative violence, and the violence of the film's resistance to interpretation."[23]

The emblematic place of the individual – character *and* spectator – within Lang's cinema would therefore *not* be that of Mabuse at the switchboard of power and control. As Gunning suggests, the signifier of the real power behind Lang's narratives is rather to be found in the many images of rooms emptied out of individual characters by a Destiny machine executing a dark scenario of modernity to which they have fallen victim. Hence, these images of absence in Lang's cinema are also the moments where the presence of the director is most strongly felt.[24] Gunning's re-readings of Lang's major films re-conceptualize the prominent features that have made them classics, but they do not turn the terms of the debate – revolving around fatality and paranoia, ornamental abstraction, narrative duplicity and identity in disguise – completely upside down. His fascination with Lang's films, as that of most of his predecessors, still revolves around what Elsaesser identifies as their "overriding concerns [...]: the relation of vision to knowledge, of knowledge to power, of power to falsehood and of duplicity to the pleasures of complicity, of 'being in the know.'"[25]

It is interesting to note how Gunning's paradoxical dialectics of authorship relate to Elsaesser's reading of Lang in other respects. On the one hand, Gunning's notion of a negative authorship seems to be in line with Elsaesser's observation that in Lang's films "it is artifice that triumphs even more than 'evil,'" and that it is this "underlying doubleness of gesture," the high degree of artifice

---

21 Elsaesser: *Weimar Cinema and After*, 149–150; cf. Gunning: *The Films of Fritz Lang*, 416.
22 Gunning: *The Films of Fritz Lang*, 476.
23 Elsaesser: *Weimar Cinema and After*, 153.
24 Gunning: *The Films of Fritz Lang*, 480.
25 Elsaesser: *Weimar Cinema and After*, 150.

and stylization, mimicry and parody, that both hides and reveals the author's signature under/in a layer of self-reflexive disguise.[26] On the other hand, with the mechanical and anonymous Destiny machine put in place of any *enunciative* act directly attributable to Lang, Gunning re-introduces another instance for which Lang's cinema is bound to become "the ultimate metaphor"[27] – not of tyranny, as for Kracauer, and not even of the cinema experience itself, as it was for the French critics of the 1950s and 1960s, but of technological modernity. It is precisely in order to avoid this notion of metaphorical or negative unity that Elsaesser introduces Sloterdijk's "enlightened false consciousness" as the "place of rupture" itself, which "implies that the opposite of disguise is not truth, immediacy or 'authenticity,' but rather, whatever it takes to instantiate this symbolic, that is, the condition of possibility of discontinuity, disjuncture, non-identity."[28]

9.4 The place of rupture

Authorship has always been one of the most prominent shapes that the "historical imaginary" takes in order to convey upon a group of films a certain sense of meaning and coherence. The attempt, famously suggested by Michel Foucault, to recognize the mark of the author in "the singularity of his absence," to "locate the space left empty by the author's disappearance [...], follow the distribution of the gaps and breaches, and watch for the openings this disappearance uncovers,"[29] has led to the question of Lang's authorship anew in the paradoxical terms of the performance of disguise and permanent deferral, residing, for Gunning, in the allegorical lure of modernity's in-between-spaces of mediation, and, for Elsaesser, in the interstices, the fissures and frictions of cinematic discourse itself: places of rupture and instances of contingency that mark what one could describe as the "historical real" and instantiate the epistemological horizon for all possible figurative meanings and imaginary investments.[30] This shift in emphasis and perspective would suggest an interpretation of Lang's films not as

---

26 Elsaesser: *Weimar Cinema and After*, 146, 153.
27 The phrase is Raymond Bellour's. Cf. Raymond Bellour: On Fritz Lang. In: Stephen Jenkins (ed.): *Fritz Lang. The Image and the Look*. London 1981, 26–37, here 29.
28 Elsaesser: *Weimar Cinema and After*, 185.
29 Foucault: What is an Author?, 207, 209.
30 The category of the "Real" understood in the (post-)Lacanian sense given to the term in the context of film and media theoretical thinking by Friedrich Kittler and Slavoj Žižek. Cf. Friedrich Kittler: *Gramophone, Film, Typewriter*. Stanford 1999; Slavoj Žižek: *The Fright of Real Tears. Krzysztof Kieslowski Between Theory and Post-Theory*. London 2001.

emblems of modernity as such, but rather as "allegories of their own problematic existence,"[31] archaeological layers indexical of their concrete time and place in history beneath the level of the symbolic.

Elsaesser has demonstrated that these historical markers are, on the very level of their material composition, also openings towards the possible futures of a film and its director perhaps nowhere more compellingly than in his book on METROPOLIS. The film was shown in Lang's intended (and now lost[32]) version only once to a select audience on January 10, 1927, before it was immediately dismembered, cut and re-edited into different national and international release versions. As Elsaesser suggests, it is exactly the uncertain, "un-authored," and "un-authorized" material and thus textual status of METROPOLIS that has turned the film into something like a "ruin-in-progress," re-sampled and re-appropriated by every new generation, renegotiating, reinventing and reinvesting, paradoxically enough, the status of its director as auteur along the way.[33]

Moments of rupture, however, occur in many other less prominent examples within (and, as the previous chapters have shown, also beyond) Lang's oeuvre. One such disorienting moment is to be found midway through DIE 1000 AUGEN DES DR. MABUSE, Lang's last film as a director. The film's central couple, the American millionaire Henri B. Travers and Marion Menil, the woman he loves and who has fallen in love with him but who is still (if involuntarily) part of a criminal scheme devised against him, sit at a table in the bar of the Hotel Luxor where most of the film's action takes place. Their conversation, held in front of the conspicuous backdrop of a wall decorated with rectangular wooden panels and buzzing ornaments of dots and broken lines producing a moiré effect of smaller rectangular units, is exposed to and monitored by the film's master criminal via a system of surveillance technologies originally installed in the hotel by the Gestapo before World War II, as we learn towards the end of the film. The fact that their conversation is overheard, known to Marion, is revealed to the spectator in a cut-away to the monitor in the secret catacomb of the hotel. There, the television image briefly collapses and breaks down into lines and dots of static interference, strongly reminiscent of the designs on the wall behind the couple. Via a zoom into the reconstituted image on the monitor, the camera view jumps back to the hotel bar. Marion and the millionaire are now

31 Thomas Elsaesser: *New German Cinema. A History*. New Brunswick 1989, 75.

32 In 2008, key scenes from the lost version were rediscovered in Buenos Aires and led, in 2010, to a new restoration of METROPOLIS that comes close – but cannot claim to be identical with – the film's 1927 premiere version.

33 Thomas Elsaesser: *Metropolis*. London 2000.

captured by the camera from a position inside the decorated wall that was previously behind them. The disorienting rupture occurs when we next see a shot of Marion from her soon-to-be lover's point of view with a completely different pattern of more harmonic and body-like, though angular and abstract, shapes surrounding her face and upper body (Fig. 9.1).

Fig. 9.1: Abstract patterns and disorienting ruptures in DIE 1000 AUGEN DES DR. MABUSE.

It is easy to discover in this sequence of shots the typical Langian labyrinth of subjective looks and uncanny gazes, the self-reflexive *mise-en-abyme* of *Jugendstil* design and the tyranny of mediated perception. In the logic of the film itself, the workings of this cinematic labyrinth are bound back to the double legacy of the Nazi past and the criminal energy of the Weimar period's Dr. Mabuse: the temporality of a historical imaginary, superimposing political and cinematic history, is literally turned into the spatial arrangement of a "double occupancy" defining the state of the present as the uncanny *Gleichzeitigkeit des*

Ungleichzeitigen and mutual interference of a multitude of (audio)visual regimes.[34] But rather than simply understand this sequence as being structured around the frozen space and static architecture of the Hotel Luxor, we could also, and perhaps more productively, interpret it as the moment of rupture itself: the instant of contradiction and epistemological shock in what first appears to be a blunt instance of false continuity on Lang's part but which may very well form "the condition of possibility of discontinuity, disjuncture, nonidentity" in order to "instantiate [a new] symbolic."[35]

To "follow the distribution of the gaps and breaches," and "watch for the openings" that the author's disappearance uncovers, as Foucault suggests, would then mean to think of the internal and the external, the contingent effect and its transcendental point of reference and coherence as being caught in the differential image of self and other, co-existing in the space between them but never coinciding: a "double vision and a dialectical reflex,"[36] the spatial design and temporal configuration of a parallax non-identity.

From the constitutive ambivalence of the place of rupture as such, an oeuvre's authorial "identity" can only emerge as the vanishing point of a "historical imaginary" that constantly renegotiates and ultimately suspends the levels of the "historical symbolic" (the norms of textual articulation imposed by the industrial structure) and the "historical real" (the materialities of cinematic discourse). Within this logic, the idea of authorial identity should be considered in terms of its "constitutive outside," both in relation to its historical "others" of industrial norms and media materialities and with respect to its temporal dislocation as the hegemonic reading strategy of an interpretive community, freezing chaos, as Lang himself envisioned, into a formula. As with all sedimented hegemonic articulations, this mode of understanding film history is, however, not only constitutive in providing some primary meaning and significance to a cultural practice and a body of work. It is also contingent insofar as it necessarily remains inside its own fantasy formation and open to be overturned by others.[37]

---

34 Cf. Thomas Elsaesser: Double Occupancy and Small Adjustments. Space, Place and Policy in the New European Cinema since the 1990s. In: Elsaesser: *European Cinema. Face to Face with Hollywood.* Amsterdam 2005, 108–130.

35 Elsaesser: *Weimar Cinema and After*, 185.

36 Elsaesser: *Weimar Cinema and After*, 152.

37 I am here drawing on a view of political hegemony developed by Ernesto Laclau and Chantal Mouffe. For a summary of their ideas, cf. Chantal Mouffe: *On the Political.* London and New York 2005, chapter 2.

Bibliography

[Anon.]: Bekanntmachung. In: *Erste Internationale Film-Zeitung* 19 (11 May 1912), n.p.

[Anon.]: Besuche in Berliner Kino-Ateliers. In: *Die Lichtbild-Bühne* 24 (15 June 1912), 18.

[Anon.]: Carver produziert für die Universal in Frankreich. In: *Film-Kurier* 100 (30 April 1931), n.p.

[Anon.]: Conrad Veidt telephoniert mit Hollywood. In: *Der Kinematograph* 240 (14 October 1929), n.p.

[Anon.]: Delog-Film-Vertriebs-G.m.b.H. (Die Filmindustrie im Handelsregister). In: *Film-Kurier* 209 (7 September 1921), n.p.

[Anon.]: Ein deutscher Tonfilm aus Hollywood. In: *Der Kinematograph* 43 (20 February 1931), n.p.

[Anon.]: Deutsche Universal verfilmt *Im Westen nichts Neues*. In: *Film-Kurier* 158 (5 July 1929), n.p.

[Anon.]: Deutschsprachige Tonfilme laufen in Amerika, aber nicht bei uns. In: *Film-Kurier* 7 (7 January 1930), n.p.

[Anon.]: Die erste Lichtspiel-Operette. In: *Der Kinematograph* 605 (7 August 1918), n.p.

[Anon.]: Die erste Lichtspiel-Operette. In: *Der Film* 32 (10 August 1918), 70.

[Anon.]: Die Filmkünstler der Lichtspieloper "Martha." In: *Delog-Post* (November 1916), 10–12.

[Anon.]: Hollywood dreht keine "Versionen" mehr. In: *Der Kinematograph* 215 (17 September 1931), n.p.

[Anon.]: "Insurrection." In: *Der Kinematograph* 250 (28 October 1931), n.p.

[Anon.]: In treuer Pflichterfüllung. In: *Illustrierte Rundschau (Hamburger Fremdenblatt)* 95 (24 April 1912), 29; reprinted in: Werner Köster and Thomas Lischeid (eds.): *Titanic. Ein Medienmythos*. Leipzig 1999, 88–89.

[Anon.]: *Jenseits des Stroms. Vollständiges Textbuch mit musikalischen Erläuterungen und Leitmotiven*. Berlin 1922). A copy is held at the Bundesarchiv-Filmarchiv, Berlin, Documentation Dept., Sign. 8244.

[Anon.]: "Liebe auf Befehl" im Deutschen Reich. In: *Der Kinematograph* 46 (24 February 1931), n.p.

[Anon.]: "Miss Venus": Die neue große Filmoperette. In: *Bühne & Film* 17 (1921), 10.

[Anon.]: Die neuen Opernfilms. In: *Der Artist* 1525 (3 May 1914), n.p.

[Anon.]: Die neue Universal-Staffel. In: *Der Kinematograph* 279 (29 November 1930), n.p.

[Anon.]: Notofilm. In: *Film-Kurier* 107 (9 October 1919), n.p.

[Anon.]: Noto-Film-Gesellschaft. In: *Film-Kurier* 143 (21 June 1921), n.p.

[Anon.]: Paul Wegener und Asta Nielsen. In: *Die Lichtbild-Bühne* 3 (15 Jan 1921), 48.

[Anon.]: Plot synopsis of Continental-Kunstfilm. In: *Erste Internationale Film-Zeitung* 25 (22 June 1912), 33.

[Anon.]: Plot synopsis of Continental-Kunstfilm. In: *Der Kinematograph* 288 (3 July 1912), n.p.

[Anon.]: Die Rache einer Tageszeitung: Der "Oberschlesische Kurier" und seine gerechte Abfuhr. In: *Die Lichtbild-Bühne* 23 (8 June 1912), n.p.

[Anon.]: Revirement bei Universal. In: *Der Kinematograph* 41 (18 February 1931), n.p.

[Anon.]: Das Rhythmoband im Dienste des Tonfilms. In: *Kinotechnische Rundschau* 42 (15 November 1930), n.p.

[Anon.]: Rhythmographie-Arbeiten. In: *Der Kinematograph* 139 (18 June 1931), n.p.

[Anon.]: Der stumme Film in U.S.A. In: *Der Kinematograph* 233 (24 September 1930), n.p.

[Anon.]: Tonfilm-Aufnahme über 10.000 Kilometer. In: *Die Lichtbild-Bühne* 245 (14 October 1929), n.p.

https://doi.org/10.1515/9783110613551-011

[Anon.]: Die Tränen der Asta Nielsen. In: *Die Lichtbild-Bühne* 49 (4 Dec 1920), 49.

[Anon.]: Universal-Kombination plant 10 Filme – für den 1. Teil der Saison. In: *Film-Kurier* 144 (22 June 1931), n.p.

[Anon.]: Universal Takes Lead in Foreign Version Films. In: *Universal Weekly* 5 (8 March 1930), n.p.

[Anon.]: Der Untergang der Titanic. In: *Die Lichtbild-Bühne* 28 (13 July 1912), n.p.

[Anon.]: Was die Delog verspricht. In: *Kinotechnische Rundschau* 38 (21 September 1929), n.p.

Abel, Richard and Rick Altman (eds.): *The Sounds of Early Cinema*. Bloomington and Indianapolis 2001.

Adam, Moritz: Das Musik-Chronometer von Carl Robert Blum im Dienste der Filmkunst. In: *Die Kinotechnik* 4 (1927), 94.

Ailbout, Hans: Musikfilme. In: *Filmland* 4 (February 1925), 64.

Allen, Robert C. and Douglas Gomery: *Film History. Theory and Practice*. New York and Boston 1986.

Altenloh, Emilie: *Zur Soziologie des Kino. Die Kinounternehmung und die sozialen Schichten ihrer Besucher*. Jena 1914.

Altenloh, Emilie: A Sociology of the Cinema. The Audience 1914. In: *Screen* 42:3 (Autumn 2001), 249–293.

Altman, Rick: General Introduction: Cinema as Event. In: Rick Altman (ed.): *Sound Theory, Sound Practice*. New York and London 1992, 1–14.

Altman, Rick: The Silence of the Silents. In: *The Musical Quarterly* 80: 4 (Winter 1996), 648–718.

Altman, Rick: Sound – All of it. In: *Iris* 27 (Spring 1999), 31–48.

Altman, Rick: *Silent Film Sound*. New York 2004.

Anderson, J.M.: Komposition durchs Telephon. In: *Der Kinematograph* 242 (16 October 1930).

Andrew, Dudley: *Concepts in Film Theory*. Oxford et al. 1984.

Aurich, Rolf, Wolfgang Jacobsen and Cornelius Schnauber: *Fritz Lang – His Life and Work. Photographs and Documents*. Berlin 2001.

Balázs, Béla: Die Erotik der Asta Nielsen 1923. In: Béla Balázs: *Schriften zum Film*, Vol. 1: *Der sichtbare Mensch / Kritiken und Aufsätze zum Film 1922–1926*, ed. by Helmut H. Diederichs, Wolfgang Gersch and Magda Nagy. Berlin 1982, 185–186.

Balázs, Béla: *Early Film Theory. Visible Man and The Spirit of Film*, ed. Erica Carter. Oxford 2010.

Baracco, Alberto: *Hermeneutics of a Film World. A Ricoerian Method for Film Interpretation*. Cham 2017.

Barnier, Martin: Le Cinéphone et l'ideal-sonore. Deux appareils sonores Gaumont des années 1920–1930. In: *1895* 24 (June 1998), 37–53.

Beck, Jacob: Wie die Lichtspiel-Oper entstand. In: *Delog-Post* (June 1917), 1–3.

Beck, Jacob: Wie die Lichtspiel-Oper entstand: Schluss. In: *Delog-Post* (July 1917), 4–8.

Bellour, Raymond: On Fritz Lang. In: Stephen Jenkins (ed.): *Fritz Lang. The Image and the Look*. London 1981, 26–37.

Bergstrom, Janet: Asta Nielsen's Early German Films. In: Paolo Cherchi Usai and Lorenzo Codelli (eds.): *Before Caligari. German Cinema, 1895–1920*. Pordenone 1990, 162–185.

Bernardy, Ernesto: Kalauer bei Tilmar Springefeld. In: *Filmland* 7 (May 1925), 64.

Biel, Steven: *Down with the Old Canoe. A Cultural History of the Titanic*. New York and London 1996.

Birett, Herbert: *Stummfilm-Musik. Materialsammlung*. Berlin 1970.

Birett, Herbert (ed.): *Verzeichnis in Deutschland gelaufener Filme. Entscheidungen der Filmzensur 1911–1920*. Munich, Berlin, Hamburg and Stuttgart 1980.

Birett, Herbert: *Das Filmangebot in Deutschland 1895–1911*. Munich 1991.

Blanchot, Maurice: *The Space of Literature*. Lincoln and London 1990.

Blum, Carl Robert: Zeit wird Raum. In: *Der Film* 11 (15 June 1927), 26.

Blum, C.R.: *Die Herstellung von Tonfilmen mittels Rhythmographie, System C.R. Blum*. Berlin 1930.

Blumenberg, Hans: *Shipwreck with Spectator: Paradigm of a Metaphor for Existence*. Cambridge, Mass. and London 1997.

Bock, Hans-Michael (ed.): *CineGraph. Lexikon des deutschsprachigen Films*. Munich 1984.

Bock, Hans-Michael (ed.): *Der komische Kintopp*. Hamburg and Berlin 1997.

Bordwell, David: Historical Poetics of Cinema. In: Richard B. Palmer (ed.): *The Cinematic Text. Methods and Approaches*. New York 1989, 369–398.

Bordwell, David: *On the History of Film Style*. Cambridge, Mass. and London 1997.

Bordwell, David: *Figures Traced in Light. On Cinematic Staging*. Berkeley, Los Angeles and New York 2005.

Bordwell, David: *Poetics of Cinema*. New York and London 2008.

Bösch, Frank: Transnationale Trauer und Technikkritik? Der Untergang der "Titanic." In: Friedrich Lenger and Ansgar Nünning (eds.): *Medienereignisse der Moderne*. Darmstadt 2000, 79–94.

Bottomore, Stephen: *The Titanic and Silent Cinema*. East Sussex 2000.

Branigan, Edward: *Point of View in the Cinem. A Theory of Narration and Subjectivity in Classical Film*. Berlin, New York and Amsterdam 1984.

Branigan, Edward: *Narrative Comprehension and Film*. London 1992.

Bratu Hansen, Miriam: America, Paris, the Alps. Kracauer (and Benjamin) on Cinema and Modernity. In: Leo Charney and Vanessa Schwartz (eds.): *Cinema and the Invention of Modern Life*. Berkeley, Los Angeles and London 1995, 362–402.

Brewster, Ben: Deep Staging in French Films 1900–1914. In: Thomas Elsaesser with Adam Barker (eds): *Early Cinema. Space, Frame, Narrative*. London 1990, 45–55.

Brewster, Ben and Lea Jacobs: *Theater to Cinema. Stage Pictorialism and the Early Feature Film*. Oxford and New York 1997.

Brockman, Stephen: *A Critical History of German Film*. Rochester 2010.

Brooks, Peter: *The Melodramatic Imagination. Balzac, Henry James, Melodrama and the Mode of Excess*. New York 1985.

Budd, Mike: Moments of "Caligari." In: Budd (ed.): *"The Cabinet of Dr. Caligari." Texts, Contexts, Histories*. New Brunswick and London 1990, 7–121.

Burch, Noël: Primitivism and the Avant-Gardes. A Dialectical Approach. In: Philip Rosen (ed.): *Narrative, Apparatus, Ideology. A Film Theory Reader*. New York 1986, 483–506.

Burckhardt, Jacob: *Gesammelte Werke*, Vol. 4: *Weltgeschichtliche Betrachtungen*. Darmstadt 1956.

Canudo, Ricciotto: The Birth of a Sixth Art [1911]. In Richard Abel (ed.): *French Film Theory and Criticism. A History / Anthology, 1907–1939*, Vol. 1. Princeton 1988, 58–66.

Caruth, Cathy: *Unclaimed Experience. Trauma, Narrative, and History*. Baltimore and London 1996.

Casetti, Francesco: *Eye of the Century. Film, Experience, Modernity*. New York 2008.

Castle, Terry: Phantasmagoria. Spectral Technology and the Metaphorics of Modern Reverie. In: *Critical Inquiry* 1 (Autumn 1988), 26–61.

Certeau, Michel de: *The Writing of History* [1975]. New York 1988.

Ch.: Optimismus der Jugend. Universal synchronisiert Sprechfilme deutsch. In: *Film-Kurier* 234 (2 October 1929).

Charney, Leo: *Empty Moments. Cinema, Modernity, and Drift*. Durham and London 1998.

Chambers, John Whiteclay II: "All Quiet on the Western Front" (1930). The Antiwar Film and the Image of the First World War. In: *Historical Journal of Film, Radio and Television* 4 (1994), 377–411.

Chapman, James, Mark Glancy and Sue Harper (eds.): *The New Film History. Sources, Methods, Approaches*. London 2009.

Chatman, Seymour: *Story and Discourse. Narrative Structure and Film*. Ithaca 1978.

Chion, Michel: *Audiovision. Sound on Screen*. New York 1994.

Choe, Steve: *Afterlives. Allegories of Film and Mortality in Early Weimar Germany*. New York et al. 2014.

Crafton, Donald: *The Talkies. America's Transition to Sound, 1926–1931*. Berkeley, Los Angeles and New York 1999.

Crary, Jonathan: *Techniques of the Observer. On Vision and Modernity in the Nineteenth Century*. Cambridge and London 1990.

Czerny, Ludwig: Film und Musik. In: *Der Film* 35 (27 August 1923), 31.

Dagrada, Elena: The Voyeur at Wilhelm's Court. In: Thomas Elsaesser with Michael Wedel (eds.): *A Second Life. German Cinema's First Decades*. Amsterdam 1996, 277–284.

Dagrada, Elena: *Between the Eye and the World. The Emergence of the Point-of-View Shot*. Brussels 2015.

Dalle Vacche, Angela: Asta Nielsen's Acting. Motion, Emotion, and the Camera-Eye. In: *Framework* 43:1 (Spring 2002), 76–94.

Dayan, Daniel and Elihu Katz: *Media Events. The Live Broadcasting of History*. Cambridge, Mass. and London 1992.

Deleuze, Gilles: *Cinema 2. The Time-Image*. London 1989.

Deranty, Jean-Philippe (ed.): *Jacques Rancière. Key Concepts*. Abingdon and New York 2010.

Deutsche Bioscop Gesellschaft m.b.H. (ed.): *Unsere Künstler*. Berlin [1913/14].

Deutsche Lichtspiel-Oper. Denkschrift Anläßlich der Erstaufführung der ersten deutschen Lichspieloper "Lohengrin" am 21. Januar 1916 in Berlin. In: *Die Film-Börse* 3 (1916), 9–10.

Dittgen, Andrea: *Franz Hofer*. Saarbrücken 1999.

Doane, Mary Ann: The Voice in Cinema. The Articulation of Body and Space. In: *Yale French Studies* 60 (1980), 33–50.

Doane, Mary Ann: *The Emergence of Cinematic Time*. Cambridge, Mass. 2003.

Dörp, Peter: Goebbels' Kampf gegen Remarque (2). Eine Untersuchung über die Hintergründe des Hasses und der Agitation Goebbels' gegen den amerikanischen Spielflm Im Westen nichts Neues nach dem gleichnamigen Bestsellerroman von Erich Maria Remarque. In: *Erich Maria Remarque-Jahrbuch* 3 (1993), 45–72.

Driessen, Barbara: *Tragödie der Technik, Triumph der Medien. Die Berichterstattung über den Untergang der Titanic in der zeitgenössischen deutschen und britischen Presse*. Münster 1999.

Dubbini, Renzo: *Geography of the Gaze. Urban and Rural Vision in Early Modern Europe*. Chicago and London 2002.

Dupont, E.A.: Kinofahrt nach Wernigerode. In: *Illustrierte Filmwoche* 43 (17 November 1916), 281.

Ďurovičová, Nataša: Translating America. The Hollywood Multilinguals 1929–1933. In: Rick Altman (ed.): *Sound Theory, Sound Practice*. New York and London 1992, 139–153.

Earle, Edward W.: *The Stereograph in America. A Cultural History*. New York 1979.

Eisenschitz, Bernard: Flüchtlingsgespräche. Die Briefe von Fritz Lang an Eleanor Rosé. In: *Filmblatt* 6:15 (Winter/Spring 2001), 54–59.

Eisenstein, Sergei M.: Unity of the Image. In: Sergei Eisenstein: *Selected Works*, Vol. 2: *Towards a Theory of Montage*. London 1994, 268–280.

Eisner, Lotte H.: *The Haunted Screen. Expressionism in the German Cinema and the Influence of Max Reinhardt*. Berkeley 2008.

Eisner, Lotte H.: *Fritz Lang*. London 1976.

Eisner, Lotte H.: *Murnau*. London 1973.

Elsaesser, Thomas: Cinema – The Irresponsible Signifier or "The Gamble with History." Film Theory or Cinema. In: *New German Critique* 40 (1987), 65–89.

Elsaesser, Thomas: *New German Cinema. A History*. New Brunswick 1989.

Elsaesser, Thomas (ed.): *Early Cinema. Space, Frame, Narrative*. London 1990.

Elsaesser, Thomas: The New German Cinema's Historical Imaginary. In: Bruce A. Murray and Christopher Wickham (eds.): *Framing the Past. The Historiography of German Cinema and Television*. Carbondale and Edvardsville 1992, 280–307.

Elsaesser, Thomas: Traps for the Mind and the Eye. Fritz Lang. In: *Sight & Sound* 7–8 (August 1997), 28–30.

Elsaesser, Thomas: *Metropolis*. London 2000.

Elsaesser, Thomas: *Weimar Cinema and After. Germany's Historical Imaginary*. London and New York 2000.

Elsaesser, Thomas: Too Big and Too Close. Alfred Hitchcock and Fritz Lang. In: *Hitchcock Annual* 12 (2003), 1–41.

Elsaesser, Thomas: The New Film History as Media Archaeology. In: *CiNéMAS* 14:2–3 (2004), 75–117.

Elsaesser, Thomas: Double Occupancy and Small Adjustments. Space, Place and Policy in the New European Cinema since the 1990s. In: Thomas Elsaesser: *European Cinema. Face to Face with Hollywood*. Amsterdam 2005, 108–130.

Elsaesser, Thomas: Early Film History and Multi-Media. An Archaeology of Possible Futures? In: Wendy Hui Kyong Chung and Thomas Keenan (eds.): *New Media, Old Media. A History and Theory Reader*. New York 2006, 13–25.

Elsaesser, Thomas: *Film History as Media Archaeology. Tracking Digital Cinema*. Amsterdam 2016.

Engelhard, W.: Hohe Politik des Tonfilms. In: *Berliner Börsen-Courier* 209 (7 May 1930).

Eyman, Scott: *The Speed of Sound. Hollywood and the Talkie Revolution, 1926–1930*. New York 1997.

Foucault, Michel: *The Archaeology of Knowledge* [1969]. New York et al. 1976.

Foucault, Michel: What is an Author? In: *Aesthetics, Method, and Epistemology*. London 1998, 205–222.

Garncarz, Joseph: Die bedrohte Internationalität des Films. Fremdsprachige Versionen deutscher Tonfilme. In: Sibylle M. Sturm and Arthur Wohlgemuth (eds.): *Hallo? Berlin? Içi Paris! Deutsch-französische Filmbeziehungen 1918–1939*. Munich 1996, 127–140.

Garncarz, Josef: *Maßlose Unterhaltung. Zur Etablierung des Films in Deutschland 1896–1914*. Frankfurt a. M. and Basel 2010.

Genette, Gérard: *Paratexts. Thresholds of Interpretation*. Cambridge, Mass., New York and Melbourne 1997, 16–36.

Glatzer, Ruth (ed.): *Das Wilhelminische Berlin. Panorama einer Metropole 1890–1918*. Berlin 1997.
Gledhill, Christine: Rethinking Genre. In: Christine Gledhill and Linda Williams (eds.): *Reinventing Film Studies*. London and New York 2000, 221–243.
Goldberg, Benjamin: *The Mirror and Man*. Charlottesville 1985.
Gombrich, Ernst H.: Norm und Form. In: Dieter Henrich and Wolfgang Iser (eds): *Theorien der Kunst*. Frankfurt a. M. 1992, 148–178.
Gombrich Ernst H.: Ambiguities of the Third Dimension. In: Ernst H. Gombrich: *Art and Illusion. A Study in the Psychology of Pictorial Representation*. London 1994, 204–244.
Gomery, Douglas: Economic Struggle and Hollywood Imperialism. Europe Converts to Sound. In: Elizabeth Weis and John Belton (eds.): *Film Sound. Theory and Practice*. New York 1985, 25–36.
Gomery, Douglas: *The Coming of Sound. A History*. New York and London 2005.
Grau, Oliver: *Virtual Art. From Illusion to Immersion*. Cambridge and London 2003.
Guerin, Frances: *A Culture of Light. Cinema and Technology in 1920s Germany*. Minneapolis and London 2005.
Gunning, Tom: Non-Continuity, Continuity, Discontinuity. A Theory of Genres in Early Film. In: *Iris* 2:1 (1984), 100–112.
Gunning, Tom: An Aesthetic of Astonishment. Early Film and the Incredulous Spectator. In: *Art & Text* 34 (1989), 31–45.
Gunning, Tom: The Cinema of Attractions. Early Film, Its Spectator and the Avantgarde. In: Thomas Elsaesser with Adam Barker (eds.): *Early Cinema. Space, Frame, Narrative*. London 1990, 56–62. First published in *Wide Angle* 8: 3–4 (Fall 1986), 63–70.
Gunning, Tom: Weaving a Narrative. Style and Economic Background in Griffith's Biograph Films. In Thomas Elsaesser with Adam Barker (eds.): *Early Cinema. Space, Frame, Narrative*. London 1990, 343–344.
Gunning, Tom: *D.W. Griffith and the Origins of American Narrative Film. The Early Years at Biograph*. Urbana and Chicago 1991, 85–129.
Gunning, Tom: Heard Over the Phone: "The Lonely Villa" and the de Lorde Tradition of the Terrors of Technology. In: *Screen* 32: 2 (Summer 1991), 184–196.
Gunning, Tom: Before Documentary. Early Nonfiction Films and the "View" Aesthetic. In: Daan Hertogs and Nico de Klerk (eds.): *Uncharted Territory. Essays on Early Nonfiction Film*. Amsterdam 1997, 9–24.
Gunning, Tom: *The Films of Fritz Lang. Allegories of Vision and Modernity*. London 2000.
Güttinger, Fritz: Franz Hofer: Ausgrabung des Jahres? In: Fritz Güttinger: *Köpfen Sie mal ein Ei in Zeitlupe. Streifzüge durch die Welt des Stummfilms*. Zurich 1992, 15–22.
Haas, Willy: "Trick-Track" – Pressevorführung in der Schauburg. In: *Film-Kurier* 216 (16 September 1921), 1.
Haas, Willy: Dirnentragödie [1927]. In: Willy Haas: *Der Kritiker als Mitproduzent. Texte zum Film 1920–1933*, ed. by Wolfgang Jacobsen, Karl Prümm and Benno Wenz. Berlin 1991.
Haas, Willy: Genialität in der Filmdarstellung [1920]. In: Willy Haas: *Der Kritiker als Mitproduzent. Texte zum Film 1920–1933*, ed. by Wolfgang Jacobsen, Karl Prümm and Benno Wenz. Berlin 1991.
Haas, Willy: Gibt es eine Schauspielermaske im Film? Filmdramaturgische Notizen [1924]. In: Willy Haas: *Der Kritiker als Mitproduzent. Texte zum Film 1920–1933*, ed. by Wolfgang Jacobsen, Karl Prümm and Benno Wenz. Berlin 1991.

Haas, Willy: Hamlet [1921]. In: Willy Haas: *Der Kritiker als Mitproduzent. Texte zum Film 1920–1933*, ed. by Wolfgang Jacobsen, Karl Prümm and Benno Wenz. Berlin 1991.

Hake, Sabine: Self-Referentiality in Early German Cinema. In: *Cinema Journal* 31:3 (Spring 1992), 37–55.

Hake, Sabine: *The Cinema's Third Machine. Writing on Film in Germany, 1907–1933*. Lincoln and London 1993, 61–88.

Hake, Sabine: *German National Cinema*. 2nd ed., New York 2008.

Hammer, Klaus: William Wauer – ein Propagandist europäischer Avantgarde. In: *Bildende Kunst* 3 (1990), 56–59.

Hansen, Miriam: Mass Culture as Hieroglyphic Writing. Adorno, Derrida, Kracauer. In: *New German Critique* 56 (Spring/Summer 1992), 43–73.

Hansen, Miriam: Early Cinema, Late Cinema: Permutations of the Public Sphere. In: *Screen* 34:3 (Autumn 1993), 197–201.

Harden, Maximilian: Titanic. Report. In: Die Zukunft (15 June 1912), 340–354; reprinted in: Werner Köster and Thomas Lischeid (eds.): *Titanic. Ein Medienmythos*.

Hartog, François: *Regimes of Historicity. Presentism and Experiences of Time*. New York 2017.

Henry, Michael: *Le cinéma expressioniste allemand. Un langage métaphorique*. Fribourg 1971.

hfr.: Die blonde Geisha. In: *Die Lichtbild-Bühne* 11 (17 March 1923), 29.

Hick, Ulrike: *Geschichte der optischen Medien*. Munich 1999.

Higson, Andrew and Richard Maltby (eds.): *"Film Europe" and "Film America." Cinema, Commerce and Cultural Exchange, 1920–1939*. Exeter 1999.

Horak, Jan-Christopher: *Making Images Move. Photographers and Avant-Garde Cinema*. Washington and London 1997.

Howells, Richard: *The Myth of the Titanic*. London 1999.

Hübel, Anke J.: *Big, bigger, Cinema! Film- und Kinomarketing in Deutschland (1910–1933)*. Marburg 2011.

Hummel, Ferdinand: Musik und Kino. In: *Delog-Post* (May 1917), 1–3.

Hummel, Ferdinand: Die Filmmusik. In: *Der Film* 36 (3 September 1922), 28–31.

Jack, Ian: Leonardo's Grave. In: *Granta* 67 (Autumn 1999), 7–38.

Jacobi, J. M.: Propaganda und Reklame. In: *Delog-Post* (Januar 1917), 4–9.

Jacobsohn, Egon: "Das Caviarmäuschen." In: *Der Kinematograph* 639 (2 April 1919), n.p.

Jäger, Ernst: "Banditen." In: *Film-Kurier* 60 (11 March 1921), n.p.

Jakobson, Roman: Two Aspects of Language and Two Types of Aphasic Disturbances. In: Jakobson: *Language in Literature*. Cambridge, Mass. 1987, 95–114.

Jossé, Harald: *Die Entstehung des Tonfilms. Beitrag zu einer faktenorientierten Mediengeschichtsschreibung*. Freiburg i. Br. and Munich 1984.

Jung, Uli: Aktualitäten und Wochenschauen. In: Uli Jung and Martin Loiperdinger (eds.), *Geschichte des dokumentarischen Films in Deutschland*, Vol. 1.: *Kaiserreich, 1895–1918*. Stuttgart 2005, 230–252.

K., Dr. F.: So geht es nicht. Die Voraussetzungen für eine deutsche Sprechfilmproduktion sind gegeben; allein die bisherigen Versuche sind untauglich. In: *Der Kinematograph* 86 (11 April 1930), n.p.

Kaes, Anton: The Debate about Cinema. Charting a Controversy (1909–1929). In: *New German Critique* 40 (Winter 1987), 7–34.

Kaes, Anton: *M*. London 2000.

Kandler, Rebecca: *Phantom. Textgenese und Vermarktung*. Munich 1996.

Kaplan, E. Ann: The "Dark Continent" of Film Noir. Race, Displacement and Metaphor in Tourneur's "Cat People" (1942) and Welles' "The Lady from Shanghai" (1948). In: Kaplan (ed.): *Women in Film Noir*. Rev. ed., London 1998, 183–201.

Kappelhoff, Hermann: And the Heart will go on and on. Untergangsphantasie und Wiederholungsstruktur in dem Film "Titanic" von James Cameron. In: *Montage AV* 8:1 (1999), 85–108.

Kappelhoff, Hermann: *The Politics and Poetics of Cinematic Realism*. New York 2015.

Kappelhoff, Hermann: *Front Lines of Community. Hollywood Between War and Democracy*. Berlin and Boston 2018.

Kappelhoff, Hermann: *Kognition und Reflexion. Zur Theorie filmischen Denkens*. Berlin and Boston 2018.

Kasten, Jürgen: Dramatik und Leidenschaft – Das Melodram der frühen zehner Jahre. Von "Abgründe" (1910) bis "Vordertreppe und Hintertreppe" (1915). In: Werner Faulstich and Helmut Korte (eds.): *Fischer Filmgeschichte*, Vol. I: *Von den Anfängen bis zum etablierten Medium 1895–1924*. Frankfurt a. M. 1994, 233–247.

Keller, F.: Universal – Paris – Berlin. In: *Film-Kurier* 86 (14 April 1931).

Kellner, Hans: Kino und Musik. In: *Die Kinotechnik* 8 (1921), 294–295.

Kelly, Andrew: "All Quiet on the Western Front." Brutal Cutting, Stupid Censors and Bigoted Politicos (1930–1984). In: *Historical Journal of Film, Radio and Television* 2 (1989), 135–150.

Kelly, Andrew: *Filming "All Quiet on the Western Front."* London and New York 1998.

Kern, Stephen: *The Culture of Time and Space, 1880–1918*. Cambridge, Mass. 1983.

Kirby, Lynn: *Parallel Tracks. The Railroad and Silent Cinema*. Exeter 1997.

Kittler, Friedrich: *Grammophone, Film, Typewriter*. Stanford 1999.

Knops, Tilo: Cinema from the Writing Desk. Detective Films in Imperial Germany. In: Thomas Elsaesser with Michael Wedel (eds.): *A Second Life. German Cinema's First Decades*. Amsterdam 1996, 132–141.

Koerber, Martin: Oskar Messter, Film Pioneer. Early Cinema between Science, Spectacle, and Commerce. In: Thomas Elsaesser with Michael Wedel (eds.): *A Second Life. German Cinema's First Decades*. Amsterdam 1996, 51–61.

Kohner, Paul: Hollywood sagt: Nur in Europa produzieren! In: *Film-Kurier* 184 (6 August 1930), n.p.

Kracauer, Siegfried: *From Caligari to Hitler. A Psychological History of the German Film*. Princeton 1947.

Kracauer, Siegfried: *History. The Last Things Before the Last* [1969]. Princeton 1995.

Kracauer, Siegfried: Über Arbeitsnachweise. Konstruktion eines Raumes [1930]. In: *Schriften*, Vol. 5.3: *Essays, Feuilletons, Rezensionen*, ed. by Inka Mülder-Bach. Frankfurt a. M. 1990, 249–257.

Kracauer, Siegfried: "Einmal um Mitternacht" [1930]. In: Siegfried Kracauer: *Werke*, Vol. 6.2: *Kleine Schriften zum Film 1928–1931*, ed. by Inka Mülder-Bach. Frankfurt a. M. 2004, 338–339.

Krause, Karl Otto: Der Lichtspielopern-Kapellmeister. In: *Delog-Post* (October-December 1917), 4–5.

Kreimeier, Klaus: Notorisch anders – Conrad Veidt. Zur schauspielerischen Repräsentation der Devianz. In: Christiane Rüffert, Irmbert Schenk, Karl H. Schmid and Alfred Tews (eds.): *Unheimlich anders. Doppelgänger, Monster, Schattenwesen im Kino*. Berlin 2005, 69–76.

Krützen, Michaela: "Esperanto für den Tonfilm." Die Produktion von Sprachversionen für den frühen Tonfilmmarkt. In: Michael Schaudig (ed.): *Positionen deutscher Filmgeschichte. 100 Jahre Kinematographie: Strukturen, Diskurse, Kontexte.* Munich 1996.

Kurtz, Rudolf: Die Geschichte des Filmmanuskripts. Die seelische Vertiefung. In: *Der Kinematograph* 71 (6 April 1934).

Laemmle, Carl: Die Internationalisierung des Films und Deutschland. In: *Film-Kurier* 1 (1 January 1928), 1.

Landauer, Gustav: Die Botschaft der Titanic. In: *Frankfurter Zeitung* (21 April 1912); reprinted in: Werner Köster and Thomas Lischeid (eds.): *Titanic. Ein Medienmythos.* Leipzig 1999, 82 and 86–87.

Landry, Harald: Der Synchronisierungs-Unfug. In: *Vossische Zeitung* (30 November 1933).

Lang, Fritz: Kitsch – Sensation – Kultur und Film. In: Edgar Beyfuss and Alex Kossowsky (eds.): *Das Kulturfilmbuch.* Berlin 1924, 28–31. Published in English as Kitsch – Sensation – Culture and Film. In: Anton Kaes, Nicholas Baer and Michael Cowan (eds.): *The Promise of Cinema. German Film Theory, 1907–1933.* Oakland 2016, 210–212.

Langdale, Allen (ed.): *Hugo Münsterberg on Film. 'The Photoplay: A Psychological Study' and Other Writings.* New York and London 2002.

Lastra, James: Reading, Writing, and Representing Sound. In: Rick Altman (ed.): *Sound Theory, Sound Practice.* New York and London 1992, 65–86.

Lastra, James: *Sound Technology and the American Cinema. Perception, Representation, Modernity.* New York 2000.

Leonhardt, Nic: "...in die Tiefe des Bildes hineingezogen." Die Stereofotografie als visuelles Massenmedium des 19. Jahrhunderts. In: Christopher Balme and Markus Moninger (eds): *Crossing Media. Theater, Film, Fotografie, Neue Medien.* Munich 2004, 99–108.

Lichtspiel-Opern-Regie. Eine Unterredung mit Rudolf Meinert. In: *Delog-Post* (June 1917), 4–6.

Lindsay, Vachel: *The Art of the Moving Picture* [1915]. New York 2000.

Loiperdinger, Martin and Uli Jung (eds.): *Importing Asta Nielsen. The International Film Star in the Making, 1910–1914.* New Barnet 2013.

[Lubitsch, Ernst:] Asta Nielsen und Ernst Lubitsch. Ein offener Brief an Asta Nielsen. In: *Lichtbild-Bühne* 43 (16 October 1920), 31–32.

Lüthge, Bobby E.: Rausch. In: *Film-Kurier* (3 August 1919).

Mack, Max: Das Motiv. Fachwissenschaftliche Hinweise. In: *Die Lichtbild-Bühne* 7:6 (7 February 1914), 11.

Mack, Max: Die Eroberung der dritten Dimension. In: *B.Z. am Mittag* 131 (8 June 1914), supplement 1. Published in English as: The Conquest of the Third Dimension. In: Anton Kaes, Nicholas Baer and Michael Cowan (eds.): *The Promise of Cinema. German Film Theory, 1907–1933.* Oakland 2016, 578–579.

Mack, Max: Die Toilette des Films. In: Max Mack (ed.): *Die zappelnde Leinwand.* Berlin 1916, 124–125.

Mack, Max: Wie ich zum Film kam. In: *Die Lichtbild-Bühne* 21 (24 May 1919), 24.

Mack, Max: *Wie komme ich zum Film?* Berlin 1919.

Mack, Max: Moderne Filmregie. In: *Die Lichtbild-Bühne* 7 (1920), 13.

Mack, Max: *With a Sigh and a Smile. A Showman Looks Back.* London 1943.

Mannoni, Laurent: *The Great Art of Light and Shadow. Archaeology of the Cinema.* Exeter 2000.

Marks, Martin Miller: *Music and the Silent Film. Contexts and Case Studies, 1895–1924.* New York 1997.

McElhaney, Joe (ed.): *A Companion to Fritz Lang*. Malden 2015.

McGilligan, Patrick: *Fritz Lang – The Nature of the Beast. A Biography*. New York 1997.

Messter, Oskar: *Mein Weg mit dem Film*. Berlin 1936.

Metz, Christian: *Psychoanalysis and Cinema. The Imaginary Signifier*. Basingstoke and London 1982.

Misu, [Mime]: Kunst und nochmals Kunst. In: *Die Lichtbild-Bühne* 23 (7 June 1913, special supplement "The Film Director"), 122.

Mitchell, G.J.: Making "All Quiet on the Western Front." In: *American Cinematographer* 66:9 (September 1985), 34–36.

Mouffe, Chantal: *On the Political*. London and New York 2005.

Mühl-Benninghaus, Wolfgang: *Das Ringen um den Tonfilm. Strategien der Elektro- und der Filmindustrie in den 20er und 30er Jahren*. Düsseldorf 1999.

Mühl-Benninghaus, Wolfgang: "Don Juan heiratet" und "Der Andere." Zwei frühe filmische Theateradaptionen. In: Thomas Elsaesser and Michael Wedel (eds.): *Kino der Kaiserzeit. Zwischen Tradition und Moderne*. Munich 2002, 336–347.

Müller, Corinna: *Frühe deutsche Kinematographie. Formale, wirtschaftliche und kulturelle Entwicklungen 1907–1912*. Stuttgart and Weimar 1994.

Müller, Corinna: Das "andere" Kino? Autorenfilme der Vorkriegsära. In: Corinna Müller and Harro Segeberg (eds.): *Die Modellierung des Kinofilms. Zur Geschichte des Kinoprogramms zwischen Kurzfilm und Langfilm (1905/6–1918)*. Munich 1998, 153–192.

Müller, Corinna: Variationen des Kinoprogramms. Filmform und Filmgeschichte. In: Corinna Müller and Harro Segeberg (eds.): *Die Modellierung des Kinofilms. Zur Geschichte des Kinoprogramms zwischen Kurzfilm und Langfilm, 1905/6–1918*. Munich 1998, 43–76.

Müller, Corinna: *Vom Stummfilm zum Tonfilm*. Munich 2003.

Müller, Cornelia and Hermann Kappelhoff (in collaboration with Sarah Greifenstein, Dorothea Horst, Thomas Scherer and Christina Schmitt): *Cinematic Metaphor. Experience – Affectivity – Temporality*. Berlin and Boston 2018.

Münsterberg, Hugo: The Photoplay. A Psychological Study. In: Allan Langdale (ed.): *Hugo Münsterberg on Film. 'The Photoplay: A Psychological Study' and Other Writings*. New York and London 2002, 43–162.

Murnau, F.W.: The Ideal Picture Needs No Titles. By Its Very Nature the Art of the Screen Should Tell a Complete Story Pictorially. In: *Theater Magazine* 47 (January 1928), 41 and 72; reprinted in Richard W. McCormick and Alison Guenther-Pal (eds.): *German Essays on Film*. New York and London 2004, 66–68.

Murr, Peter: Film als Mißton. Diktatur der Patente. In: *Vossische Zeitung* 232 (18 May 1930) n.p.

Musicus: Die Lichtspiel-Oper. In: *Illustrierte Filmwoche* 43 (17 November 1916), 278.

Musser, Charles: The Nickelodeon Era Begins. Establishing the Framework for Hollywood's Mode of Representation. In: Thomas Elsaesser with Adam Barker (eds.): *Early Cinema. Space, Frame, Narrative*. London 1990, 256–273.

Narath, Albert: Oskar Messter and his Work. In: Raymond Fielding (ed.): *A Technological History of Motion Pictures and Television. An Anthology from the Pages of the Journal of the Society of Motion Picture and Television Engineers*. Berkeley, Los Angeles and London 1967, 109–117.

Naremore, James: *More than Night. Film Noir in Its Contexts*. Rev. ed., Berkeley, Los Angeles, London 2008.

Neumann, Dr.E. : Die Technik der Opernfilms. In: *Illustrierte Filmwoche* 43 (17 November 1916), 280.

Nielsen, Asta: *Die schweigende Muse. Lebenserinnerungen*. Berlin 1977.

Odin, Roger: Film documentaire, lecture documentarisante. In: Jean Charles Lyant and Roger Odin (eds.): *Cinémas et réalités*. St. Etienne 1984, 263–280.

Ottenheym, Konrad: *Film und Musik bis zur Einführung des Tonfilms. Beiträge zu einer Geschichte der Filmmusik*. Diss., Berlin 1925.

Quaresima, Leonardo: Dichter Heraus! The Autorenfilm and the German Cinema of the 1910s. In: *Griffithiana* 38–39 (1990), 101–126.

Paech, Joachim: *Literatur und Film*. Stuttgart 1988.

Palme, E.: Das Rhythmographie-Verfahren. In: *Kinotechnische Rundschau* 28-29 (12 and 19 July 1930), n.p.

Panagia, Davide: *Jacques Rancière's Sentiments*. Durham and London 2018.

Pander, Hans: Die Illusion beim Tonfilm. In: *Die Kinotechnik* 17 (5 September 1930), 471.

Parikka, Jussi: *What is Media Archaeology?* Cambridge, Mass. 2012.

Paul, William: Uncanny Theater. The Twin Inheritances of the Movies. In: *Paradoxa* 3–4 (1997), 321–347.

Pearson, Roberta E.: *Eloquent Gestures. The Transformation of Performance Style in the Griffith Biograph Films*. Berkeley, Los Angeles and London 1992.

Pearson, Roberta: Transitional Cinema. In: Geoffrey Nowell-Smith (ed.): *The Oxford History of World Cinema*. Oxford 1996, 23–42.

Prévot, René: "Einmal um Mitternacht." In: *Deutsche Filmzeitung* 45 (8 November 1929). Reprinted in Gero Gandert (ed.): *Der Film der Weimarer Republik. Ein Handbuch der zeitgenössischen Kritik*, Vol. 1: 1929. Berlin and New York 1993, 144.

Prinzler, Hans Helmut and Enno Patalas (eds.): *Lubitsch*. Munich and Lucerne 1987.

Pulch, Harald : Messters Experiment der Dirigentenfilme. In: *KINtop* 3 (1994), 53–64.

R., St.: Die erste Filmoper. In: *Allgemeine Kino-Börse* 36 (1922), 5.

Rancière, Jacques: *The Names of History. On the Poetics of Knowledge*. Minneapolis and London 1994.

Rancière, Jacques: Die Geschichtlichkeit des Films [1998]. In: Eva Hohenberger and Judith Keilbach (eds.): *Die Gegenwart der Vergangenheit. Dokumentarfilm, Fernsehen und Geschichte*. Berlin 2003, 230–246.

Rancière, Jacques: *The Politics of Aesthetics. The Distribution of the Sensible*. London and New York 2005.

Rancière, Jacques: *Film Fables*. Oxford and New York 2006.

Rancière, Jacques: *Ist Kunst widerständig?* Berlin 2008.

Rancière, Jacques: *Aesthetics and Its Discontents*. Cambridge and Malden 2009.

Rancière, Jacques: *Mute Speech. Literature, Critical Theory, and Politics*. New York 2011.

Rancière, Jacques: *The Intervals of Cinema*. London and New York 2014.

Reiff, Johann E.: Quellen der Liebe. *Film-Kurier* 249 (25 October 1921).

Richter, Hans: *Kinobriefe* 9 (16 April 1919).

Rohbeck, Johannes: *Technik, Kultur, Geschichte. Eine Rehabilitierung der Geschichtsphilosophie* Frankfurt a. M. 2000.

Rohwaldt, K.: Photoskulptur. In: *Die Umschau* 6 (1900), 5–7; reprinted in: Albert Kümmel and Petra Löffler (eds): *Medientheorie 1888–1933. Texte und Kommentare*. Frankfurt a. M. 2002, 57–61.

Roland, Marc: Gleichlaufsysteme. In: *Die Filmtechnik* 17 (1926), 348–349.

Ropars-Wuilleumier, Marie-Claire: The Function of Metaphor in Eisenstein's "October." In: *Film Criticism* 2:2 (1978), 109–127.

Rosen, Philip: *Changed Mummified. Cinema, Historicity, Theory*. Minneapolis and London 2001.

Rosenstone, Robert: *Visions of the Past. The Challenge of Film to Our Idea of History*. Cambridge and London 1995.

Sadowski, Piotr: *The Semiotics of Light and Shadows. Modern Visual Arts and Weimar Cinema*. London, Oxford, New York, New Delhi and Sydney 2018.

Salt, Barry: Film Form, 1900–1906. In: Thomas Elsaesser with Adam Barker (eds): *Early Cinema. Space, Frame, Narrative*. London 1990, 31–44.

Salt, Barry: *Film Style & Technology. History & Analysis*. 2nd ed. London 1992.

Salt, Barry: Early German Film. The Stylistics in Comparative Context. In: Thomas Elsaesser with Michael Wedel (eds.): *A Second Life. German Cinema's First Decades*. Amsterdam 1996, 225–236.

Saunders, Thomas: *Hollywood in Berlin. American* Cinema *and Weimar Germany*. Berkeley, Los Angeles and London 1994.

Sbt.: Eine neue Filmoperette – Das berliner Ereignis der Woche. In: *Der Film* 32 (1919), 24.

Scheunemann, Dietrich: The Double, the Décor, and the Framing Device. Once More on Robert Wiene's "The Cabinet of Dr. Caligari." In: Scheunemann (ed.): *Expressionist Film. New Perspectives*. Rochester 2003, 125–156.

Schivelbusch, Wolfgang: *The Railway Journey. Trains and Travel in the 19th Century*. New York 1979.

Schlüpmann, Heide: Cinema as Anti-Theater. Actresses and Female Audiences in Wilhelminian Germany. In: *Iris* 11 (Summer 1990), 77–93.

Schlüpmann, Heide: Melodrama and Social Drama in Early German Cinema. In: *Camera Obscura* 22 (January 1990), 73–89.

Schlüpmann, Heide: The Sinister Gaze. Three Films by Franz Hofer from 1913. In Paolo Cherchi Usai and Lorenzo Codelli (eds.): *Before Caligari. German Cinema, 1895–1920*. Pordenone 1990, 452–472.

Schlüpmann, Heide: *Unheimlichkeit des Blicks. Das Drama des frühen deutschen Kinos*. Basel and Frankfurt a. M. 1990 (engl.: *The Uncanny Gaze. The Drama of Early German Cinema*. Urbana-Champaign et al. 2010)

Schlüpmann, Heide: *Abendröthe der Subjektphilosophie. Eine Ästhetik des Kinos*. Frankfurt a. M. 1998.

Schlüpmann, Heide, Carola Gramann, Eric de Kuyper, Sabine Nessel and Michael Wedel (eds.): *Unmögliche Liebe. Asta Nielsen, ihr Kino*. Vienna 2009.

Schrader, Bärbel (ed.): *Im Westen nichts Neues – Eine Dokumentation*. Leipzig 1992.

Schüler, Bernhard: *Der Ullstein Verlag und der Stummfilm. Die Uco-Film GmbH als Ausdruck einer innovativen Partnerschaft*. Wiesbaden 2013.

Schweinitz, Jörg: "Wie im Kino!" Die autothematische Welle im frühen Tonfilm. Figurationen des Selbstreflexiven. In: Thomas Koebner (ed.): *Diesseits der dämonischen Leinwand. Neue Perspektiven auf das späte Weimarer Kino*. Munich 2003, 373–392.

Sellmann, Adolf: *Der Kinematograph als Volkserzieher?* Langensalza 1912.

Simmel, Georg: Zur Philosophie des Schauspielers [1920/21]. In: Georg Simmel: *Das individuelle Gesetz. Philosophische Exkurse*, ed. by Michael Landmann. Frankfurt a. M. 1987, 75–95. English translation by Philip Lawton: *Toward the Philosophy of the Actor*. https://papers.ssrn.com/sol3/papers.cfm?abstract_id=2897044 (15 April 2018).

Simmel, Georg: Die Großstädte und das Geistesleben. In: Georg Simmel: *Aufsätze und Abhandlungen 1901–1908*. Frankfurt a.M. 1995, 116–131.

Simmons, J.: Film and International Politics. The Banning of "All Quiet on the Western Front." In: *Historian* 52 (1989), 40–60.

Sinnerbrink, Robert: *Stimmung*. Exploring the Aesthetics of Mood. In: *Screen* 53: 2 (Summer 2012), 148–163.

Sloterdijk, Peter: *Critique of Cynical Reason*. Minneapolis 1988. Originally published as *Kritik der zynischen Vernunft*. Frankfurt a. M. 1983.

Spieker, Markus: *Hollywood unterm Hakenkreuz. Der amerikanische Spielfilm im Dritten Reich*. Trier 1999.

Stein, Otto Th.: Ueber Regiekunst im Lichtbildtheater. In: *Erste Internationale Film-Zeitung* 48 (30 November 1912), 51.

Steinthal, Walter: Bei Asta Nielsen. In: *Die Lichtbild-Bühne* 41 (9 October 1920).

Strauven, Wanda (ed.): *The Cinema of Attractions Reloaded*. Amsterdam 2006.

Thompson, Kristin: *Exporting Entertainment. America in the World Film* Market, *1907–1914*. London 1985.

Thompson, Kristin: *"Im Anfang war. . . ."* Some Links between German Fantasy Films of the Teens and the Twenties." In: Paolo Cherchi Usai and Lorenzo Codelli (eds.): *Before Caligari. German Cinema, 1895–1920*. Pordenone 1990, 138–161.

Thompson, Kristin: *Herr Lubitsch Goes to Hollywood. German and American Film After World War I*. Amsterdam 2005.

Trotter, David: Stereoscopy. Modernism and the "Haptic." In: *Critical Quarterly* 4 (December 2004), 38–58.

Tsivian, Yuri: Portraits, Mirrors, Death. On Some Decadent Clichés in Early Russian Films. In: *Iris* 14–15 (Autumn 1992), 67–83.

Tsivian, Yuri: Cutting and Framing in Bauer's and Kuleshov's Films. In: *KINtop* 1 (1993), 103–113.

Tsivian, Yuri: Two "Stylists" of the Teens. Franz Hofer and Yevgenii Bauer. In: Thomas Elsaesser with Michael Wedel (eds.): *A Second Life. German Cinema's First Decades*. Amsterdam 1996, 264–275.

Urgiß, Julius: William Wauer. In: *Illustrierte Kino-Woche* 32–33 (25 August 1916), 210.

Urgiß, Julius: Die Aufnahmen für die Film-Oper "Martha" in Wernigerode a. Harz. In: *Der Kinematograph* 510 (4 October 1916).

Uricchio, William: Stereography. In: Richard Abel (ed.): *Encyclopedia of Early Cinema*. London and New York 2005, 610–611.

Vasey, Ruth: *The World According to Hollywood, 1918–1939*. Exeter 1997.

Vierhaus, Rudolf: Zum Problem historischer Krisen. In: Karl-Georg Faber and Christian Meier (eds.): *Historische Prozesse. Beiträge zur Historik*, Vol. 2. Munich 1978, 313–329.

Vogl-Bienek, Ludwig: Die historische Projektionskunst. Eine offene geschichtliche Perspektive auf den Film als Aufführungsereignis. In: *KINtop* 3 (1994), 11–32.

Volz, Robert: Die Filmoperette. In: *Der Bildwart* 2 (1925). Reprinted in: Katja Uhlenbrok (ed.): *. . . aus dem Geiste der Operette. Musiktheater und Tanzkultur im deutschen Film 1922–1937*. Hamburg 1997, 4–7.

Waltz, Gwendolyn: 2-D? 3-D? The Technology and Aesthetics of Dimension in Early Cinema and Turn-of-the-Century Stage Performance. In: *Cinema & Cie* 3 (Fall 2003), 26–38.

Wauer, William: *Der Kunst eine Gasse! Kritische Beiträge zur Theaterreform*. Berlin 1906.

Wauer, William: *Die Kunst im Theater. Bemerkungen und Gedanken*. Berlin 1909.

Wauer, William: Die Theaterkunst. In: *Der Sturm* 76 (September 1911), 605.

Wauer, William: Die künstlerischen Grundlagen des Films. In: *Erste Internationale Filmzeitung* 21 (1915), 15–21.

Wauer, William: Die Wirklichkeit des Films. In: *Illustrierte Filmwoche* 27 (6 Juli 1918), 184–185.

Wauer, William: Filmkunst: Kunst oder Nicht-Kunst? In: *Illustrierte Filmwoche* 38 (21 September 1918), 271.

Wauer, William: *Theater als Kunstwerk*. Berlin 1919.

Weber-Robine, Friedrich: Das Tonbild und die Sprechmaschine. Eine knappe Darstellung der Kontrollmittel des Tonbild-Theaters. In: *Der Kinematograph* 196, 198, 200, 204 (28 September 1910 – 23 November 1910).

Wedel, Michael: *Max Mack. Showman im Glashaus*. Berlin 1996.

Wedel, Michael: Filmform und Filmformat. Bausteine zu einer Mediengeschichte des frühen deutschen Kinos. In: *KINtop* 8 (1999), 189–194.

Wedel, Michael: Klärungsprozesse. Tobis, Klangfilm und die Tonfilmumstellung 1928–1932. In: Jan Distelmeyer (ed.): *Tonfilmfrieden / Tonfilmkrieg. Die Geschichte der Tobis vom Technik-Syndikat zum Staatskonzern*. Munich 2003, 34–43.

Wedel, Michael: Okkupation der Zeit. In: *Schnitt* 29 (Winter 2003), 10–15.

Wedel, Michael: *Der deutsche Musikfilm. Archäologie eines Genres 1914–1945*. Munich 2007.

Wedel, Michael: Film als Rhythmus der Gemeinschaft. Zu einer Denkfigur bei Rancière. In: Drehli Robnik, Thomas Hübel and Siegfried Mattl (eds.): *Das Streit-Bild. Film, Geschichte und Politik bei Jacques Rancière*. Vienna 2010, 145–160.

Wedel, Michael: The Beginnings / Die Anfänge (1912–1921). In: Michael Wedel, Chris Wahl and Ralf Schenk: *100 Years Studio Babelsberg. The Art of Filmmaking*. Kempen 2012, 234–251.

Wedel, Michael: *Kollision im Kino. Mime Misu und der Untergang der "Titanic."* Munich 2012.

Wedel, Michael: Grausame Geschichte. Kracauer, *Visual History* und Film. In: Bernhard Groß, Vrääth Öhner and Drehli Robnik (eds.): *Film und Gesellschaft denken mit Siegfried Kracauer*. Vienna 2018, 107–119.

Wellmann, Marc (ed.): *William Wauer und der Berliner Kubismus. Die Plastischen Künste um 1920*. Cologne 2011.

White, Hayden: The Modernist Event. In: Vivian Sobchack (ed.): *The Persistence of History. Cinema, Television, and the Modern Event*. New York and London 1996, 17–38.

Whittock, Trevor: *Metaphor and Film*. Cambridge 1990.

Williams, Linda: The Prologue to "Un Chien Andalou." A Surrealist Film Metaphor. In: *Screen* 17:4 (December 1976), 24–33.

Williams, Linda: *Figures of Desire. A Theory and Analysis of Surrealist Film*. Berkeley, Los Angeles, Oxford 1981.

Williams, Linda: Dream Rhetoric and Film Rhetoric. Metaphor and Metonymy in "Un Chien Andalou." In: *Semiotica* 33 (1981): 87–103.

Williams, Linda: Corporealized Observers. Visual Pornographies and the "Carnal Density of Vision." In: Patrice Petro (ed.): *Fugitive Images. From Photography to Video*. Bloomington 1995, 3–41.

Wolffsohn, Karl (ed.): *Jahrbuch der Filmindustrie*, vol. 4. Berlin 1930.

Wolffsohn, Karl (ed.): *Jahrbuch der Filmindustrie*, Vol. 5. Berlin 1933.

Yacavone, Daniel: *Film Worlds. A Philosophical Aesthetics of Cinema*. New York 2015.

Zglinicki, Friedrich von: *Der Weg des Films*. Hildesheim and New York 1979.

Zimmerschied, Karl: *Die deutsche Filmindustrie. Ihre Organisation und Stellung im deutschen Staats- und Wirtschaftsleben*. Stuttgart 1922.

Zizek, Slavoj: *The Fright of Real Tears. Krzysztof Kieslowski Between Theory and Post-Theory*. London 2001.

Filmography

A Narrow Escape or The Physician of the Castle. Dir. unknown. 1908.

Abend – Nacht – Morgen (Evening – Night – Morning). Dir. F.W. Murnau. 1920.

Afgrunden (The Abyss). Dir. Urban Gad. 1910.

All Quiet on the Western Front. Dir. Lewis Milestone. 1930.

Atlantis. Dir. August Blom. 1913.

Banditen. Dir. Edwin Carewe. 1923.

Berlin – Die Sinfonie der Grossstadt (Berlin, Symphony of a Big City). Dir. Walter Ruttmann. 1927.

Broadway. Dir. Pál Fejos. 1929.

Cabiria. Dir. Giovanni Pastrone. 1914.

Captain of the Guard. Dir. John S. Robertson, Pál Fejos. 1930.

Cat People. Dir. Jacques Tourneur. 1942.

Das alte Lied (The Old Song). Dir. Karl Otto Krause. 1919.

Das Cabinet des Dr. Caligari (The Cabinet of Dr. Caligari). Dir. Robert Wiene. 1920.

Das Caviarmäuschen (The Caviar Mouse). Dir. Gerhard Dammann. 1919.

Das fremde Mädchen (The Strange Girl). Dir. Mauritz Stiller. 1913.

Das indische Grabmal (The Indian Tomb). Dir. Fritz Lang. 1959.

Das Kussverbot (Kissing Prohibited). Dir. Ludwig Czerny. 1920.

Das Mädel von Pontecuculi (The Girl from Pontecuculi). Dir. Ludwig Czerny. 1924.

Das Menuett. Dir. Ludwig Czerny. 1919.

Das rosa Pantöffelchen (The Pink Slipper). Dir. Franz Hofer. 1913.

Das schwarze Los (The Black Lot). Dir. John Gottowt. 1913.

Das Testament des Dr. Mabuse (The Testament of Dr. Mabuse). Dir. Fritz Lang. 1932.

Das Weib ohne Herz (The Woman Without a Heart). Dir. Walter Schmidthässler. 1912.

Der Andere (The Other One). Dir. Max Mack. 1913.

Der Blusenkönig (The Blouse King). Dir. Ernst Lubitsch. 1917.

Der brennende Acker (The Burning Soil). Dir. F.W. Murnau. 1923.

Der Freischütz (The Marksman). Dir. Rudolf Meinert. 1918.

Der Gang in die Nacht (Journey into the Night). Dir. F.W. Murnau. 1920.

Der Golem (The Golem). Dir. Henrik Galeen, Paul Wegener. 1914.

Der Golem, wie er in die Welt kam (The Golem How He Came into the World). Dir. Carl Boese, Paul Wegener. 1920.

Der Januskopf (The Head of Janus). Dir. F.W. Murnau. 1920.

Der letzte Mann (The Last Laugh). Dir. F.W. Murnau. 1924.

Der müde Tod (Destiny). Dir. Fritz Lang. 1921.

Der Rebell (The Rebel). Dir. Kurt Bernhardt, Luis Trenker. 1932.

Der Steckbrief (The 'Wanted' Poster). Dir. Franz Hofer. 1913.

Der Student von Prag (The Student of Prague). Dir. Paul Wegener, Stellan Rye. 1913.

Der Tiger von Eschnapur (The Tiger of Eschnapur). Dir. Fritz Lang. 1959.

Der Waffenschmied (The Armourer). Dir. Rudolf Meinert. 1918.

Der Zug des Herzens (The Pull of the Heart). Dir. Walter Schmidthässler. 1912.

Des Alters erste Spuren (First Traces of Age). Dir. Franz Hofer. 1913.

Die 1000 Augen des Dr. Mabuse (The Thousand Eyes of Dr. Mabuse). Dir. Fritz Lang. 1960.

Die Augen des Ole Brandis (The Eyes of Ole Brandis). Dir. Stellan Rye. 1914.

Die blonde Geisha (The Blonde Geisha). Dir. Ludwig Czerny. 1923.

https://doi.org/10.1515/9783110613551-012

DIE BRIGANTIN VON NEW YORK (THE BRIGANTINE FROM NEW YORK). Dir. Hans Werckmeister. 1924.

DIE FINANZEN DES GROSSHERZOGS (THE FINANCES OF THE GRAND DUKE). Dir. F.W. Murnau. 1923.

DIE FLEDERMAUS (THE BAT). Dir. Max Mack. 1923.

DIE FRAU IM MOND (WOMAN IN THE MOON). Dir. Fritz Lang. 1929.

DIE GROSSE SEHNSUCHT (THE GREAT LONGING). Dir. Steve Sekely. 1930.

DIE HERRIN VON ATLANTIS. Dir. G.W. Pabst. 1932.

DIE INSEL DER SELIGEN (THE ISLAND OF THE HAPPY ONES). Dir. Max Reinhardt. 1913.

DIE LUSTIGEN WEIBER VON WINDSOR (THE MERRY WIVES OF WINDSOR). Dir. William Wauer. 1918.

DIE NIBELUNGEN (NIBELUNGEN). Dir. Fritz Lang. 1924.

DIE SCHWARZE KATZE (THE BLACK CAT). Dir. Viggo Larsen. 1910.

DIE SCHWARZE KUGEL ODER DIE GEHEIMNISVOLLEN SCHWESTERN (THE BLACK BOWL, OR, THE MYSTERIOUS
    SISTERS). Dir. Franz Hofer. 1913.

DIE SCHWARZE NATTER (THE BLACK VIPER). Dir. Franz Hofer. 1913.

DIE SCHWIMMENDEN EISBERGE (THE FLOATING ICEBERGS). Der Tag im Film (German newsreel). 1912.

DIE UNSICHTBARE FRONT (THE INVISIBLE FRONT). Dir. Richard Eichberg. 1932.

DIE VENEZIANISCHE NACHT (THE VENETIAN NIGHT). Dir. Max Reinhardt. 1914.

DIE WEISSE SKLAVIN (THE WHITE SLAVE). Dir. August Blom. 1910.

DIRNENTRAGÖDIE (TRAGEDY OF A WHORE). Dir. Bruno Rahn. 1927.

DRESSUR ZUR EHE (TRAINING FOR MARRIAGE). Dir. Franz Hofer. 1916.

DR. MABUSE – DER SPIELER (DR. MABUSE – THE GAMBLER). Dir. Fritz Lang. 1922.

DR. SCHOTTE. Dir. William Wauer. 1918.

EINMAL UM MITTERNACHT (ONCE AT MIDNIGHT). Dir. Karl Otto Krause. 1929.

EIN WALZERTRAUM (A WALTZ DREAM). Dir. Ludwig Berger. 1925.

FAUST. Dir. F.W. Murnau. 1926.

FURY. Dir. Fritz Lang. 1936.

GRANDMA'S READING GLASS. Dir. George Albert Smith. 1900.

GRETCHEN SCHUBERT. Dir. Karl Moos. 1926.

HANNEMANN, ACH HANNEMANN (HANNEMANN, OH, HANNEMANN). Dir. Edmund Edel. 1919.

HEARD OVER THE PHONE. Dir. Edwin S. Porter. 1908.

HEIDENRÖSLEIN. Dir. Franz Hofer. 1916.

HELL'S HEROES. Dir. William Wyler. 1929.

HILDE WARREN UND DER TOD (HILDE WARREN AND DEATH). Dir. Joe May. 1917.

HOUSE BY THE RIVER. Dir. Fritz Lang. 1950.

HURRAH! EINQUARTIERUNG! (HURRAH! QUARTERING). Dir. Franz Hofer. 1913.

ICH GEH AUS UND DU BLEIBST DA. Dir. Hans Behrendt. 1931.

ICH HAB DICH LIEB (I AM FOND OF YOU). Dir. Karl Otto Krause. 1926.

ICH HAB' MEIN HERZ IM AUTOBUS VERLOREN (I HAVE LOST MY HEART IN A BUS). Dir. Carlo Campogalliani,
    Domenico Gambino. 1929.

IM BEWUSSTSEIN DER SCHULD (CONSCIOUS OF GUILT). Dir. William Wauer. 1916.

IN EINEM KÜHLEN GRUNDE (DOWN IN THE COOL VALLEY). Dir. Max Agerty. 1921.

JENSEITS DES STROMES (BEYOND THE STREAM). Dir. Ludwig Czerny. 1922.

KAMMERMUSIK (CHAMBER MUSIC). Dir. Franz Hofer. 1915.

KATASTROPHE DER „TITANIC" ("TITANIC" DISASTER). Gaumont. 1912.

LACHENDE HERZEN (LAUGHING HEARTS). Dir. Carlo Emerich. 1919.

LA MUJER DE MEDIANOCHE (MIDNIGHT WOMAN). Dir. Carlo Campogalliani. 1925.

L'ARRIVÉE D'UN TRAIN À LA CIOTAT (ARRIVAL OF A TRAIN AT LA CIOTAT). Dir. Auguste & Louis Lumière.
    1895.

LIEBELEI. Dir. August Blom. 1914.

LIEBESFRÜHLING (SPRING OF LOVE). Dir. Karl Otto Krause. 1933.

LUCREZIA BORGIA. Dir. Richard Oswald. 1922.

M. Dir. Fritz Lang. 1931.

MARTHA ODER DER MARKT VON RICHMOND (MARTHA, OR, THE MARKET AT RICHMOND). Dir. Gustav
    Schönwald. 1916.

METROPOLIS. Dir. Fritz Lang. 1927.

MISS VENUS. Dir. Ludwig Czerny. 1921.

MONNA VANNA. Dir. Richard Eichberg. 1922.

NOSFERATU. Dir. F.W. Murnau. 1922.

PAPRIKA. Dir. Carl Boese. 1932.

PETER LUMP. Dir. William Wauer. 1916.

PHANTOM. Dir. F.W. Murnau. 1922.

QUELLEN DER LIEBE (FOUNTAINS OF LOVE). Dir. Grete Massé. 1920.

RAUSCH. Dir. Ernst Lubitsch. 1919.

RESURRECTION. Dir. Edwin Carewe. 1931.

RICHARD WAGNER. Dir. Carl Froelich, William Wauer. 1913.

SAVED FROM THE TITANIC (WAS DIE TITANIC SIE LEHRTE). Dir. Étienne Arnaud. 1912.

SCARLET STREET. Dir. Fritz Lang. 1945.

SCHATTEN (WARNING SHADOWS). Dir. Arthur Robison. 1923.

SCHLOSS VOGELÖD. Dir. F.W. Murnau. 1921.

SCHUHPALAST PINKUS (SHOE PALACE PINKUS). Dir. Ernst Lubitsch. 1916.

SECRET BEYOND THE DOOR. Dir. Fritz Lang. 1948.

SHOWBOAT. Dir. Harry A. Pollard. 1929.

SKANDAL IN BUDAPEST (SCANDAL IN BUDAPEST). Dir. Steve Sekely. 1933.

SO RÄCHT SICH DIE SONNE (HOW THE SUN TAKES REVENGE). Dir. William Wauer. 1915.

S.O.S. EISBERG (SOS Iceberg). Dir. Arnold Fanck. 1933.

STEUERMANN HOLK (HELMSMAN HOLK). Dir. Rochus Gliese, Ludwig Wolff. 1920.

STORMS. Dir. William Wyler. 1930.

SUNRISE – A SONG OF TWO HUMANS. Dir. F.W. Murnau. 1927.

TABU. Dir. F.W. Murnau. 1930.

TARTÜFF (TARTUFFE). Dir. F.W. Murnau. 1925.

THE BIG HEAT. Dir. Fritz Lang. 1953.

THE BOUDOIR DIPLOMAT. Dir. Malcolm St. Clair, John M. Stahl. 1930.

THE GAY SHOE CLERK. Dir. Edwin S. Porter. 1906.

THE GIRL AND HER TRUST. Dir. D.W. Griffith. 1912.

THE GRIT OF THE GIRL TELEGRAPHER. Dir. J.P. McGowan. 1912.

THE KING OF JAZZ. Dir. John Murray Anderson. 1930.

THE LADY FROM SHANGHAI. Dir. Orson Welles. 1948.

THE LAST PERFORMANCE. Dir. Pál Fejos. 1929.

THE LONEDALE OPERATOR. Dir. D.W. Griffith. 1911.

THE LONELY VILLA. Dir. D.W. Griffith. 1909.

THE MATRIX. Dir. Lana& Lilly Wachowski. 1999.

TITANIC. Dir. James Cameron. 1997.

TITANIC – IN NACHT UND EIS (TITANIC – IN NIGHT AND ICE). Dir. Mime Misu. 1912.

TRICK-TRACK. Dir. Emil Albes. 1921.

UN CHIEN ANDALOU. Dir. Luis Buñuel. 1929.

UNHEIMLICHE GESCHICHTEN (UNCANNY TALES). Dir. Richard Oswald. 1919.

UNTER FALSCHER FLAGGE (UNDER THE WRONG BANNER). Dir. Johannes Meyer. 1932.

VAMPYRE DER GROSSSTADT (VAMPIRES OF THE CITY). Dir. Franz Hofer. 1914.

VANINA. Dir. Arthur von Gerlach. 1922.

VARIETÉ. Dir. E.A. Dupont. 1925.

WEIHNACHTSGLOCKEN 1914 (CHRISTMAS BELLS 1914). Dir. Franz Hofer. 1914.

WENN DIE LIEBE NICHT WÄR (IF LOVE DIDN'T EXIST). Dir. Joseph Max Jacobi. 1921.

WENN MÄNNER STREIKEN (WHEN MEN GO ON STRIKE). Dir. Edmund Edel. 1919.

WENN VIER DASSELBE TUN (WHEN FOUR DO THE SAME). Dir. Ernst Lubitsch. 1917.

WER IN DER JUGEND NICHT KÜSST (WHO HASN'T KISSED WHEN YOUNG). Dir. Karl Otto Krause. 1918.

WHILE THE CITY SLEEPS. Dir. Fritz Lang. 1955.

WIR ARMEN KLEINEN MÄDCHEN (WE POOR LITTLE GIRLS). Dir. Karl Otto Krause. 1926.

WO IST COLETTI? (WHERE IS COLETTI?). Dir. Max Mack. 1913.

YOU ONLY LIVE ONCE. Dir. Fritz Lang. 1937.

ZAPFENSTREICH AM RHEIN (TATTOO AT THE RHINE). Dir. Jaap Speyer. 1930.

ZIGEUNERBLUT (GYPSY BLOOD). Dir. Karl Otto Krause. 1920.

ZUM PARADIES DER DAMEN (THE LADIES' PARADISE). Dir. Max Mack. 1914.

ZWEIMAL GELEBT (LIVED TWICE). Dir. Max Mack. 1912.

Subject Index

https://doi.org/10.1515/9783110613551-013

Name Index

https://doi.org/10.1515/9783110613551-014

Film Index

https://doi.org/10.1515/9783110613551-015

www.ingramcontent.com/pod-product-compliance
Lightning Source LLC
Chambersburg PA
CBHW020531270326
41927CB00006B/527